Advanced Information and Knowledge Processing

Springer
London
Berlin
Heidelberg
New York
Hong Kong
Milan
Paris
Tokyo

Also in this series

Shichao Zhang, Chengqi Zhang and
Xindong Wu

Knowledge Discovery in Multiple Databases

With 21 Figures

Springer

Shichao Zhang, PhD, MSc
Chengqi Zhang, PhD, MSc, BSc, DSc
FIT, University of Technology Sydney, Australia

Xindong Wu, PhD, MSc
Department of Computer Science, University of Vermont, USA

Series Editors
Xindong Wu
Lakhmi Jain

British Library Cataloguing in Publication Data
Zhang, Shichao
   Knowledge discovery in multiple databases. – (Advanced information and knowledge processing)
   1. Data mining 2. Distributed databases
   I. Title II. Zhang, Chengqi III. Wu, Xindong
   005.7′58

   ISBN 1852337036

Library of Congress Cataloging-in-Publication Data
Zhang, Shichao.
   Knowledge discovery in multiple databases / Shichao Zhang, Chengqi Zhang, Xindong Wu.
     p. cm.
   Includes bibliographic references and index.
   ISBN 1-85233-703-6 (alk. paper)
   1. Database management. 2. Database searching. I. Zhang, Chengqi, 1957– II. Wu, Xindong
   III. Title
   QA76.9.D3Z54 2004
   005.74–dc22   2004048100

AI&KP ISSN 1610-3947

ISBN 1-85233-703-6 Springer-Verlag London Berlin Heidelberg
Springer-Verlag is part of Springer Science+Business Media
springeronline.com

Typesetting: Electronic text files prepared by authors
Printed and bound in the United States of America
34/3830-543210 Printed on acid-free paper SPIN 10894388

Preface

Many organizations have an urgent need of mining their multiple databases inherently distributed in branches (distributed data). In particular, as the Web is rapidly becoming an information flood, individuals and organizations can take into account low-cost information and knowledge on the Internet when making decisions. How to efficiently identify quality knowledge from different data sources has become a significant challenge.

This challenge has attracted a great many researchers including the authors who have developed a local pattern analysis, a new strategy for discovering some kinds of potentially useful patterns that cannot be mined in traditional multi-database mining techniques. Local pattern analysis delivers high-performance pattern discovery from multiple databases. There has been considerable progress made on multi-database mining in such areas as hierarchical meta-learning, collective mining, database classification, and peculiarity discovery. While these techniques continue to be future topics of interest concerning multi-database mining, this book focuses on these interesting issues under the framework of local pattern analysis.

The book is intended for researchers and students in data mining, distributed data analysis, machine learning, and anyone else who is interested in multi-database mining. It is also appropriate for use as a text supplement for broader courses that might also involve knowledge discovery in databases and data mining.

The book consists of ten chapters. Chapter 1 states the multi-database mining problem and its importance. Chapter 2 lays a common foundation for subsequent material. This includes the preliminaries on data mining and multi-database mining, as well as necessary concepts, previous efforts, and applications. Chapter 3 introduces the framework of local pattern analysis. The later chapters are essentially self-contained and may be read selectively, and in any order. Chapters 4, 5, and 6 develop techniques for preprocessing the data in multi-databases. Chapters 7, 8, and 9 presents techniques for identifying interesting patterns from multi-databases based on local pattern analysis. And Chapter 10 presents a summary of the previous chapters and demonstrates some open problems.

Beginners should read Chapters 1 and 2 before selectively reading other chapters. Although the opening problems are very important, techniques in

other chapters may be helpful for experienced readers who want to attack
such problems.

Shichao Zhang   March 2004

Chengqi Zhang

Xindong Wu

Acknowledgments

We are deeply indebted to Jenny Wolkowicki for the carefully proofreading, as well as many colleagues for the advice and support they gave during the writing of this book. We are especially grateful to Tony King for his editorial efforts when he worked with Springer.

For many suggested improvements and discussions on the material, we thank Professor Geoffrey Webb from Monash University, Mr. Zili Zhang from Deakin University, Dr. Huan Liu from Arizona State University, President Hong Liang and Ms. Yanchun Zhou from Guangxi Teachers University, Ms. Li Liu and Mr. Xiaowei Yan from the University of Technology, Sydney, Professor Xiaopei Luo from the Chinese Academy of Sciences;, and Professor Guoxi Fan from the Education Bureau of Quanzhou.

Contents

1. Importance of Multi-database Mining

This book focuses on developing new techniques for multi-database mining. In Chapter 1, we outline the importance, and existing limitations, of multi-database mining, and explain why there is an urgent need for efficient analysis of data in such databases. We point out, too, that there are essential differences between mono- and multi-database mining. An existing process of multi-database mining is included in this chapter, and some practical issues involving mining multi-databases, including application-independent database classification, local pattern analysis, and local pattern synthesis, are briefly discussed.

1.1 Introduction

The increasing use of multi-database technology, such as in computer communication networks, distributed database systems, federated database systems, language systems, and homogeneous information processing systems, has led to the increased development of multi-database systems for real-world applications. For decision-making, many organizations need to mine the multiple databases distributed throughout their branches. On the other hand, as the Web is rapidly being inundated with information, individuals and organizations can utilize low-cost information and knowledge on the Internet when making decisions. Therefore, the efficient identification of quality knowledge from different data sources presents a significant challenge.

A multi-database environment consists of a group of databases or datasets. The goal of multi-database mining is to identify potentially useful patterns from multi-databases.

Traditional multi-database mining utilizes mono-database mining techniques, which consist of a two-step approach. The databases most relevant to an application are selected in the first step. Then all the data from these databases are pooled to amass a huge dataset. This dataset is used to search for useful patterns based upon mono-database mining techniques.

The first step constitutes an effective means of identifying patterns by searching for the dataset comprised of the databases relevant to an application (Liu-Lu-Yao 1998). This step is typically application-dependent. The second step constitutes putting all the data from the relevant databases into a single dataset, and mining the dataset. This can destroy some patterns, such as, for example, the pattern that 70% of the branches within a company agree that a married customer usually has at least 2 cars if they are aged between 45 and 65. Such patterns might have assisted in decision-making at the company head office level. Thus mono-database mining techniques fail in this regard.

In particular, much work on multi-database mining has been built on quality data. That is, the input to the mining algorithms assumes that the data in multi-databases are nicely distributed, containing no missing, inconsistent, and/or incorrect values. This can lead to (1) disguising useful patterns, (2) low performance, and (3) poor-quality outputs, if the assumption is not true.

On the other hand, there are essential differences between mono- and multi-database mining. Both data and patterns in multi-databases present more challenges than those in mono-databases. For example, unlike in mono-databases, data in multi-databases may pose the following problems: data may have different names in different branches; data may have different formats in different branches; data may have different structures in different branches; and data may conflict, or even be impure, in different branches. Patterns in multi-database problems exhibit the following features: local patterns, (global) high-vote patterns, (global) exceptional patterns, and (global) suggested patterns.

In this chapter we define the process of multi-database mining, and discuss practical problems that can arise. We also briefly illustrate the importance of multi-database mining in real-world applications, describe the multi-database problems, analyze differences between mono- and multi-database mining, and discuss the limitations of traditional multi-database mining.

With this in mind, the rest of this chapter is organized as follows. Section 1.2 illustrates the role of multi-database mining in real-world applications. Section 1.3 describes multi-database mining problems. Section 1.4 analyzes the differences between mono- and multi-database mining by demonstrating the features of data in mono- and multi-databases. Section 1.5 recalls the evolution of multi-database mining. Section 1.6 discusses the limitations of traditional multi-database mining. Section 1.7 defines a process for multi-database mining. Section 1.9 briefly outlines the major contributions of this book. Section 1.10 defines the structure of the book.

1.2 Role of Multi-database Mining in Real-world Applications

Private business, government, and academic sectors have all implemented measures to computerize all, or part of, their daily functions (Hurson-BP 1994). Generally, an interstate (or international) company consists of multiple branches. For example, the Bank of China has many branches in different locations. Each branch has its own database. This means that data are widely distributed and thus a multi-database problem emerges (see Figure 1.1). For the purpose of this book, we take as a convenient example of a multi-database facility an interstate company with a head office where global decisions are made, and a number of branches that contribute to these decisions in various ways. Therefore the terms "head office" and "branches" are used throughout this book.

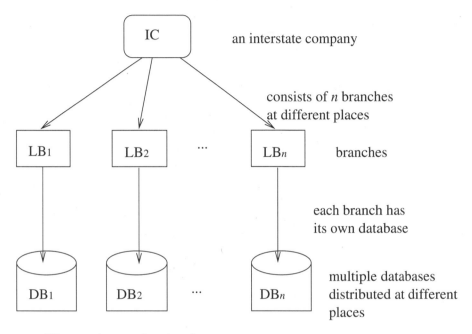

IC: an international or interstate company
LBi: the ith branch of a company
DBi: database of the ith branch

Fig. 1.1. An interstate company and its branches

In Figure 1.1, the top level is a head office (IC). This central company is responsible for the development and decision-making of the entire company. The middle level consists of n branches LB_1, LB_2, ..., LB_n. The lower level consists of n local databases DB_1, DB_2, ..., DB_n of the n branches.

Figure 1.1 illustrates the structure of a dual-level interstate company. In the real world, the structure of an interstate company is usually more complicated. It may consist of a central company and multiple branches. However, each branch may also have multi-level subbranches.

Many organizations have a pressing need to manipulate all the data in each of their branches rapidly and reliably. This need is very difficult to satisfy when the data are stored in many independent databases, and all the data are of importance to an organization. Formulating and implementing queries requires the consideration of data from more than one database. It requires knowledge of where all the data are stored, mastery of all the necessary interfaces, and the ability to correctly incorporate partial results from individual queries into a single result.

To satisfy these demands, researchers and practitioners have intensified efforts to develop appropriate techniques for utilizing and managing multiple database systems. Hence, developing multi-database systems has become an important research area within the database community.

The computing environment is becoming increasingly widespread through the use of the Internet and other computer communication networks. In this environment, it has become more critical to develop methods for building multi-database systems that can combine relevant data from many sources and present the data in a form that is comprehensible to users. It has also become important that tools be developed to facilitate the efficient growth and maintenance of information systems in a highly dynamic and distributed environment. One important technique within the environment is the development of multi-database systems. This includes managing and querying data from the collections of heterogeneous databases.

The increased use of multi-database technology has meant that a great many multi-database systems are now being developed for real-world applications. For example, the French Teletel system has 1500 separate databases (Hurson-BP 1994) and Woolworth Safeway Ltd. has a number of databases in branches distributed all over the world.

From the above observations, it is obvious that many large organizations have multi-level branches. While present multi-database technology can support many multi-database applications within these organizations, it must be possible in the mining of these multi-databases to enable efficient utilization of the data. Thus, the development of multi-database mining is both a challenging and critical task.

Some essential differences between mono- and multi-database mining are demonstrated shortly. We also show that traditional multi-database mining techniques are inadequate for dual-level applications within organizations such as interstate companies. Thus, solving multi-database mining problems will have a great impact on both private and public enterprises.

1.3 Multi-database Mining Problems

As explained earlier, an interstate company often consists of multi-level branches. For the purpose of this book, we define each interstate company as a dual-level organization (a head office with multiple branches), as depicted in Figure 1.1. Each branch has a database, and the database is a relation or a table.

In Figure 1.1 we demonstrate that there are fundamental differences between mono- and multi-database mining. For example, multi-database mining may be restricted by requirements imposed by decisions made on two levels: by the head office (global applications) or by branches (local applications). For global applications, and for corporate profitability, the head office is more interested in high-vote patterns that have the support of most of its branches, rather than the original raw data. In local applications, a branch manager needs to analyze the data to make local decisions.

Dual-level applications in an interstate company are depicted in Figure 1.2.

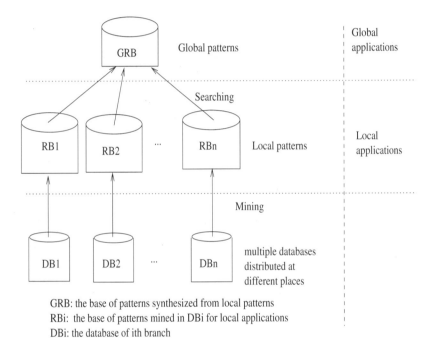

GRB: the base of patterns synthesized from local patterns
RBi: the base of patterns mined in DBi for local applications
DBi: the database of ith branch

Fig. 1.2. Two-level applications in an interstate company

In Figure 1.2, the lower level consists of n local databases DB_1, DB_2, ..., DB_n of n branches within an interstate company. The middle level consists of n sets RB_1, RB_2, ..., RB_n of local patterns discovered from databases DB_1, DB_2, ..., DB_n, respectively. These local patterns can be used for decision-making within branches (local applications). At the top level is a set of global patterns that are synthesized from the n sets RB_1, RB_2, ..., RB_n. These global patterns are used for an overall decision by the head office (global applications).

Traditional multi-database mining integrates all the data from these databases to amass a huge dataset for investigation by mono-database mining techniques. However, there are important challenges involved in applying this model to real-world applications. These include re-mining the data and loss of useful information.

Figure 1.2 illustrates where each database has been mined at each branch for use in local applications. Collecting all data together from different branches might produce a huge database, and lose some important patterns necessary for the purpose of centralized processing. However, forwarding the local patterns (rather than the original raw data) to the head office provides a feasible means of dealing with multiple database problems. The patterns forwarded from branches are called *local patterns*.

On the other hand, the number of forwarded patterns may be so large that browsing the pattern set and finding interesting patterns can be rather difficult for the head office. Therefore, it might be difficult to identify which of the patterns (including different and identical ones) are really useful at the top level.

1.4 Differences Between Mono- and Multi-database Mining

In the previous sections we have indicated that there are essential differences between mono- and multi-database mining. This section illustrates the differences between mono- and multi-database mining using the features of data and patterns in mono- and multi-databases.

1.4.1 Features of Data in Multi-databases

There are many ways to model a given real-world object (or relationships to other objects) in, for example, an interstate company, depending on how the model will be used (Hurson-BP 1994). Because local databases are developed independently, with differing local requirements, a multi-database system is likely to have many different models, or representations, for similar objects. Formally, a multi-database system is a federation of autonomous, and possibly heterogeneous, database systems used to support global applications and concurrent accesses to data stored in multiple databases (Hurson-BP 1994).

Data in a multi-database situation can have the following features:

(1) they may have different names in different branches;
(2) they may have different formats in different branches;

(3) they may have different structures in different branches;
(4) they may conflict, and even be impure in different branches;
(5) they is distributed in different branches;
(6) they could be shared by branches; and
(7) the same data might be used for two-level applications.

We now illustrate these features of data in multi-databases.

1. *Name differences.* Local databases may have different conventions for the naming of objects, leading to problems with synonyms and homonyms.

A synonym is when the same data item has a different name in different databases. The global system must recognize the semantic equivalence of the items, and map the different local names to a single global name. A homonym is when different data items have the same name in different databases. The global system must recognize the semantic difference between items and map the common names to different global names.

2. *Format differences.* Many analysis, or visualization, tools require that data be in particular formats within branches. Format differences include differences in data type, domain, scale, precision, and item combinations.

An example is when a part number is defined as an integer in one database and as an alphanumeric string in another. Sometimes data items are broken into separate components in one database, while the combination is recorded as a single quantity in another.

Multi-databases typically resolve format differences by defining transformation functions between local and global representations. Some functions may consist of simple numeric calculations such as converting square feet to acres. Others may require lookup tables or algorithmic transformations. A problem in this area is that the local-to-global transformation (required if updates are supported) may be very complex.

3. *Structural differences.* Depending on how an object is used by a database, it may be structured differently in different local databases.

A data item may have a single value in one database, and multiple values in another. An object may be represented as a single relation in one location or as multiple relations in another. The same item may be a data value in one location, an attribute in another, and a relation in a third. So the data often have discrepancies in structure and content that must be cleaned.

4. *Conflicting data.* Databases that model the same real-world object may have conflicts within the actual data values recorded.

One system may lack some information due to incomplete updates, system errors, or insufficient demand to maintain such data. A more serious problem arises when two databases record the same data item but assign it different values. The values may differ because of an error, or because of valid differences in the underlying semantics.

5. *Distributed data.* In most organizations, data are stored in various formats, in various storage media, and with various computers.

In this case, data might be created, retrieved, updated, and deleted using various access mechanisms.

6. *Data sharing.* A major advantage of multi-database systems is the means by which branch data and sources can be shared.

In an interstate company, each of its branches has individual functions, data, and sources. These branches can interact and share their data when they are confronted with problems beyond their individual capabilities.

7. *Data servers for both local and global applications.* All comprehensive organizations have dual-level decisions: head office (global applications) and branch decisions (local applications).

The above clearly demonstrates that data in multi-databases are very different from data in mono-databases.

1.4.2 Features of Patterns in Multi-databases

The branch managers of an interstate company need to consider original raw data in their databases to identify local patterns for local applications. However, the head office is generally interested in local patterns, rather than original raw data, for global applications. This is because the branches and the central headquarters serve at two different application levels. Patterns represent different granularities at each of these levels. At branch level, a local pattern is often uncertain. At head office level, the local pattern is taken as certain.

Generally, patterns in multi-databases can be divided into (1) local patterns, (2) high-vote patterns, (3) exceptional patterns, and (4) suggested patterns.

1. *Local patterns.* In many interstate companies, the branch managers need to consider original raw data in their databases so they can identify local patterns for local-level decisions.

Each branch of an interstate company has certain individual functions. The branch managers must design their own plans and policies for development and competition within their branches. They therefore need to analyze data only in their local databases to identify local patterns. Each branch can then share these patterns with other branches. More important, they can forward their local patterns to the head office of the company when global decisions need to be made.

2. *High-vote patterns.* These are patterns that are supported/voted for by most branches. They reflect common characteristics among branches, and are generally used to make global decisions.

When an interstate company makes a global decision, the head office is usually interested in local patterns rather than original raw data. Using local patterns, it can be ascertained what their branches are supporting. High-vote patterns are helpful in making decisions for the common good.

3. *Exceptional patterns.* These are patterns that are strongly supported (voted for) by only a few branches. They reflect the individuality of branches, and are generally used to create special policies specifically for those branches.

Although high-vote patterns are useful in reaching common decisions, head offices are also interested in viewing the exceptional patterns used for making special decisions at only a few of the branches. Exceptional patterns may also be useful in predicting (testing) the sale of new products.

4. *Suggested patterns.* These are patterns that have less votes than the minimal vote (written as *minvote*) but are very close to *minvote*.

Minimal votes are given by users or experts. If a local pattern has votes equal to, or greater than, *minvote*, the local pattern is said to be a global pattern, and is known as a high-vote pattern. Under the threshold *minvote*, there may be some local patterns that have less votes than *minvote* but are very close to it. We call these patterns "suggested patterns", and they are sometimes useful in making global decisions.

It is important to note that *local patterns also inherit the features of data in multi-databases.* In particular, there are some fundamental issues that make patterns in multi-databases different from those in mono-databases: (1) pattern trustworthiness and (2) pattern inconsistency. The first issue results from collected data, and the second is caused by negative association rule mining (Wu-Zhang-Zhang 2002).

The above differences in data and patterns in multi-database systems clearly demonstrate that multi-database mining differs from mono-database mining. This invites the exploration of efficient mining techniques for identifying novel patterns in multi-databases such that patterns can serve dual-level applications.

1.5 Evolution of Multi-database Mining

Data mining techniques, such as those described in (Agrawal-Imielinski-Swami 1993, Han-Pei-Yin 2000, Liu-Motoda 1998, Webb 2000), have been successfully used in many diverse applications. These include medical diagnosis, risk prediction, credit card fraud detection, computer security break-in and misuse detection, computer user identity verification, aluminum and steel smelting control, pollution control in power plants, and fraudulent income tax return detection. The techniques developed are oriented towards mono-databases.

Multi-database mining has been recently recognized as an important research topic in the data mining community. Yao and Liu have proposed a means of searching for interesting knowledge in multiple databases according to a user query (Yao-Liu 1997). The process involves selecting all interesting information from many databases by retrieval. In this case, mining only works on selected data.

Liu et al. have proposed another mining technique in which relevant databases are identified (Liu-Lu-Yao 1998]). Their work has focused on the first step in multi-database mining, which is the identification of databases that are most relevant to an application. A relevance measure was proposed to identify relevant databases for mining, with the objective of finding patterns, or regularities, within certain attributes. This can overcome the drawbacks that result from pooling all databases into a single, very large, database upon which existing data mining techniques or tools are applied. (For details, please see (Liu-Lu-Yao 1998, Yao-Liu 1997))

Zhong et al. have proposed a method of mining peculiarity rules from multiple statistical and transaction databases based on previous work (Zhong-Yao-Ohsuga 1999). A peculiarity rule is discovered from peculiar data by searching for relevance among such data. Roughly speaking, data are peculiar if they represent a peculiar case described by a relatively small number of objects, and are very different from other objects in a dataset. Although it appears to be similar to the exception rule from the viewpoint of describing a relatively small number of objects, the peculiarity rule represents a well-known fact with common sense, which is a feature of the general rule.

According to (Liu-Lu-Yao 1998, Yao-Liu 1997, Zhong-Yao-Ohsuga 1999), the process of multi-database mining can be depicted as shown in Figure 1.3.

Figure 1.3 illustrates the functions used in the process of multi-database mining. It is known as the traditional process of multi-database mining to distinguish it from the process described in this book. The area 'A' contains n sets of local databases in an interstate company. Here, 'localDBs' stands for a set of local databases, and 'databaseselection' is a procedure of application-dependent database classification that identifies databases most relevant to an application. The area 'B' contains all databases that are relevant to an application, and 'dataintegration' is a procedure that integrates all data in the relevant databases into a mono-dataset, known as a 'mono-dataset'. Meanwhile, 'mono-DBmining' is a procedure that uses mono-database mining techniques to discover the mono-dataset integration, and 'patternset' is a set of the patterns searched for in the mono-dataset integration.

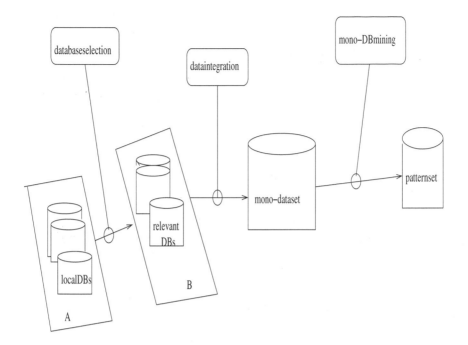

Fig. 1.3. The process of traditional multi-database mining

Other related research projects are now briefly reviewed. Wu and Zhang have advocated an approach for identifying patterns in multi-databases by weighting (Wu-Zhang 2003). Ribeiro et al. have described a way of extending the INLEN system for multi-database mining by incorporating primary and foreign keys, as well as developing and processing knowledge segments (Ribeiro-Kaufman-Kerschberg 1995). Wrobel has extended the concept of foreign keys to include foreign links, since multi-database mining also involves accessing non-key attributes (Wrobel 1997). Aronis et al. have introduced a system, WoRLD, that uses spreading activation to enable inductive learning from multiple tables in multiple databases spread across the network (Aronis et al. 1997). Kargupta et al. have built a collective mining technique for distributed data (Kargupta-HSPW 2000, Kargupta-HSJ 2001). Grossman et al. have established a system, known as Papyrus, for distributed data mining (Grossman-BRMT 2000, Turinsky-Grossman 2001). Existing parallel mining techniques can also be used to deal with multi-databases (Chattratichat et al. 1997, Cheung-Ng-Fu-Fu 1996, Prodromidis-Stolfo 1998, Prodromidis-Chan-Stolfo 2000, Shintani-Kitsuregawa 1998).

The above efforts provide a good insight into multi-database mining. However, they are inadequate for identifying two new kinds of patterns: high-vote patterns and exceptional patterns, which reflect the distributions of local patterns. These patterns are very useful in global applications. Other limitations of traditional multi-database mining are detailed in the next section.

1.6 Limitations of Previous Techniques

As explained previously, despite there being many methods of multi-database mining, most are still closely modeled on techniques for mono-database mining. This leads to (1) expensive search costs and (2) the loss of patterns. Further limitations are discussed below.

1. The input to traditional mining algorithms assumes that the data in multi-databases are nicely distributed, containing no missing, inconsistent, and incorrect values. This leads to (1) disguising useful patterns, (2) low performance, and (3) poor-quality outputs.

Existing data preparation is focused on a single dataset. Because there is an essential difference between multi- and mono-databases, it generates a significant need to prepare the data in multi-databases.

2. Database selection (Liu-Lu-Yao 1998) is an application-dependent technique that is inadequate in many applications. It needs to be carried out multiple times in order to identify relevant databases for two or more real-world applications. In particular, when users need to mine their multi-databases without reference to any specific application, application-dependent techniques are not efficient.

Indeed, identifying patterns in data is often application-independent. A running application is delayed if multi-databases are mined, due to the huge amounts of data being processed.

3. Putting all the data from relevant databases into a single database can destroy some important information that might reflect the distribution of patterns. These patterns might be more important than the patterns present in the single database for the purpose of global decision-making by a centralized company. Hence, existing techniques for multi-database mining are inadequate for many applications.

In some cases, each branch of an interstate company, large or small, has equal power within voting patterns that have an impact on global decisions. For global applications, it is natural for the head office to be interested in the patterns voted for by most of the branches or in exceptional patterns. It is therefore inadequate in multi-database mining to utilize existing techniques used for mono-database mining.

4. Collecting all data from multi-databases can amass a huge database for centralized processing using parallel mining techniques.

This is unnecessary as there are many techniques, such as sampling and parallel algorithms, for dealing with large databases.

A better approach is to first classify the multiple databases. The data from a class of databases can then be put into a single database for discovery, utilizing the existing techniques.

It may be an unrealistic proposition to collect data from different branches for centralized processing because of the huge volume of data. For example, different branches of Wal-Mart receive 20 million transactions a day. This is more than the rate at which data can be feasibly collected and analyzed using today's computing power.

5. Forwarding all rules mined in branches to a central company. The number of forwarded rules may be so large that browsing the rule set, and finding interesting rules from it, can be a difficult task. In particular, it is more difficult to identify which of the forwarded rules are genuinely useful to their applications.

One strategy may be to reuse all the promising rules discovered in branches, because the local databases have been mined for local applications. However, to reuse the local rules and select from them, a method must be developed to: (1) determine valid rules for the overall organization from the amassed database, and (2) reduce the size of the candidate rules from multi-databases. The following problems arise: (a) any rule from a database has the potential to contribute in the construction of a valid rule for the overall organization, and (b) the number of promising rules from multi-databases can be very large before it is determined which ones are of interest.

6. Because of data privacy, and related issues, it is possible that some databases of an organization may share their association rules but not their original databases.

Privacy is a very sensitive issue, and safeguarding its protection in a multi-database is of extreme importance. Most multi-database designers take privacy very seriously, and allow for some protection facility. For source sharing in real-world applications, sharing patterns is a feasible way of achieving this. This is because: (1) certain data, such as commercial data, are secret for competitive reasons; (2) reanalyzing data is costly; and (3) inexperienced decision-makers do not know how to confront huge amounts of data. The branches of an interstate company must search their databases for local applications. Hence, forwarding the patterns (rather than the original raw data) to centralized company headquarters presents a feasible way of dealing with multi-database problems.

Even though all the above limitations might not be applicable to some organizations, efficient techniques, such as sampling and parallel and distributed mining algorithms, are needed to deal with the amassed mono-databases. However, sampling models depend heavily upon the transactions of a given database being randomly appended to the database in order to hold the binomial distribution. Consequently, mining association rules upon paralleling (MARP), which employs hardware technology such as parallel machines to implement concurrent data mining algorithms, is a popular choice (Agrawal-Shafer 1996, Chattratichat et al. 1997, Cheung-Ng-Fu-Fu 1996, Park-Chen-Yu 1995, Parthasarathy-Zaki-Li 1998, Shintani-Kitsuregawa 1998). Existing MARP developments endeavor to scale up data mining algorithms by changing existing sequential techniques into parallel versions. These algorithms are effective and efficient, and have played an important role in mining very large databases. However, as well as the above five limitations, MARP has two other limitations when executing data mining with different data sources.

7. MARP does not make use of local rules at branches; nor does it generate these local rules. In real-world applications, these local rules are useful to the local data sources, and should be generated in the first instance.
8. Parallel data mining algorithms require greater computing resources (such as massive parallel machines) and additional software to distribute components of parallel algorithms among processors of parallel machines. And, most important, it is not always possible to apply MARP to existing data mining algorithms. Some data mining algorithms are sequential in nature, and cannot make use of parallel hardware.

From the above observations, it is clear that traditional multi-database mining is inadequate for dual-level applications. This prompts the need to develop new techniques for multi-database mining.

1.7 Process of Multi-database Mining

As previously explained, there are three factors that illustrate the importance of multi-database mining: (1) there are a great many multi-databases already serving organizations; (2) there are essential differences between mono- and multi-database mining; and (3) there are some limitations in existing multi-database mining techniques. For these reasons, a process of multi-database mining (MDM) (Zhang-Wu-Zhang 2003) is defined below. We also advocate the development of some new techniques.

1.7.1 Description of Multi-database Mining

There are various existing data mining algorithms that can be used to discover local patterns in local databases (Agrawal-Imielinski-Swami 1993, Webb 2000). These include the paralleling algorithms mentioned above (Prodromidis-Stolfo 1998, Shintani-Kitsuregawa 1998). The process of our multi-database mining (MDM) focuses on local pattern analysis described as follows.

Given n databases within, say, an interstate company, MDM is performed at several levels: (i) identifying quality data (see Chapters 4 and 6); (ii) searching for a good classification of the databases (see Chapter 5); (iii) identifying two kinds of new patterns, high-vote patterns and exceptional patterns, from local patterns (see Chapters 7 and 8); and (iv) synthesizing patterns in local patterns by weighting (see Chapter 9).

The major technical challenge in multi-database mining is how to adapt it to serve dual-level applications. However, the traditional process of multi-database mining shown in Figure 1.3 cannot serve dual-level applications. To meet dual-level requirements, our process of MDM is depicted in Figure 1.4.

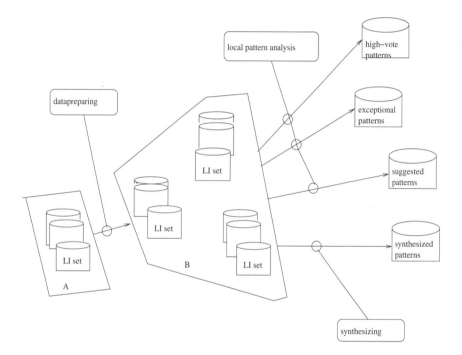

Fig. 1.4. The process of multi-database mining

In Figure 1.4, the area 'A' contains n sets of local instances of an interstate company, where 'LIset' stands for local instance set; and 'datapreparation' is a procedure of quality data preparation and application-independent database classification. After classifying the multi-databases, the local instance sets are divided into several groups in the area 'B'. For each group of local instances, we can use the procedure 'localinstanceanalysis' to search for patterns, such as high-vote patterns, exceptional patterns, and suggested patterns. The procedure 'synthesizing' can also be used to aggregate the patterns from the local instances in each group.

1.7.2 Practical Issues in the Process

In Figure 1.4, three specific procedures: 'datapreparation', 'localinstanceanalysis', and 'synthesis' are required, as well as other procedures, to unify names of items and remove noise. Although the problem of unifying names of items and removing noise must also be encountered by multi-database systems (Hurson-BP 1994), this process focuses only on issues raised from the three procedures in Figure 1.4. The functions of the procedures are now detailed.

1. Data preparation can be more time consuming, and can present more challenges, in multi-database mining. The importance of data preparation can be illustrated from several perspectives: (1) real-world data are impure; (2) high-performance mining systems require quality data; and (3) quality data yield concentrative patterns. Thus the development of data preparation technologies and methodologies is both a challenging and critical task.

There are several key problems in data preparation: (i) developing techniques for cleaning data; (ii) constructing a logical system for identifying quality knowledge; (iii) constructing a logical system for resolving knowledge conflicts; and (iv) designing application-independent database clustering.

(a) **Developing techniques for cleaning data**. Data cleaning techniques have been widely studied and applied in pattern recognition, machine learning, data mining, and Web intelligence. For multi-database mining, distributed data cleaning presents more challenges than does traditional data cleaning for single datasets. For example, data may conflict within multi-databases. This book adapts existing data cleaning techniques so as to generate quality data for multi-database mining, which mainly includes:

– Recovering incomplete data: filling the values missed, or expelling ambiguity;
– Purifying data: consistency of data name, consistency of data format, correcting errors, or removing outliers (unusual or exceptional values); and
– Resolving data conflicts: using domain knowledge or expert decision to settle discrepancy.

(b) **Constructing a logical system for identifying quality knowledge**. As we argued previously, sharing knowledge (rather than original raw data) presents a feasible way to deal with different data-source problems (Wu-Zhang 2003). Accordingly, we assume that a data-source is taken as a knowledge base. A company is viewed as a data-source, and a rule has two values in a data-source that are true (the data-source supports the rule) and false (otherwise). (Note: If a data-source contains only data, we can transform it into knowledge by existing mining techniques.)

However, external knowledge may be subject to noise. Thus, if a data-source (company) wants to form its own knowledge for data mining applications the data- source must have the ability to refine external knowledge (see Chapter 4).

(c) **Constructing a logical system for resolving knowledge conflicts** (see Chapter 6). Traditional (positive) association rules can only identify companionate correlations among items. It is desirable in decision-making to catch the mutually-exclusive correlations among items—referred to as negative associations. In a previous paper we presented a new method for identifying negative association rules in databases (Wu-Zhang-Zhang 2002). Negative association rules can increase the quality of decisions. However, in a multi-database environment, negative association rules cause knowledge conflicts within databases.

(d) **Designing application-independent database clustering** (see Chapter 5). To perform effective application-independent database classification our system deals with several key problems: (d1) how to construct measurements of relevant databases, (d2) how to construct measurements of good classifications, and (d3) how to design effective algorithms for application-independent database classification.

(d1) *Constructing measurements of relevance of databases.* There are many well-known techniques for data clustering, and data clustering techniques have been extended to classify text databases through query probing in information retrieval. For multi-database mining, a general-purpose database classification presents more challenges than both data clustering and text database classification. In that sense, existing clustering techniques are far from adequate when applied to multi-database mining. This book extends present techniques of database classification by designing new clustering strategies. For data clustering, the database classification problem can be described as follows.

Let $DS = \{D_1, D_2, ..., D_m\}$ be a set of m databases from the branches of an interstate company. A classification of DS into n clusters is presented by mutually disjoint sets $DS_1, DS_2, ..., DS_n$, such that $DS = DS_1 \cup DS_2 \cup \cdots \cup DS_n$ or, equivalently, by the classifiers $f_1, f_2, ..., f_n$, such that $f_i(D) = 1$, if D is in DS_i and $f_i(D) = 0$, if D is not in DS_i, for all $i = 1, 2, ..., n$. The set of classifier functions $\{f_1, f_2, ..., f_n\}$ is a hard n-classification of clustering DS into n clusters.

To generate application-independent database classifications in this system, we have presented a new clustering strategy based on two of our previous research results. The first is an effective technique for data partitioning developed in (Zhang 2001). Using this technique we can significantly reduce the overheads of indexing interesting features in databases.

The second is an effective technique for identifying quality data as developed in (Zhang-Zhang 2001b). This technique can determine the relationships between two datasets by pre- and post-analysis. Using pre- and post-analysis, we are able to measure the relevance of databases. The key problem to be solved in this new clustering strategy is how to construct appropriate classifiers $f_1, f_2, ..., f_n$ for DS.

(d2) *Constructing measurements of good classifications.* We may obtain many different classifications by changing classifiers $f_1, f_2, ..., f_n$ for DS. However, we need to know how many classes are appropriate for a set of databases in an application. For some special applications, we must consider their requirements on classifications so as to select an appropriate classification. For general-purpose mining, a good database classification should be determined by the structure and distribution of the data in multi-databases. Therefore, an evaluation metric must be designed for searching for good database classification.

In this system, we construct an assessor that is a set of evaluation functions, such as uncontradiction, idealization, and goodness, for measuring a database classification. One of the distinct features of our classification should be that it takes factors, such as uncontradiction, idealization, and goodness, into consideration. This strategy can greatly improve the work in (Zhang 2001).

(d3) *Designing effective algorithms for application-independent database classification.* To generate a good classification from given multiple databases, we have designed a two-step searching strategy in this system. The first step is to design a procedure for generating a database classification. For a set of databases, the procedure generates a database classification under a set of classifiers $f_1, f_2, ..., f_n$.

The second step is to develop an efficient algorithm to search for a good classification by a set of evaluation functions, such as uncontradiction, idealization, and goodness. In the algorithm, by changing classifiers $f_1, f_2, ..., f_n$, we can search for a good database classification supported by a set of evaluation functions.

2. Our system uses the following four approaches to hunt effective multi-database mining strategies for identifying new patterns.

As argued in the previous sections we develop four techniques to search for new patterns from local patterns. That is, (a) we design a local pattern analysis, (b) we identify high-vote patterns, (c) we find exceptional patterns, and (d) we synthesize patterns by weighting.

(a) *Designing a local pattern analysis.* Using traditional multi-database mining techniques, we can identify patterns, such as frequent itemsets, association patterns, and classification patterns, by analyzing all the data in a database cluster. However, these techniques are inadequate for finding some patterns: for example, if 80% of 15 supermarket branches reported the amounts of their sales increased 9% when bread and milk were frequently purchased. Therefore, analyzing local patterns is very important for mining novel and useful patterns in multi-databases.

However, for a large company, the number of local patterns may be so large that browsing the pattern set, and finding interesting patterns from it, can be a difficult task for a head office. In particular, it is harder to identify which local patterns are genuinely useful to their applications. Therefore, analyzing local patterns is also a difficult task.

In a multi-database environment, a pattern has attributes: for example, the name of the pattern, the vote rate of branches, and supports (and confidences for a rule) in branches that vote for the pattern. In other words, a pattern is a super-point of the form

$$P(name, vote, vsupp, vconf),$$

where *name* is the dimension of the name of the pattern; *vote* is the dimension of the vote rate of the pattern; *vsupp* is a vector that indicates the m dimensions of supports in m branches (the support dimensions), and *vconf* is a vector that indicates the m dimensions of confidence in m branches (the confidence dimensions).

In our MDM process, we have innovated the local pattern analysis strategy in (Zhang 2001) by using the techniques in (Zhang-Zhang 2001a). The key problem to be solved in this innovative strategy is how do we analyze the diverse projections of patterns in a multi-dimension space that consists of local patterns within a company?

(b) *Identifying high-vote patterns.* Within a company, each branch, large or small, has an equal power to vote for patterns that are used in global decision-making. Some patterns receive votes from most of the branches. These patterns are referred to as high-vote patterns. High-vote patterns represent the commonness of the branches. Therefore, these patterns may be paramount in terms of global decision-making within the company.

Because traditional mining techniques cannot identify high-vote patterns, these patterns are regarded as novel patterns in multi-databases. In this system, we have designed a mining strategy for identifying high-vote patterns of interest, based on a local pattern analysis. The key problem to be solved in this mining strategy is how to post-analyze high-vote patterns. Using our techniques in (Zhang 2001), we have proposed a new means of post-analyzing high-vote patterns so that they can be easily understood and applied.

(c) *Finding exceptional patterns.* Like high-vote patterns, exceptional patterns are also regarded as novel patterns in multi-databases. But an exceptional pattern receives votes from only a few branches. While high-vote patterns are useful when a company is reaching common decisions, headquarters are also interested in viewing exceptional patterns to be utilized when special decisions are made at only a few of the branches, perhaps for predicting the sales of a new product. Exceptional patterns can capture the individuality of branches. Therefore, these patterns are also very important.

Because exceptional patterns differ from high-vote patterns, in our MDM process we have also designed a new strategy for identifying exceptional patterns by analyzing local patterns.

(d) *Synthesizing patterns by weighting.* Although each branch has equal power to vote for patterns for decision making, branches may each be of different value to their company. For example, if sales of branch A are 4 times that of branch B, branch A is certainly more important than branch B to the company. Thus the decisions of the company would tend to lean towards branches with higher sales. Also, local patterns may have different supports in a branch. For example, let the supports of patterns X_1 and X_2 be 0.9 and 0.4 in a branch, respectively. Pattern X_1 is far more believable than pattern X_2. These two examples demonstrate the importance of branches and patterns for the decision-making of a company. Therefore, synthesizing patterns is very useful.

In our MDM process, we have developed a new strategy for synthesizing local patterns based on one of our previous research results. The research is an efficient model for synthesizing patterns from local patterns by weighting (Wu-Zhang 2003). Using this technique we can significantly improve the performance of multi-database mining systems.

3. To incorporate the proposed strategies to form an effective multi-database mining system, we have undertaken extensive experiments.

We have clustered the presented techniques above into a prototype system. The proposed approaches have also been evaluated and optimized by the actual databases of a chain of supermarkets.

1.8 Features of the Defined Process

The defined process of MDM has delivered a new method for building multi-database mining systems. The main features of this process are now described.

– New mining techniques and methodologies developed in our MDM process can significantly increase the ability of multi-database mining systems.

Previously, techniques in multi-database mining were developed to search for patterns using existing mono-database mining. Although data in multi-databases can be merged into a single dataset, such merging can lead to many problems, such as tremendous amounts of data, the destruction of data distributions, and the infiltration of uninteresting attributes. In particular, some concepts, such as regularity, causal relationships, and patterns cannot be discovered if we simply search a single dataset, since the knowledge is essentially hidden within the multi-databases (Zhong-Yao-Ohsuga 1999). It is a difficult task to effectively exploit the potential ability of mining systems and it is one of the key issues essential to designing an effective mining strategy.

Our multiple-data-source mining strategy aims to identify quality patterns (including high-vote patterns), exceptional patterns, and synthesizing patterns, based on local pattern analysis. Because previous techniques can only search patterns in multiple-data-sources the same as in single-databases, they cannot discover high-vote patterns, exceptional patterns, and synthesizing patterns in multiple data-sources. Therefore, these patterns are regarded as novel patterns. In particular, our data preparation techniques will deliver quality data and knowledge. This is especially useful for the making of quality decisions.

– The new mining techniques and methodologies developed in our MDM process can significantly improve the performance of multi-database mining systems.

As we argued previously, an interstate company must confront dual-level decisions: the company's decisions (global applications) and the branches' decisions (local applications). For global applications, the company headquarters must tackle huge amounts of data and local patterns. Therefore, the development of high-performance systems for mining multi-databases is very important.

In our MDM process we develop group pattern discovery systems for identifying potentially useful patterns from multiple data-sources based on local pattern analysis. As we have shown, previous techniques are inadequate for mining these patterns. Our local pattern analysis leads to greatly reduced search costs and much more useful information is generated. In particular, our work on data preparation significantly cuts down on the amount of data necessary for a multiple-data-source mining application. Further efficiency is accomplished by our pattern selection strategies.

– In our MDM process we have created several multi-database mining techniques and methodologies to deal with key problems that have not been satisfactorily solved before.

We deal with two problems concerning multi-database mining. The first problem is how to classify multi-databases. Database selection is an application-dependent technique that is inadequate in real-world applications (see (Liu-Lu-Yao 1998)). For example, database selection must be carried out multiple times in order to identify relevant databases for two or more real-world applications. In particular, when a mining task is without reference to any specific application, application-dependent techniques are not efficient. The second problem is how to effectively identify useful patterns. Existing multi-database mining strategies collect all the data from these databases to amass a huge database for discovery by the available mono-database mining techniques. This leads to not only an expensive search, but also the possible disguising of useful patterns.

For efficient multiple-data-source mining, the key problem is finding a way to identify quality patterns to support various kinds of applications. We have designed two new strategies to deal with this very difficult problem. First we design group data preparation systems to improve the quality of data and knowledge. Then we develop some group pattern discovery systems based on our existing local pattern analysis used to identify novel and useful patterns. The new strategies in our MDM process differ greatly from existing multiple-data-source mining strategies.

– In our MDM process we have created a multi-database mining system for general-purpose, high-performance, pattern discovery.

In this new strategy, we combine mining strategies to be developed for our MDM process with other acceptable strategies used in existing multi- and mono-database mining systems. Note that simply combining various mining strategies will not work because certain strategies may conflict. We have effectively incorporated good mining strategies to resolve any conflict issues, so as to make a significant breakthrough in the development of effective multi-database mining systems. This multi-database mining system aims at supporting general-purpose, high-performance, pattern discovery and dual-level applications for companies and organizations.

In addition, the defined process of MDM advocates the development of new techniques for multi-database mining.

– *Theoretical innovation.* In this process, new theories for such as application-independent database classification and local pattern analysis are proposed. These theories exhibit essential differences from those used in mono-database mining, as well as in traditional multi-database mining.

– *Requirements for applications.* With the growth of multi-database technology, a great many multi-database systems have been developed for real-world applications. Businesses, such as interstate companies, must often confront dual-level decisions: central company decisions (global applications) and branch decisions (local applications). Developing multi-database mining techniques is therefore critical.

– *Potential benefits.* As stated previously, when making overall decisions, new patterns that reflect the distribution of local patterns may be more important than the patterns discovered from a single database. Hence, identifying the two kinds of new patterns is an imperative issue. It delivers two direct benefits: greatly reduced search costs by the reusing of local patterns, and the availability of more useful information for global applications. Thus, high-vote patterns can be used to construct strategies for global development. Also, exceptional patterns can be used to construct strategies for the improved development of special branches and new products.

– *Novel patterns.* Previous techniques in multi-database mining have been developed to search for patterns using existing mono-database mining. They were found to be inadequate for discovering new patterns that reflected the distributions of local patterns. Therefore, high-vote and exceptional patterns are novel patterns that differ from the patterns previously searched for by multi-database mining.

- *Novel techniques.* Unlike traditional multi-database mining techniques that follow upon the techniques for mono-database mining, it is argued here that pattern discovery in global applications can also become a local pattern analysis. An new application-independent database classification algorithm is designed by similarity. Also, we propose the development of techniques for local pattern analysis by reusing. This is different from the previous techniques for multi-database mining which put all data from relevant databases into a single database for centralized discovery.

- *New challenges.* Local pattern analysis can be regarded as a new problem. A number of potential and diverse patterns within local patterns need to be satisfactorily extracted to support the decisions made by global applications. Therefore, local pattern analysis presents more challenges than does pattern analysis in a massed mono-database. Thus, this book advocates a change in approach to the problem of how to best analyze multi-databases. It also presents new mining techniques for appropriate applications.

1.9 Major Contributions of This Book

With the advance of multi-database system techniques, a great many multi-databases have been constructed. Consequently, multi-database mining is now a very important and significant topic in data mining. As mentioned in Sections 1.5 and 1.6, there have been many research efforts on multi-database mining. However, at present, all the data from multi-databases are assumed to be available for centralized examination with existing methods.

This book argues that, for central decision-making, pattern discovery in global applications must also involve the analyzing of local patterns.

There are diverse data mining algorithms that can be used to identify association rules in a mono-database. This book focuses on analyzing local patterns as a means of discovering new patterns in multi-databases. These work have an impact on both industry and academia. Our major contributions are:

1. We develop an efficient and effective application-independent database classification for mining multi-databases based on their similarity to each other (Chapter 3).
2. We advocate techniques for identifying high-vote patterns from local patterns. These are regarded as novel patterns. For example, high-vote patterns can reflect commonness in various branches of a company. To use these patterns efficiently, a high-vote pattern analysis is also presented (Chapter 4).

3. We design an algorithm for identifying exceptional patterns in local patterns also regarded as novel patterns. Exceptional patterns reflect the individuality of branches. This is useful when making special decisions for individual branches, for example, predicting the sales of a new product (Chapter 5).
4. We present an approach for synthesizing patterns from local patterns by weighting, rather than searching all data in a certain class of related databases. A rule selection is therefore established for an improved synthesizing model (Chapter 6).

Our proposed techniques are very different from traditional multi-database mining because we focus on local pattern analysis. Each approach has been implemented experimentally to evaluate the effectiveness and efficiency of these techniques, and the results show promise.

1.10 Organization of the Book

So far, we have discussed the importance of multi-database mining, and have advocated the need for the development of improved techniques in multi-database mining. The remainder of this book focuses on new techniques for use within the process of multi-database mining, based on the authors' recent research papers. The work is organized as follows.

In Chapter 2, we present some of the basic concepts of multi-database mining. We also briefly discuss previous research efforts.

In Chapter 3, we design a framework for local pattern analysis to deal with multi-database mining problems. Local instance, local pattern, global pattern, and local pattern analysis are formally defined in this chapter.

Chapters 4, 5, and 6 tackle issues of data preparation. In Chapter 4, a data-source (or dataset) is taken as a knowledge base. A framework is thus presented for identifying quality knowledge (Zhang-WZS 2003) obtained from different data-sources (multi-databases). Our logical system for identifying quality knowledge is focused on the following epistemic properties:

(*Veridicality*) Knowledge is true.
(*Introspection*) A data-source is aware of what it supports and of what it does not support.
(*Consistency*) The knowledge of a data-source is noncontradictory.

(Consistency is dealt with in Chapter 6.)

To reduce search costs, certain techniques for identifying relevant databases are developed. These techniques are typically application-dependent, and will be referred to as database selection . However, database selection has to be carried out multiple times to identify the databases relevant to two, or more, real-world applications. As we have said, when users need to mine their multi-databases without reference to any specific application, existing techniques are not effective. In Chapter 5, an application-independent database classification (Wu-Zhang-Zhang 2004) for mining multi-databases is presented based on the similarity of the databases.

In Chapter 6, a framework is presented to resolve conflict within multiple databases. Having recognized the importance of negative association rule mining, there are many reports on the subject. This generates a crucial challenge in mining multiple databases: negative association rules cause knowledge conflicts within databases.

Chapters 7, 8, and 9 deal with efficient algorithms for pattern discovery from multiple databases.

Forwarding mined association rules from branches to a central headquarters provides a feasible way of dealing with multi-database problems, as it avoids the volume of the original raw data. However, the rules forwarded may also be too numerous for dealing with by central headquarters. Chapter 7 presents techniques for searching for specific patterns, or high-vote patterns, from local patterns, to assist in the solving of this problem.

For the same reasons, Chapter 8 presents techniques for discovering *exceptional patterns*, from local patterns. As we described earlier, exceptional patterns are so called because they are strongly supported by only a few branches of a company. They reflect the individuality of the branches.

Mining association rules at branches and forwarding these rules (rather than the original raw data) to central company headquarters provides a feasible way to deal with multi-database mining problems. Meanwhile, the association rules at each branch may be required for that branch in the first instance, so association analysis within each branch is also important and useful. However, as mentioned above, the rules forwarded from branches may be too numerous for the central company headquarters to use. Chapter 9 presents a weighting model for synthesizing high-frequency association rules (Wu-Zhang 2003) from branches. There are certain reasons for focusing on high-frequency rules. First, they are of interest to a head office because they are supported by most branches. This can enhance corporate profitability. Second, high-frequency rules have a greater probability of becoming valid rules in the union of all data-sources. In order to extract high-frequency rules efficiently, a procedure of rule selection is also constructed to enhance the weighting model to deal with low-frequency rules.

In Chapter 10, we summarize the work carried out in this book.

2. Data Mining and Multi-database Mining

2.1 Introduction

This chapter provides an introduction to data mining, reviews existing research into multi-database mining, and describes some required concepts.

The pressure to enhance corporate profitability has caused companies to spend more time identifying diverse opportunities in areas such as sales and investment. To this end, huge amounts of data are collected in company databases for decision-support purposes. Also, amalgamations, new partnerships, and takeovers have resulted in the formation of particularly large companies, or organizations, that utilize increasingly larger multi-database systems. Government enterprises and academic research are also generating, and making use of, growing amounts of data.

The examples below should be sufficient to put the current situation into perspective.

- NASA's Earth Observing System (EOS), for orbiting satellites and other space-borne instruments, sends one terabyte of data to receiving stations each day.
- By the year 2000 a typical Fortune 500 company was projected to possess more than 400 trillion characters in their electronic databases, requiring 400 terabytes of mass storage.

With the increasing use of databases the need to be able to digest large volumes of data is now critical. Therefore, data mining techniques are being widely researched as new innovations become imperative.

As we have stated, this book presents new techniques for multi-database mining. By way of a preliminary discussion, this chapter briefly introduces data mining techniques, existing research into multi-database mining, and basic concepts.

We begin by summarizing the process of knowledge discovery. Then, in Section 2.3, we introduce some of the basic concepts, the knowledge of which is required for understanding this book. In Section 2.4, we outline past research into mono-database mining and, in Section 2.5, past research into multi-database mining. Finally we summarize the chapter.

2.2 Knowledge Discovery in Databases

Knowledge discovery in databases (KDD) (also referred to as data mining), is the extraction of hidden predictive information from large databases. It is a powerful new technology with great potential to help companies, for example, to focus on the most important information in their data warehouses. KDD tools predict future trends and behavior, allowing businesses to make proactive, knowledge-driven decisions. The automated prospective analyses offered by KDD move beyond the analysis of past events provided by retrospective tools typical of decision-support systems. KDD tools can answer business questions that were traditionally too time consuming to resolve. They scour databases for hidden patterns, finding predictive information that experts might miss because it lies outside their expectations.

Most companies already collect and refine massive quantities of data. KDD techniques can be implemented rapidly on existing software and hardware platforms to enhance the value of existing information resources, and can be integrated with new products and systems as they are brought online. When implemented on high performance client/server or parallel processing computers, KDD tools can analyze massive databases to deliver answers to questions such as: Which clients are most likely to respond to my next promotional mailing, and why?

A widely accepted definition of KDD is given by Fayyad et al. in which KDD is defined as the nontrivial process of identifying valid, novel, potentially useful, and ultimately understandable patterns in data (Fayyad-Piatetsky-Smyth 1996). The definition regards KDD as a complicated process comprising a number of steps. Data mining is one step in the process.

2.2.1 Processing Steps of KDD

In general, the process of knowledge discovery in databases consists of an iterative sequence of the following steps (Han-Huang-Cercone-Fu 1996, Han 1999, Liu-Motoda 1998, Wu 1995, Zhang 1989).

Defining the problem. The goals of the knowledge discovery project must be identified and must be verified as actionable. For example, if the goals are met, a business can then put newly discovered knowledge to use. The data to be used must also be identified.

Data preprocessing. This includes data collection, data cleaning, data integration, data selection, and data transformation.

- Data collection obtains necessary data from various internal and external sources; resolves representation and encoding differences; and joins data from various tables to create a homogeneous source.
- Data cleaning checks and resolves data conflicts, outliers (unusual or exception values), noisy, erroneous, missing data, and ambiguity; and uses conversions and combinations to generate new data fields, such

as ratios or rolled-up summaries. These steps require considerable effort, often as much as 70 percent, or more, of the total data mining effort.

- Data integration integrates multiple, heterogeneous data-sources into a single source.

- Data selection is where data relevant to the analysis task is retrieved from the database. In other words, it selects a dataset, or focuses on a subset of variables or data samples, on which discovery is to be performed.

- Data transformation is where data are transformed or consolidated into forms appropriate for mining, by performing summary, or aggregation, operations.

Data mining is an essential process where intelligent methods are applied in order to extract data patterns. It searches for patterns of interest in a particular representational form, or a set of such representations, including classification rules or trees, regression, clustering, sequence modeling, dependency, and so forth. The user can significantly aid the data mining method by correctly performing the preceding steps.

Post data mining includes pattern evaluation, deployment of the model, maintenance, and the presentation of knowledge.

- Pattern evaluation identifies the truly interesting patterns representing knowledge, based on certain *interesting measures*, tests the model for accuracy on an independent dataset — one that has not been used to create the model; assesses the sensitivity of a model, and pilot tests the model for usability. For example, if a model is used to predict customer response, then a prediction can be made and a test mailing done to a subset in order to check how closely the responses match predictions.

- Deployment of the model. A predictive model is used to predict results for new cases. The prediction is then used to improve organizational behavior. Deployment may require building computerized systems that capture the appropriate data and generate a prediction in real time so that a decision maker can apply the prediction. For example, a model can determine whether a credit card transaction is likely to be fraudulent.

- Maintenance. Whatever is being modeled, things are likely to change over time. The economy changes, competitors introduce new products, or the news media comes up with a new hot topic. Any of these forces can alter customer behavior. So the model that was correct yesterday and today might no longer be appropriate tomorrow. Maintaining models requires constant revalidation of the model using new data to assess whether it is still appropriate.

- The presentation of knowledge is where visualization and knowledge representation techniques are used to present mined knowledge to users.

The knowledge discovery process is iterative. For example, while cleaning and preparing data you might discover that data from a certain source are unusable, or that you require data from a previously unidentified source to be merged with other data. Often, the first time through, the data mining step will reveal that additional data cleaning is required.

2.2.2 Data Pre-processing

The ability to analyze and understand massive datasets lags far behind the ability to gather and store the data. Therefore, knowledge discovery and data mining are rapidly becoming an important field of research. No matter how powerful computers are now, or will be in the future, KDD researchers and practitioners must consider ways of efficiently managing the ever-growing data generated by the extensive use of computers and ease of data collection. Many different approaches have been introduced to address the data explosion issue. These include algorithm scale-up and data reduction (by data pre-processing). As a result, data pre-processing can be more time consuming, and can present more challenges than can data mining (Fayyad-Simoudis 1997).

Data collection is a very important step in knowledge discovery within databases. This step obtains necessary data from various internal and external data-sources that are relevant to a mining application. This can take advantage of the remarkable possibilities of access to information and knowledge that the Internet provides. Web technologies, such as HTTP and HTML, have dramatically changed enterprise information management. The vast amount of information available on the World Wide Web has great potential to improve the quality of decision-making (Lesser 1998, 2000). A corporation can benefit from intranets and the Internet to gather, manage, distribute, and share data, inside and outside the corporation.

Real-world data often have to be transformed in many ways for use in different situations. Also, the data can have discrepancies in structure and content that must be cleaned. In addition, many visualization tools, or tools for analysis, require the data to be in particular formats. Traditionally, such transformation has been done through ad hoc scripts, or through cookie-cutter transformation tools that require much laborious and errorprone programming. Moreover, the transformation process is typically decoupled from the analysis process. On large datasets, such transformation and analysis is quite timeconsuming. Users often need to perform many iterations of analysis and transformation, and have to endure many long, frustrating delays.

Data integration joins all relevant internal and external data to create a single homogeneous dataset. When internal and external data are joined into a single dataset for mining tasks all of the data play an equal role in data mining. However, because some collected data may be untrustworthy (even fraudulent), useful patterns can be disguised. If external data are not pre-processed before they are applied, patterns identified from the data can result in a high-risk application. For example, a stock investor might need to collect information from outside data-sources to make an investment decision. If the investor gathers fraudulent information, and the information is directly applied to investment decisions, he or she might lose money. Hence, it is very important to collect quality data.

Data often contain noise and erroneous components, and can have missing values. There is also the possibility that redundant or irrelevant variables have been recorded, while important features have been overlooked. Data cleaning includes provision for correcting inaccuracies, removing anomalies, eliminating duplicate records, filling holes in the data, and checking entries for consistency. Cleaning is required to make the necessary transformation of the original into a format suitable for use by data mining tools.

Another important requirement with the KDD process is feature selection (Liu-Motoda 1998, Wu 2000). KDD is a complicated task and often depends on the proper selection of features. Feature selection is the process whereby features are chosen that are necessary and sufficient to represent the data. There are several issues that influence feature selection. These include: masking variables, the number of variables employed in the analysis, and relevancy of variables.

Masking variables hides, or disguises, patterns in data. Numerous studies have shown that inclusion of irrelevant variables can hide real clustering of the data, so only those variables which help discriminate the clustering should be included in the analysis.

The number of variables used in data mining is also an important consideration. There is generally a tendency to use more and more variables. However, increased dimensionality has an adverse effect because, for a fixed number of data patterns, increased dimensionality makes the multi-dimensional data space sparse.

However, failing to include relevant variables also causes failure in identifying the clusters. A practical difficulty in mining some industrial data is knowing whether all important variables have been included in the data records.

2.2.3 Data Mining

Data mining has been popularly treated as a synonym of knowledge discovery in databases, although some researchers even view data mining as the kernel step of knowledge discovery. Data mining derives its name from similarities between searching for valuable business information in a large database and mining a mountain for a vein of valuable ore. Both processes require either sifting through an immense amount of material, or intelligently probing it to find exactly where the value resides.

> Strictly speaking, *data mining is the process of discovering interesting knowledge, such as patterns, associations, changes, anomalies and significant structures, from large amounts of data stored in databases, data warehouses, or other information repositories.* This valuable information can be in the form of patterns, associations, changes, anomalies, and significant structures (Fayyad-Piatetsky-Smyth 1996). In other words, data mining attempts to extract potentially useful knowledge from data.

Given databases of sufficient size and quality, data mining technology can generate new business opportunities as follows.

1. **Prediction of trends and behaviors**. Data mining seeks predictive information in large databases. Questions that traditionally required extensive hands-on analysis can now be quickly answered directly from the data. A typical example of a predictive problem is targeted marketing. Data mining uses data on past promotional mailings to identify the targets most likely to maximize return on investment in future mailings. Other predictive problems include forecasting bankruptcy and other forms of default, and identifying segments of a population likely to respond similarly to given events.

2. **Discovery of previously unknown patterns**. Data mining tools sweep through databases and, in one step, identify previously hidden patterns. An example of pattern discovery is the analysis of retail sales data to identify seemingly unrelated products that are often purchased together. Other pattern discovery problems include detecting fraudulent credit card transactions and identifying anomalous data that could represent data entry keying errors.

Data mining techniques can yield the benefits of automation on existing software and hardware platforms, and can be implemented on new systems as existing platforms are upgraded and new products developed. When data mining tools are implemented on high-performance parallel processing systems, they are able to analyze massive databases in minutes. Faster processing means that users can automatically experiment with more models to understand complex data. This makes it practical for users to analyze huge quantities of data. Larger databases, in turn, yield improved predictions. With the rapid advance in data capture, transmission, and storage, large-system users will increasingly need to implement new and innovative ways to mine the after-market value of their vast stores of detailed data, employing MPP (massive parallel processing) systems to create new sources of business advantage.

The most commonly used techniques in data mining are as follows.

Decision trees: Tree-shaped structures that represent sets of decisions. These decisions generate rules for the classification of a dataset. Specific decision tree methods include Classification and Regression Trees (CART) and Chi-Square Automatic Interaction Detection (CHAID).

Nearest neighbor method: A technique that classifies each record in a dataset based on a combination of the classes of k record(s) most similar to it in an historical dataset, sometimes known as the k-nearest neighbor technique.

Rule induction: The extraction of useful if-then rules from data, based on statistical significance.

Genetic algorithms: Optimization techniques that use processes such as genetic combination, mutation, and natural selection in a design based on the concepts of evolution.

Artificial neural networks: Nonlinear predictive models that learn through training, and resemble biological neural networks in structure.

Many of these technologies have been in use for more than a decade with specialized analysis tools that work with relatively small volumes of data. These capabilities are now evolving to integrate directly with industry-standard data warehouses and OLAP platforms.

One of the important topics in data mining is association rule mining. Since its introduction in 1993 (Agrawal-Imielinski-Swami 1993) the method of association rule mining has received a great deal of attention. It has been mainly developed to identify the relationships among itemsets that have high frequency and strong correlation. Association rules enable us to detect the items that often occur together in an application. This book illustrates proposed techniques for mining multi-databases, using association rules.

2.2.4 Post Data Mining

Post data mining is used to analyze, cluster, and maintain the patterns discovered from databases. Pattern analysis and clustering are helpful in improving efficiency when using patterns. Pattern maintenance is necessary to identify the changes of patterns in real-world applications.

However, even when patterns have been identified from a database, it does not mean that the mining process can be terminated. We must analyze and cluster the mined patterns so as to detail a way to use the patterns. On the other hand, the number of patterns discovered may be so large that browsing the pattern set and finding interesting patterns can be somewhat difficult for users. It can be hard to identify which of the patterns are really useful to applications. One of the tasks required in post data mining is to improve efficiency when using the patterns.

In many applications, the databases are dynamic, that is, transactions are continuously being added. There is much work that focuses on mining frequent itemsets in market basket datasets (e.g., (Agrawal-Imielinski-Swami

1993, Brin-Motwani-Silverstein 1997)). However, many items such as suits, toys and some foods, represent smart model in market basket data. For example, jeans and white shirt may have often been purchased at one time from a department store, and black trousers and blue T-shirt often purchased at another time. The department store may have made different decisions when buying according to such different purchasing models. This means that certain goods are very often purchased at one time according to market basket data, and they are solely purchased at another time. These items are called *fashionable goods*. Although most fashionable items may not be large itemsets in a market basket dataset, such itemsets are useful when making decisions on buying. Consequently, mining fashionable patterns is an important issue when mining market basket data. Indeed, since new data may represent a changing trend of customer buying patterns, we should intuitively have more confidence in the new data than in the old. Thus, novelty of data should be highlighted in mining models. However, although mining customer buying patterns based on the support-confidence framework can reflect the frequency of itemsets, it cannot catch the stylishness of data. Another task of post data mining is to maintain patterns and identify trend patterns.

2.2.5 Applications of KDD

KDD is potentially valuable in virtually any industrial and business sector where database and information technology are used. A wide range of companies has deployed successful applications of data mining. While early adopters of this technology have tended to be in information-intensive industries such as financial services and direct-mail marketing, the technology is applicable to any company looking to leverage a large data warehouse to better manage their customer relations. Two critical factors for success with data mining are: a large, well-integrated data warehouse and a well-defined understanding of the business process within which data mining is to be applied (such as customer prospecting, retention, campaign management, and so on).

Some successful application areas include the followings.

1. A pharmaceutical company can analyze its recent sales force activities and its results to improve its targeting of high-value physicians and to determine which marketing activities will have the greatest impact in the next few months. The data need to include competitor market activity as well as information about the local health-care systems. The results can be distributed to the sales force via a wide-area network that enables the representatives to review the recommendations from the perspective of the key attributes in the decision process. The ongoing dynamic analysis of the data warehouse allows best practices from throughout the organization to be applied in specific sales situations.

2. A credit card company can leverage its vast warehouse of customer transaction data to identify customers most likely to be interested in a new

credit product. Using a small test mailing, the attributes of customers with an affinity to the product can be identified. Recent projects have indicated more than a twenty-fold decrease in costs for targeted mailing campaigns over conventional approaches.

3. A diversified transportation company, with a large direct sales force, can apply data mining to identify the best prospects for its services. Using data mining to analyze its own customer experience, this company can build a unique segmentation identifying the attributes of high-value prospects. Applying this segmentation to a general business database, such as those provided by Dun and Bradstreet, can yield a prioritized list of prospects by region.

4. A large consumer package goods company can apply data mining to improve its sales process to retailers. Data from consumer panels, shipments, and competitor activity can be applied to understand the reasons for brand and store switching. Through this analysis, the manufacturer can select promotional strategies that best reach their target customer segments.

Each of these examples has a clear common ground. They leverage the knowledge about customers implicit in a data warehouse to reduce costs and improve the value of customer relations. These organizations can now focus their efforts on the most important (profitable) customers and prospects, and design targeted marketing strategies to best reach them.

One of the most popular and successful applications of database systems is in the area of marketing, where a great deal of information about customer behavior is collected. Marketers are interested in finding customer preferences so as to target them in future campaigns (Berry, 1994, Fayyad-Simoudis 1997).

There are various applications reported in recent data mining conferences and journals and in various journal special issues on data mining. The following are some applications reported in (Fayyad-Simoudis 1997, Piatetsky-Matheus 1992).

– The SKICAT (Sky Image Cataloging and Analysis Tool) system concerns an automation of reduction and analysis of the large astronomical dataset known as the Palomar Observatory Digital Sky Survey (POSS-II) (Fayyad-Piatetsky-Smyth 1996). The database is huge: three terabytes of images containing on the order of two billion sky objects. This research was initiated by George Djorgovski from the California Institute of Technology who realized that new techniques were required in order to analyze such huge amounts of data. He teamed up with Jet Propulsion Laboratory's Usama Fayyad and others. The result was SKICAT.

– Health-KEFIR (Key Findings Reporter) is a knowledge discovery system used in health care as an early warning system (Fayyad-Piatetsky-Smyth 1996). The system concentrates on ranking deviations according to measures of how interesting these events are to the user. It focuses on discovering and explaining key findings in large and dynamic databases. The system performs an automatic drill-down through data along multiple dimensions to determine the most interesting deviations of specific quantitative measures relative to their previous and expected values. The deviation technique is a powerful tool used in KEFIR to identify interesting patterns from the data. The deviations are then ranked, using some measure of interestingness, such as looking at the actions that can be taken in response to the relevant deviations. They might even generate recommendations for corresponding actions. KEFIR uses Netscape to present its findings in a hypertext report, using natural language and business graphics.

- TASA (Telecommunication Network Alarm Sequence Analyzer) was developed for predicting faults in a communication network (Fayyad-Piatetsky-Smyth 1996). A typical network generates hundreds of alarms per day. The TASA system generates rules like if a certain combination of alarms occurs within (...) time, then an alarm of another type will occur within (...) time. The time periods for the "if" part of the rules are selected by the user, who can rank or group the rules once they are generated by TASA.

- R-MINI system uses both deviation detection and classification techniques to extract useful information from noisy domains (Fayyad-Piatetsky-Smyth 1996). It uses logic to generate a minimal size rule set that is both complete and consistent.

- Knowledge Discovery Workbench (KDW) (Piatetsky-Matheus 1992) is a collection of methods used for interactive analysis of large business databases. It includes many different methods for clustering, classification, deviation detection, summarization, dependency analysis, and so forth. It is the user, however, who needs to guide the system in searches. Thus, if the user is knowledgeable in both the domain and the tools used, the KDW system can be domain independent and versatile.

- Experiment result analysis summarizes experiment results and predictive models.

- Clementine is a commercial software package for data mining (Integrated Solutions, Ltd.) (Fayyad-Piatetsky-Smyth 1996). Basically, it is a classifier system based on neural networks and inductive machine learning. It has been applied for the prediction of viewing audiences for the BBC, selection of retail outlets, anticipating toxic health hazards, modeling skin corrosivity, and so on.

2.3 Association Rule Mining

This section recalls some concepts required for association rule mining in this book.

Let $I = \{i_1, i_2, ..., i_m\}$ be a set of literals, or *items*. For example, goods such as milk, sugar, and bread for purchase in a store are items; and $A_i = v$ is an item, where v is a domain value of attribute A_i in a relation $R(A_1, ..., A_n)$.

X is an *itemset* if it is a subset of I. For example, a set of items for purchase from a store is an itemset; and a set of $A_i = v$ is an itemset for the relation $R(PID, A_1, A_2, ..., A_n)$, where PID is a key.

$D = \{t_i, t_{i+1}, ..., t_n\}$ is a set of transactions, called the *transaction database*, where each transaction t has a *tid* and a *t*-itemset: $t = (tid, t\text{-itemset})$. For example, the shopping cart of a customer going through checkout is a transaction; and a tuple $(v_1, ..., v_n)$ of the relation $R(A_1, ..., A_n)$ is a transaction.

A transaction t contains an itemset X if, and only if, (iff) for all items, $i \in X$, i is in *t*-itemset. For example, a shopping cart contains all items in X when going through checkout; and for each $A_i = v_i$ in X, v_i occurs at position i in the tuple $(v_1, ..., v_n)$.

An itemset X in a transaction database D has a *support*, denoted as $supp(X)$ (we also use $p(X)$ to stand for $supp(X)$), that is, the ratio of transactions in D contains X. Or

$$supp(X) = |X(t)|/|D|,$$

where $X(t) = \{t \text{ in } D | t \text{ contains } X\}$.

An itemset X in a transaction database D is called a large (frequent) itemset if its support is equal to, or greater than, a threshold of minimal support $(minsupp)$, which is given by users or experts.

An *association rule* is an implication $X \rightarrow Y$, where itemsets X and Y do not intersect.

Each association rule has two quality measurements: *support* and *confidence*, defined as

– the support of a rule $X \rightarrow Y$ is the support of $X \cup Y$, where $X \cup Y$ means both X and Y occur at the same time;
– the confidence of a rule $X \rightarrow Y$ is $conf(X \rightarrow Y)$ as the ratio $|(X \cup Y)(t)|/|X(t)|$ or $supp(X \cup Y)/supp(X)$.

That is, support = frequencies of occurring patterns; confidence = strength of implication.

The *support-confidence framework* (Agrawal-Imielinski-Swami 1993): Let I be the set of items in database D, $X, Y \subseteq I$ be itemsets, $X \cap Y = \emptyset$, $p(X) \neq 0$, and $p(Y) \neq 0$. Minimal support $(minsupp)$ and minimal confidence $(minconf)$ are given by users or experts. Then $X \rightarrow Y$ is a valid rule if

(1) $supp(X \cup Y) \geq minsupp,$
(2) $conf(X \rightarrow Y) = \frac{supp(X \cup Y)}{supp(X)} \geq minconf,$

where $conf(X \to Y)$ stands for the confidence of the rule $X \to Y$.

Mining association rules can be broken down into the subproblems:

(1)   generating all itemsets that have support greater than, or equal to, the user-specified minimum support; that is, generating all large itemsets;

(2)   generating all the rules that have minimum confidence in the following naive way: for every large itemset X, and any $B \subset X$, let $A = X - B$. If the confidence of a rule $A \to B$ is greater than, or equal to, the minimum confidence (or $supp(X)/supp(A) \geq minconf$), then it can be extracted as a valid rule.

To demonstrate the use of the support-confidence framework, we detail the process of mining association rules by an example as follows.

Let the item universe be $I = \{A, B, C, D, E\}$; and a transaction database be $TID = \{100, 200, 300, 400\}$. The data in the transactions are listed in Table 2.1.

Table 2.1 *Sample transaction database*

TID	Items				
100	A		C	D	
200		B	C		E
300	A	B	C		E
400		B			E

In Table 2.1, 100, 200, 300, 400 are the unique identifiers of the four transactions; and A = sugar, B = bread, C = coffee, D = milk, and E = cake.

Each row in Table 2.1 can be taken as a transaction. We can discover association rules from these transactions using the support-confidence framework. Let

$minsupp = 50\%$ (to be frequent, an itemset must be in at least two transactions);

$minconf = 60\%$ (to be a high-confidence (valid) rule, at least 60% of the time the antecedent is found in the transaction, the consequent must also be found there).

By the support-confidence framework, we present the two-step association rule mining as follows.

(1)   The first step is to count the frequencies of k-itemsets.

For Table 2.1, item $\{A\}$ occurs in two transactions $TID = 100$ and $TID = 300$, its frequency is 2, and its support $(supp(A))$ is 50%, which is equal to $minsupp = 50\%$; item $\{B\}$ occurs in three transactions $TID = 200$, $TID = 300$, and $TID = 400$, its frequency is 3, and its support $supp(B)$ is

75%, which is greater than *minsupp*; item $\{C\}$ occurs in three transactions $TID = 100$, $TID = 200$ and $TID = 300$, its frequency is 3, and its support $supp(C)$ is 75%, which is greater than *minsupp*; item $\{D\}$ occurs in one transaction $TID = 100$, its frequency is 1, and its support $supp(D)$ is 25%, which is less than *minsupp*; item $\{E\}$ occurs in three transactions $TID = 200$, $TID = 300$, and $TID = 400$, its frequency is 3, and its support $supp(E)$ is 75%, which is greater than *minsupp*. They are summarized in Table 2.2.

Table 2.2 *1-itemsets in the database*

Itemsets	Frequency	> minsupp
$\{A\}$	2	y
$\{B\}$	3	y
$\{C\}$	3	y
$\{D\}$	1	n
$\{E\}$	3	y

We now consider 2-itemsets. For Table 2.1, itemset $\{A, B\}$ occurs in one transaction $TID = 300$, its frequency is 1, and its support $supp(A \cup B)$ is 25%, which is less than $minsupp = 50\%$, where $A \cup B$ is used to stand for $\{A, B\}$ in formulas in this book; itemset $\{A, C\}$ occurs in two transactions $TID = 100$ and $TID = 300$, its frequency is 2, and its support $supp(A \cup C)$ is 50%, which is equal to $minsupp = 50\%$; itemset $\{A, D\}$ occurs in one transaction $TID = 100$, its frequency is 1, and its support $supp(A \cup D)$ is 25%, which is less than $minsupp = 50\%$; itemset $\{A, E\}$ occurs in one transaction $TID = 300$, its frequency is 1, and its support $supp(A \cup E)$ is 25%, which is less than $minsupp = 50\%$; itemset $\{B, C\}$ occurs in two transactions $TID = 200$ and $TID = 300$, its frequency is 2, and its support $supp(B \cup C)$ is 50%, which is equal to *minsupp*; and so on. This is summarized in Table 2.3.

Table 2.3 *2-itemsets in the database*

Itemsets	Frequency	> minsupp
$\{A, B\}$	1	n
$\{A, C\}$	2	y
$\{A, D\}$	1	n
$\{A, E\}$	1	n
$\{B, C\}$	2	y
$\{B, E\}$	3	y
$\{C, D\}$	1	n
$\{C, E\}$	2	y

Also, we can obtain 3-itemsets and 4-itemsets as listed in Table 2.4 and Table 2.5.

Table 2.4 *3-itemsets in the database*

Itemsets	Frequency	$>minsupp$
$\{A, B, C\}$	1	n
$\{A, B, E\}$	1	n
$\{A, C, D\}$	1	n
$\{A, C, E\}$	1	n
$\{B, C, E\}$	2	y

Table 2.5 *4-itemsets in the database*

Itemsets	Frequency	$>minsupp$
$\{A, B, C, E\}$	1	n

Here, 5-itemsets in the database is empty. According to the above definitions, $\{A\}$, $\{B\}$, $\{C\}$, $\{E\}$, $\{A, C\}$, $\{B, C\}$, $\{B, E\}$, $\{C, E\}$, and $\{B, C, E\}$ in the dataset are frequent itemsets.

(2)   The second step is to generate all association rules from the frequent itemsets.

Because there is no frequent itemset in Table 2.5, 4-itemsets do not contribute any valid association rule. In Table 2.4, there is one frequent itemset, $\{B, C, E\}$, with $supp(B \cup C \cup E) = 50\% = minsupp$. For frequent itemset $\{B, C, E\}$, because $supp(B \cup C \cup E)/supp(B \cup C) = 2/2 = 100\%$ is greater than $minconf = 60\%$, $B \cup C \rightarrow E$ can be extracted as a valid rule; because $supp(B \cup C \cup E)/supp(B \cup E) = 2/3 = 66.7\%$ is greater than $minconf$, $B \cup E \rightarrow C$ can be extracted as a valid rule; because $supp(B \cup C \cup E)/supp(C \cup E) = 2/2 = 100\%$ is greater than $minconf$, $C \cup E \rightarrow B$ can be extracted as a valid rule; and because $supp(B \cup C \cup E)/supp(B) = 2/3 = 66.7\%$ is greater than $minconf$, $B \rightarrow C \cup E$ can be extracted as a valid rule; and so on. The generated association rules from $\{B, C, E\}$ are in Tables 2.6 and 2.7.

Table 2.6 *For frequent 3-itemsets, start with 1-item consequences*

RuleNo	Rule	Confidence	support	$>minconf$
Rule1	$B \cup C \rightarrow E$	100%	50%	y
Rule2	$B \cup E \rightarrow C$	66.7%	50%	y
Rule3	$C \cup E \rightarrow B$	100%	50%	y

Table 2.7 *Form all 2-item consequences from high-conf 1-item consequences*

RuleNo	Rule	Confidence	support	$>minconf$
Rule4	$B \rightarrow C \cup E$	66.7%	50%	y
Rule5	$C \rightarrow B \cup E$	66.7%	50%	y
Rule6	$E \rightarrow B \cup C$	66.7%	50%	y

Also, we can generate all association rules from frequent 2-itemsets as shown in Table 2.3. They are illustrated in Tables 2.8 through 2.11.

Table 2.8 *For 2-itemsets, start with 1-item consequences for $\{A, C\}$*

RuleNo	Rule	Confidence	support	$> minconf$
Rule7	$A \rightarrow C$	100%	50%	y
Rule8	$C \rightarrow A$	66.7%	50%	y

Table 2.9 *For 2-itemsets, start with 1-item consequences for $\{B, C\}$*

RuleNo	Rule	Confidence	support	$> minconf$
Rule9	$B \rightarrow C$	66.7%	50%	y
Rule10	$C \rightarrow B$	66.7%	50%	y

Table 2.10 *For 2-itemsets, start with 1-item consequences for $\{B, E\}$*

RuleNo	Rule	Confidence	support	$> minconf$
Rule11	$B \rightarrow E$	100%	75%	y
Rule12	$E \rightarrow B$	100%	75%	y

Table 2.11 *For 2-itemsets, start with 1-item consequences for $\{C, E\}$*

RuleNo	Rule	Confidence	support	$> minconf$
Rule13	$C \rightarrow E$	66.7%	50%	y
Rule14	$E \rightarrow C$	66.7%	50%	y

According to the above definitions, the 14 association rules listed in the above data set can be extracted as valid rules.

2.4 Research into Mining Mono-databases

Association rule mining is one of the most prevailing research topics in mono-database mining. We now briefly introduce some well-known research into mining association rules.

1. The support-confidence framework measures the uncertainty of an association rule with two factors: support and confidence.

However, this measure is inadequate for modeling some uncertainties of association rules. For instance, the measurement does not provide a test to capture the correlation of two itemsets, and some of the association rules mined are not of interest. In order to improve this framework, some measures on the support and confidence of association rules, such as the chi-squared test model (Brin-Motwani-Silverstein 1997) and the collective-strength-based measure (Aggarawal-Yu 1998), have recently been proposed. These different measurements on support and confidence lead to different models for mining association rules. Hence, the measuring of uncertainty of association rules has recently become one of the crucial problems in mining association rules.

In fact, measurement of the uncertainty of an event is a well-known topic. Mathematical probability theory and statistics offer many mature techniques for measuring uncertainty. Thus, there are a great many measuring models that can be applied to estimate the uncertain factors (*supp* and *conf*) of an association rule. Below, we briefly recall some of the familiar methods for measuring association rules, which are relevant to the work in this book.

2. Piatetsky-Shapiro (Piatetsky 1991) argued that a rule $X \rightarrow Y$ is not interesting if

$$support(X \rightarrow Y) \approx support(X) \times support(Y)$$

where $support(X \rightarrow Y) = support(X \cup Y)$.

According to probability interpretation, $support(X \cup Y) = p(X \cup Y)$ and $confidence(X \rightarrow Y) = p(Y|X) = p(X \cup Y)/p(X)$. Then Piatetsky-Shapiro's argument can be denoted as

$$p(X \cup Y) \approx p(X)p(Y).$$

This means that $X \rightarrow Y$ cannot be extracted as a rule if $p(X \cup Y) \approx p(X)p(Y)$. In fact, in probability theory, $p(X \cup Y) \approx p(X)p(Y)$ denotes X is approximately independent of Y.

3. A statistical definition of (Brin-Motwani-Silverstein 1997) for the dependence of the sets X and Y is

$$Interest(X,Y) = \frac{p(X \cup Y)}{p(X)p(Y)},$$

with the obvious extension to more than two sets. This formula, which we refer to as the *interest* of Y, given X, is one of the main measurements of uncertainty for association rules. Certainly, the further the value is from 1, the more the dependence. Or, for $1 > mininterest > 0$, if $|\frac{p(X \cup Y)}{p(X)p(Y)} - 1| \geq mininterest$, then $X \rightarrow Y$ is a rule of interest.

By Piatetsky-Shapiro's argument, we can divide $Interest(X,Y)$ into several cases as follows:

(1) if $p(X \cup Y)/(p(X)p(Y)) = 1$, or $p(X \cup Y) = p(X)p(Y)$, then Y and X are independent;
(2) if $p(X \cup Y)/(p(X)p(Y)) > 1$, or $p(X \cup Y) > p(X)p(Y)$, then Y is positively dependent on X;
(3) if $p(X \cup Y)/(p(X)p(Y)) < 1$, or $p(X \cup Y) < p(X)p(Y)$, then Y is negatively dependent on X, or $\neg Y$ is positively dependent on X.

In this way, we can define another form of interpretation of rules of interest as follows. For $1 > mininterest > 0$, (a) if

$$\frac{p(X \cup Y)}{p(X)p(Y)} - 1 \geq mininterest$$

then $X \Rightarrow Y$ is a rule of interest; and (b) if

$$-(\frac{p(X \cup Y)}{p(X)p(Y)} - 1) \geq mininterest$$

then $X \to \neg Y$ is a rule of interest, where $\neg Y$ is the logical "not" of Y, or Y is not contained for transactions in a database.

This leads to two new definitions of association rules of interest as follows.

Definition 2.1 (*Piatetsky-Shapiro's argument*) *Let I be the set of items in database TD, $X, Y \subseteq I$ be itemsets, $X \cap Y = \emptyset$, $p(X) \neq 0$, and $p(Y) \neq 0$. $minsupp, minconf,$ and $mininterest > 0$ are given by users or experts. Then, $X \to Y$ can be extracted as a valid rule of interest if*

(1) $p(X \cup Y) \geq minsupp$,
(2) $p(Y|X) \geq minconf$, and
(3) $|p(X \cup Y) - p(X)p(Y)| \geq mininterest$.

Definition 2.2 (*Brin, Motwani, and Silverstein's argument*) *Let I be the set of items in database D, $X, Y \subseteq I$ be itemsets, $X \cap Y = \emptyset$, $p(X) \neq 0$, and $p(Y) \neq 0$. The thresholds minimum support ($minsupp$), minimum confidence ($minconf$), and minimum interest ($mininterest > 0$) are given by users or experts. Then, $X \to Y$ can be extracted as a valid rule of interest if*

(1) $p(X \cup Y) \geq minsupp$,
(2) $p(Y|X) \geq minconf$, and
(3) $|\frac{p(X \cup Y)}{p(X)p(Y)} - 1| \geq mininterest$.

Here, condition (3) ensures that $X \to Y$ is a rule of interest.

According to the above framework, we can take

(1) $X \cap Y = \emptyset$;
(2) $p(X \cup Y) \geq minsupp$;
(3) $p(Y|X) \geq minconf$ (e.g., $conf(X \to Y) \geq minconf$); and
(4) $|\frac{p(X \cup Y)}{p(X)p(Y)} - 1| \geq mininterest$

as the *conditions* under which association rule $X \to Y$ can be extracted as a valid rule of interest in this book, where the thresholds *minimum support* ($minsupp$), *minimum confidence* ($minconf$), and *minimum interest* ($mininterest > 0$) are given by users or experts.

4. The J-measure is as

$$J(X;Y) = p(Y)[p(X|Y)\log(\frac{p(X|Y)}{p(X)}) + (1 - p(X|Y))\log(\frac{1 - p(X|Y)}{1 - p(X)})]$$

for a rule $X \to Y$, where the term inside the square brackets is the relative (or cross) entropy. (Relative entropy is the similarity, or goodness of fit, of two probability distributions.)

The J-measure is the average information content of a probabilistic classification rule (Smyth-Goodman 1991). It is used to find the best rules relating to discrete attributes. A probabilistic classification rule is a logical implication $X \to Y$ with some probability p, where the left- and right-hand sides correspond to a single attribute. The right-hand side is restricted to simple, single-valued, assignment expressions, while the left-hand side may be a conjunction of these simple expressions.

High values for $J(X;Y)$ are desirable, but are not necessarily associated with the best rule. For example, rare conditions may be associated with the highest values for $J(X;Y)$ (i.e., where a particular Y is highly unlikely), but the resulting rule is insufficiently general to provide any new information. Consequently, analysis may be required in which the accuracy of a rule is traded for some level of generality or goodness-of-fit.

5. The distance metric between two rules R_1 and R_2 is defined in (Dong-Li 1998) as

$$D(R_1, R_2) = \delta_1 \times |(X_1 \cup Y_1)\Theta(X_2 \cup Y_2)| + \delta_2 \times |X_1\Theta X_2| + \delta_3 \times |Y_1\Theta Y_2|,$$

where $R_1 = X_1 \to Y_1$, $R_2 = X_2 \to Y_2$, δ_1, δ_2, and δ_3 are parameters to weight the relative importance of all three terms, and Θ is an operator denoting the symmetric difference between X and Y (i.e., $(X - Y) \cup (Y - X)$).

Dong and Li's interestingness is used to evaluate the importance of an association rule by considering its unexpectedness in terms of other association rules in its neighborhood. The *neighborhood* of an association rule consists of all association rules within a given distance. An r-neighborhood of a rule is given by the set

$$N(R_0, r) = \{R|D(R, R_0) \leq r, R \text{ is a potential rule}\}.$$

The set is used to define the interestingness of a rule. Two types of interestingness are unexpected confidence and isolation. *Unexpected confidence interestingness* is defined as

$$UCI = \begin{cases} 1, & \text{if } ||c(R_0) - ac(R_0, r)| - sc(R_0, r)|, \\ 0, & \text{otherwise,} \end{cases}$$

where $c(R_0)$ is the confidence of R_0, $ac(R_0, r)$ are the average confidence and standard deviation of the rules in the set $M \cap N(R_0, r) - \{R_0\}$ (M being the set of rules satisfying the minimum support and confidence), and t_1 is a threshold. *Isolated interestingness* is defined as

$$II = \begin{cases} 1, & \text{if } ||N(R_0, r)| - |M \cap N(R_0, r)| > t_2, \\ \\ 0, & \text{otherwise,} \end{cases}$$

where $|N(R_0, r)|$ is the number of potential rules in an r-neighborhood, $|M \cap N(R_0, r)|$ is the number of rules generated from the neighborhood, and t_2 is a threshold.

6. The ratio $\frac{p(Y|X) - p(Y)}{1 - p(Y)}$ of the conditional probability and the priori probability to describe the increased degree of $p(Y|X)$ relative to $p(Y)$, referred to as the *CPIR* model, is defined in (Wu-Zhang-Zhang 2002) as

$$CPIR(Y|X) = \frac{supp(X \cup Y) - supp(X)supp(Y)}{supp(X)(1 - supp(Y))}.$$

CPIR is taken as a metric for the confidence measure *conf* of the rule $X \Rightarrow Y$ in the following discussion. Here, $supp(X \cup Y) \geq supp(X)supp(Y)$ and $supp(X)(1 - supp(Y)) \neq 0$, where $supp(Y|X) = p(Y|X)$ in the model is replaced with $supp(X \cup Y)/supp(X)$ for the convenience of mining association rules.

While positive association rules that enable us to detect the *companionate* correlations among items are useful in decision-making, it is also desirable in applications to capture the *mutually exclusive* correlations among items. These mutually exclusive correlations are referred to as *negative association rules*, and are hidden in infrequent itemsets. The development of negative association rule mining will mean that companies will gain more business opportunities through using infrequent itemsets of interest than will those that only take into account frequent itemsets.

The interestingness in (Wu-Zhang-Zhang 2002) is used for identifying both positive and negative association rules in databases. This method extends traditional associations to include association rules of the forms $A \Rightarrow \neg B$, $\neg A \Rightarrow B$, and $\neg A \Rightarrow \neg B$, which indicate negative associations between itemsets.

With the increasing use and development of data mining techniques and tools, much work has recently focused on finding alternative patterns, including unexpected patterns (Padmanabhan 1998, 2000), exceptional patterns (Hussain 2000, Hwang 1999, Liu 1999, Suzuki 1996, 1997), and strong negative associations (Savasere 1998).

Unexpected patterns and exceptional patterns are referred to as *exceptions of rules*, also known as *surprising patterns*. An exception, which is defined as a deviational pattern to a well-known fact, exhibits unexpectedness.

For example, while $bird(x) \Rightarrow flies(x)$ is a well-known fact, mining exceptional rules is used to find patterns such as $bird(x), penguin(x) \Rightarrow \neg flies(x)$. This means unexpected patterns and exceptional patterns are default rules as well as not being negative rules.

A strong negative association is referred to as a *negative relation* between two itemsets. This negative relation really implies a negative rule between the two itemsets. However, strong negative association only reveals the existence in a hidden representation. For example, $X \nRightarrow Y$ is a strong negative association. Obviously, this rule cannot be used in an automated reasoning system.

Unlike existing mining techniques, the interestingness in (Wu-Zhang-Zhang 2002) extends traditional associations to include association rules of forms $A \Rightarrow \neg B$, $\neg A \Rightarrow B$, and $\neg A \Rightarrow \neg B$, which indicate negative associations between itemsets. We call rules of the form $A \Rightarrow B$ *positive rules*, and rules of the other forms *negative rules*. This work differs from existing work in association analysis in two aspects. Infrequent itemsets in databases are of interest to us for mining negative association rules. The following constraints have been defined for identifying interesting negative rules of the form $A \Rightarrow \neg B$.

(1) $A \cap B = \emptyset$;
(2) $supp(A) \geq minsupp$, $supp(B) \geq minsupp$, and $supp(A \cup \neg B) \geq minsupp$;
(3) $supp(A \cup \neg B) - supp(A)supp(\neg B) \geq mininterest$;
(4) $supp(A \cup \neg B)/supp(A) \geq minconf$.

Also, to design an efficient model for mining both positive and negative association rules, the $CPIR$ model was designed to estimate the confidence of association rules. This uses the increasing degree of the rule's conditional probability relative to its priori probability.

7. An anytime framework for mining very large databases shared by multi-users has been designed by (Zhang-Zhang 2002b). It generates approximate results that can be accessed at any time while the system is autonomously mining a database.

Mining *approximate frequent itemsets* from the sample of a large database can reduce computation costs significantly. For example, we can select a sample from a large database for estimating the support of candidates using Chernoff bounds (Srikant-Agrawal 1997, Toivonen 1996). This technique is effective for *mono-user applications*, where mono-user applications are those that can work well under a unique precision on frequent itemsets. However, *multi-user applications* require different precisions.

In real-world applications, a database is developed to be shared by multi-users. Therefore, data mining must be developed to serve multi-user applications. For a very large database, multi-users might demand different precisions on results for different applications. For example, a short-term stock investor might demand approximate frequent itemsets quickly from a shared stock database for high-profits as time may mean money. A long-term stock investor is more likely to wait for more accurate results.

Using traditional instance-selection (sampling) techniques, one must re-sample a database multiple times, and mine the selected instance sets for different precisions when the database is very large. For example, consider a very large database TD, shared by five users. For the time/performance tradeoff, the five users require 0.85, 0.90, 0.92, 0.95, and 0.98 precisions when estimating frequent itemsets. Existing instance selection based approaches are efficient for meeting the requirements of a user when identifying approximate frequent itemsets by sampling (Liu 2001-Motoda, Srikant-Agrawal 1997, Toivonen 1996, Zhang-Zhang 2001c). However, for the five different precisions, we need to select five instance sets, and mine them.

Zhang and Zhang's anytime mining framework can support inquiries from multiple users at any time. In this way, users can make tradeoff decisions when they choose, depending upon the required accuracy of results. Our approach is different from traditional mining techniques because it aims at attacking the multi-user application problem.

As there are a great many large databases shared by multi-users, the mining of large databases for serving multi-user applications is a new and pressing topic in data mining research. Because of the essential differences between mining tasks for multi- and mono-user applications, research into the multi-user application problem will have an impact on both industry and academia.

8. Han et al. have proposed a novel frequent pattern mining model, based on the frequent pattern tree (FP-tree) (Han-Pei-Yin 2000).

An FP-tree is a tree structure as defined below.

It consists of one root labeled *null*, a set of item prefix subtrees, which are the children of the root, and a frequent-item header table.

Each node in the item prefix subtree consists of three fields: item-name, count and node-link, where item-name registers which item the particular node represents, count registers the number of transactions represented by the portion of the path reaching the node, and node-link links to the next node in the FP-tree which carries the same item-name; or it is null if there are none.

Each entry in the frequent-item header table consists of two fields, item-name and head of node-link, which points to the first node in the FP-tree carrying the item-name.

The process of the FP-tree-based model is as follows.

First, an FP-tree is constructed, which is an extended prefix-tree structure storing crucial quantitative information about frequent patterns. Only frequent length-1 items will have nodes in the tree, and the tree nodes are arranged in such a way that more frequently occurring nodes will have a better chance of sharing nodes than less frequently occurring ones.

Second, an FP-tree-based pattern fragment growth mining method is developed, which starts from a frequent length-1 pattern (as an initial suffix pattern), and examines only its conditional pattern base (a subdatabase which consists of the set of frequent items co-occurring with the suffix pattern). It then constructs its (conditional) FP-tree, and performs mining recursively with such a tree. The pattern growth is achieved via concatenation of the suffix pattern with the new patterns generated from a conditional FP-tree. Since a frequent itemset in any transaction is always encoded in the corresponding path of the frequent pattern trees, pattern growth ensures the completeness of the result. In this context, the method is not an *Apriori*-like restricted generation-and-test, but a restricted test only. The major operations of mining are count accumulation and prefix path count adjustment, which are usually much less costly than the candidate generation and pattern-matching operations performed in most *Apriori*-like algorithms.

Third, the search technique employed in mining is a partitioning-based, divide-and-conquer method, rather than the *Apriori*-like bottom-up generation of frequent itemset combinations. This dramatically reduces the size of the conditional pattern base generated at the subsequent level of search, as well as the size of its corresponding conditional FP-tree. Moreover, it transforms the problem of finding long frequent patterns into looking for shorter ones, and then concatenating the suffix. It employs the least frequent items as the suffix, which offers good selectivity. All these techniques contribute to a substantial reduction in search costs.

9. Zhang and Zhang have proposed a method for identifying causality between variables X and Y, represented in the form $X \to Y$ with conditional probability matrix $M_{Y|X}$ (Zhang-Zhang 2002e).

While there has been much work done on discovering item-based association rules and quantitative association rules, some work has focused on mining causal rules in databases (Cooper 1997, Heckerman 1995, Silverstein 1998). Mining models for causality, such as the LCD algorithm (Cooper 1997) and the CU-path algorithm (Silverstein 1998), which are used for constraint-based causal discovery, have been proposed for mining causal relationships in market basket data. In fact, the CU-path algorithm is an improved model of the LCD algorithm, which applies the chi-squared formula to test the dependence, independence, and conditional independence between variables so as to discover the possible causal relationships between those variables.

However, these models are only suitable for mining causal rules among simple variables, such as "*states* → *united*" for words in the *clari.world* news hierarchy (Silverstein 1998). They are inadequate for discovering causal rules among multi-value variables in large databases, and for representing them. In fact, mining causality among multi-value variables in many applications, such as decision-making, diagnosis, and planning, is useful for solving application problems.

Another distinct difference with Zhang and Zhang's model is that it offers a method for optimizing conditional probability matrices for causal rules, which merges unnecessary information for the extracted causal rules. Obviously, this model can be used to optimize the knowledge in intelligent systems.

10. Webb has presented an alternative approach to a direct search for association rules for some applications (Webb 2000). This method applies the OPUS search to prune the search space on the basis of interrelationships between itemsets.

In Webb's model, association rule mining is tackled as a search process that starts with general rules (rules with one condition on the left-hand side (LHS)) and searches through successive specializations (rules formed by adding additional conditions to the LHS). Such a search is unordered. That is, the order in which successive specializations are added to an LHS is not significant, and $A \wedge B \wedge C \to X$ is the same as $C \wedge B \wedge A \to X$. An important component of an efficient search in this context is minimizing the number of association rules that need to be considered. A key technique used to eliminate potential association rules from consideration is "optimistic pruning".

Optimistic pruning operates by forming an optimistic evaluation of the highest rule value that might occur in a region of the search space. An optimistic evaluation is one that cannot be lower than the actual maximum value. If the optimistic value for the region is lower than the lowest value that is of interest, then that region can be pruned. If a search seeks the top m association rules, then it can maintain a list of the top m rules encountered at that point during the search. If an optimistic evaluation is lower than the lowest value of a rule in the top m, then the corresponding region of the search space may be pruned. Other pruning rules could perhaps identify regions that could be pruned if they contained only rules that failed to meet pre-specified constraints such as:

- minimum support (the frequency in the data of the right-hand side (RHS) or of the RHS and LHS in combination);
- minimum *lift*; or
- being one of the top m association rules on some specified criterion.

Here, $lift$ is a frequently utilized measure of association rule utility. The lift of an association rule $= \frac{|LHS \wedge RHS|}{|LHS|} / \frac{|RHS|}{n}$, where $|X|$ is the number of cases with conditions X, and n is the total number of cases in the dataset.

The term *credible rule* is used to denote association rules for which, at some given point in a search, it is possible that the rule will be of interest, using whatever criterion of interest applies for the given search.

If we restrict association rules to having a single condition on the RHS, these search strategies are plausible:

(1) *for each potential RHS, the condition explores the space of possible LHS conditions*; or

(2) *for each potential LHS combination of conditions, the space of possible RHS conditions is explored.*

The former strategy leads to the most straightforward implementation, as it involves a simple iteration through a straightforward search for each potential *RHS* condition. However, this implies accessing the count of the number of cases covered by the *LHS* many times, once for each *RHS* condition for which an *LHS* is considered. At the very least, this entails computational overheads for caching information. At worst, it requires a pass through the data each time the value is to be utilized. While a pass through the data has lower overheads when the data are stored in memory rather than on disk, it is still a time-consuming operation that must be avoided if computation is to be efficient.

The algorithm, which applies the OPUS search algorithm to obtain an efficient search for association rules, is designed as a recursive procedure with these arguments:

(1) **CurrentLHS**: the set of conditions in the LHS of the rule currently being considered;

(2) **AvailableLHS**: the set of conditions that may be added to the LHS of rules to be explored below this point; and

(3) **AvailableRHS**: the set of conditions that may appear on the RHS of a rule in the search space at this point and below.

This algorithm is computationally efficient for an association rule analysis during which the number of rules to be found can be constrained and all data can be maintained in memory.

A number of efforts on research into efficient algorithms for mining association rules (Agrawal-Srikant 1994, Park-Chen-Yu 1997), measures of itemsets (Aggarawal-Yu 1998), parallel data mining for association rules (Han-Karypis-Kumar 1997), FP-tree-based model (Han-Pei-Yin 2000), and OPUS-based algorithm (Webb 2000), have been reported.

There has also been much work on mining special databases. For example, spatial data mining is the discovery of novel and interesting relationships and characteristics that may exist implicitly in spatial databases (Cai et al. 1991, Ester et al. 1997, Han 1997, Ng 1994); temporal database mining (Chen 1998), image data mining for multi-dimensional remotely sensed images (Cromp 1993); probabilistic database mining (Zhang-Zhang 2004); mining time-series databases (Tsumoto 1999); text mining (Feldman et al. 1999); and Web mining for the discovery and application of usage patterns from Web data (Srivastava 2000).

2.5 Research into Mining Multi-databases

As we have seen, knowledge discovery in databases aims at the discovery of useful information from large collections of data. The discovered knowledge can consist of rules describing properties of the data, frequently occurring patterns, clustering of objects in the database, and so on. These can be used to support various intelligence activities, such as decision-making, planning, and problem-solving.

Recently, it has been recognized in the KDD community that multi-database mining is an important research topic (Zhong-Yao-Ohsuga 1999). So far, most of the KDD methods that have been developed are on the single universal relation level. Although, theoretically, any multi-relational database can be transformed into a single universal relation, in fact this can lead to many complications such as universal relations of unmanageable size, infiltration of uninteresting attributes, the loss of useful relation names, unnecessary join operations, and inconveniences inherent in distributed processing. In particular, certain concepts, regularities, causal relationships, and rules cannot be discovered if we just search a single database, since some basic knowledge hides in multiple databases.

Multi-database mining involves many related topics, including interestingness checking, relevance, database reverse engineering, granular computing, and distributed data mining. For example, Liu et al. have proposed an interesting method for relevance measurement, and an efficient implementation for identifying relevant databases, as the first step for multi-database mining (Liu-Lu-Yao 1998, Yao-Liu 1997). Zhong et al. have proposed a way of mining peculiarity rules from multiple statistical and transaction databases (Zhong-Yao-Ohsuga 1999). Ribeiro et al. have described a method for extending the INLEN system for multi-database mining by the incorporation of primary and foreign keys, as well as the development and processing of knowledge segments (Ribeiro-Kaufman-Kerschberg 1995). Wrobel has extended the concept of foreign keys into foreign links, because multi-database mining is also concerned with getting to non-key attributes (Wrobel 1997). Aronis et al. have introduced a system called WoRLD that uses spreading activation to enable inductive learning from multiple tables in multiple databases spread across the network (Aronis et al. 1997).

In this section, we briefly recall some related work, including the multi-database mining techniques in (Liu-Lu-Yao 1998, Yao-Liu 1997, Zhong-Yao-Ohsuga 1999).

2.5.1 Parallel Data Mining

Due to the size of large databases, and the amount of intensive computation involved in association analysis, parallel and distributed data mining has been a crucial mechanism for large-scale data mining applications. Existing research in this area has focused on the study of the degree of parallelism, synchronization, data locality issues, and optimization techniques necessary for global association computation.

For example, Cheung et al. have proposed some strategies to leverage the skew of association patterns in a distributed database environment, and have offered some optimizations to efficiently generate global frequent sets (Cheung-Ng-Fu-Fu 1996). Their main idea is to use local pruning to support count exchange to achieve efficient association analysis.

As discussed in Chapter 1, there are some limitations in applying parallel and distributed data mining techniques when searching for patterns from multi-databases. However, parallel and distributed data mining can be combined with our synthesizing model by weighting, for very large database mining applications, as we demonstrate in Chapter 6. If each of the databases is still large, we can apply an association rule mining technique upon the paralleling (MARP) algorithm to discover the local associations from each data-source,. We can then analyze local patterns.

2.5.2 Distributed Data Mining

Distributed data mining (DDM) deals with different possibilities of data distribution. A well-known method is hierarchical meta-learning, which has a similar goal of efficiently processing large amounts of data (Chan 1996, Prodromidis-Stolfo 1998, Prodromidis-Chan-Stolfo 2000). Meta-learning starts with a distributed database, or a set of data subsets of an original database, concurrently running a learning algorithm (or different learning algorithms) on each of the subsets. It combines the predictions from classifiers learned from these subsets by recursively learning "combiner" and "arbiter" models in a bottom-up tree manner. The focus of meta-learning is to combine the predictions of learned models from the partitioned data subsets in a parallel and distributed environment.

In addition, Kargupta et al. have built a collective mining technique for distributed data (Kargupta-HS 1997, Kargupta-HSPW 2000, Kargupta-HSJ 2001); and Grossman et al. have established a system, known as Papyrus, for distributed data mining (Grossman-BRMT 2000, Turinsky-Grossman 2001).

However, unlike the mining strategy in this book, meta-learning, collective mining, and Papyrus do not produce a global learning model from classifiers from different data subsets.

Meta-learning Strategy for Mining Multi-databases. Meta-learning is a technique that seeks to compute higher-level classifiers (or classification models), referred to as meta-classifiers, that integrate in a certain basic fashion multiple classifiers, which compute separately over different databases (Prodromidis-Stolfo 1998, Prodromidis-Chan-Stolfo 2000). Meta-learning starts with a distributed database, or a set of data subsets of an original database, concurrently running a learning algorithm (or different learning algorithms) on each of the subsets. It combines the predictions from classifiers learned from these subsets by recursively learning combiner and arbiter models in a bottom-up tree manner. The focus of meta-learning is to combine the predictions of learned models from the partitioned data subsets in a parallel and distributed environment.

Given a set of training examples, that is, $\{(x_1, y_1), ..., (x_n, y_n)\}$, for some unknown function, $y = f(x)$, with each x_i interpreted as a set of attribute (feature) vectors x_i of the form $\{x_{i1}, x_{i2}, ..., x_{ik}\}$, and with each y_i representing the class label associated with each vector ($y_i \in \{y_1, y_2, ..., y_m\}$), the task is to compute a classifier or model $\hat{f}$ that approximates f, and correctly labels any feature vector drawn from the same source as the training set. It is common to refer to the body of knowledge that classifies data with the label y as the concept of class y.

Some of the common representations used for the generated classifiers are decision trees, rules, version spaces, neural networks, distance functions, and probability distributions. In general, these representations are associated with different types of algorithms that extract different types of information from the database. They also provide alternative capabilities besides the common ability to classify unseen exemplars drawn from a certain domain. For example, decision trees are declarative, and thus more comprehensible to humans than weights computed within a neural network architecture. However, both are able to compute concept y, and classify unseen records (examples).

Meta-learning is loosely defined as learning from learned knowledge. In this case, we concentrate on learning from the output of concept learning systems. This is achieved by learning from the predictions of these classifiers on a common validation dataset. Thus, we are interested in the output of the classifiers, not the internal structure and strategies of the learning algorithms themselves. Moreover, in some of the schemes defined, the data presented to the learning algorithms may also be available to the meta-learner. The different stages in a simplified meta-learning scenario are listed below.

1. The classifiers (base classifiers) are trained from the initial (base-level) training sets.
2. Predictions are generated by the learned classifiers on a separate validation set.
3. A meta-level training set is composed from the validation set, and the predictions generated by the classifiers on the validation set.
4. The final classifier (meta-classifier) is trained from the meta-level training set.

In meta-learning, a learning algorithm is used to learn how to integrate the learned classifiers. That is, rather than having a predetermined and fixed integration rule, the integration rule is learned based on the behavior of the trained classifiers.

For example, let x be an instance whose classification we seek, and $C_1(x), C_2(x), ..., C_k(x)$ be the predicted classifications of x from the k base classifiers, C_i, $i = 1, 2, ..., k$. Then, $class(x)$ and $attrvec(x)$ denote the correct classification and attribute vector of example x, respectively.

In the combiner strategy, the predictions of the learned base classifiers on the validation set form the basis of the meta-learner's training set. A composition rule, which varies in different schemes, determines the content of training examples for the meta-learner. From these examples, the meta-learner generates a meta-classifier, that we call a combiner. In classifying an instance, the base classifiers first generate their predictions. Based on the same composition rule, a new instance is generated from the predictions, which is then classified by the combiner. The aim of this strategy is to "coalesce" the predictions from the base classifiers by learning the relationship, or correlation, between these predictions and the correct prediction. A combiner computes a prediction that may be entirely different from any proposed by a base classifier, whereas an arbiter chooses one of the predictions from the base classifiers and the arbiter itself.

Several schemes for the composition rule are evaluated. First, the predictions $C_1(x), C_2(x), ..., C_k(x)$, for each example x in the validation set of examples, E, are generated by the k base classifiers. These predicted classifications are used to form a new set of "meta-level training instances" T, which is used as input to a learning algorithm that computes a combiner. The manner in which T is computed varies, as defined below.

class-combiner: The meta-level training instances consist of the correct classification and predictions; that is, $T = \{(class(x), C_1(x), C_2(x), ..., C_k(x)) \mid x \in E\}$. This "stacking" scheme was also proposed by Wolpert (Wolpert 1992).

class-attribute-combiner: The meta-level training instances are formed as in a class-combiner, with the addition of the attribute vectors; that is, $T = \{(class(x), C_1(x), C_2(x), ..., C_k(x), attrvec(x)) \mid x \in E\}$.

binary-class-combiner: The meta-level training instances are composed in a manner similar to that in the class-combiner scheme, except that each prediction $C_i(x)$ has l binary predictions, $C_{i1}(x), ..., C_{il}(x)$, where l is the number of classes. Each prediction $C_{ij}(x)$ is produced from a binary classifier, which is trained on examples that are labeled with classes j and $\neg j$. In other words, we are using more specialized base classifiers and attempting to learn the correlation between the binary predictions and the correct prediction. For concreteness, $T = \{(class(x), C_{11}(x), ..., C_{1l}(x), C_{21}(x), ..., C_{2l}(x), ..., C_{k1}(x), ..., C_{kl}(x)) \mid x \in E\}$.

These three schemes for the composition rule are defined in the context of forming a training set for the combiner. These composition rules are also used in a similar manner during classification after a combiner has been computed. Given an instance where classification is sought, we first compute the classifications predicted by each of the base classifiers. The composition rule is then applied to generate a single meta-level test instance, which is then classified by the combiner to produce the final predicted class of the original test datum.

Meta-learning improves efficiency by executing in parallel the base-learning processes (each implemented as a distinct serial program) on (possibly disjoint) subsets of the training data set (a data reduction technique). This approach has the advantage, first, of using the same serial code without the time-consuming process of parallelizing it and, second, of learning from small subsets of data that fit in the main memory.

Meta-learning improves predictive performance by combining different learning systems, each having a different inductive bias (e.g., representation, search heuristics, search space). By combining separately learned concepts, meta-learning is expected to derive a higher-level model that explains a large database more accurately than any of the individual learners. Furthermore, meta-learning constitutes a scalable machine-learning method, since it can be generalized to hierarchical, multi-level meta-learning.

Meta-learning is particularly suitable for distributed data mining applications, such as fraud detection in financial information systems. Financial institutions today typically develop custom fraud detection systems targeted to their own asset bases. Recently though, banks have come to search for unified and global approaches that would also involve the periodic sharing with each other of information about attacks.

The key difficulties in this approach are: financial companies avoid sharing their data for a number of competitive and legal reasons; the databases that companies maintain on transaction behavior are huge, and growing rapidly; real-time analysis is highly desirable to update models when new events are detected; and easy distribution of models in a networked environment is essential to maintain up-to-date detection capability. Meta-learning is a general strategy that provides the means of learning how to combine and integrate a number of classifiers, or models, learned separately at different financial institutions. The designed system JAM allows financial institutions to share their models of fraudulent transactions that each computes separately, while not disclosing their own proprietary data.

Determining the optimal set of classifiers for meta-learning is a combinatorial problem. Hence, the objective of pruning is to utilize heuristic methods to search for partially grown meta-classifiers (meta-classifiers with pruned subtrees) that are more efficient and scalable, and at the same time, achieve comparable or better predictive performance results than fully grown (unpruned) meta-classifiers. Two stages of pruning meta-classifiers are: the a priori pruning, or pre-training pruning, and the a posteriori pruning, or post-training pruning, stages. Both levels are essential, and complementary to each other, with respect to the improvement of accuracy and efficiency of the system.

A priori pruning, or pre-training pruning, refers to the filtering of the classifiers before they are combined. Instead of combining classifiers in a brute force manner, with pre-training pruning we introduce a preliminary stage for analyzing the available classifiers and qualifying them for inclusion in a combined meta-classifier. Only those classifiers that appear, according to one or more pre-defined metrics, to be most "promising" participate in the final meta-classifier. Here, we adopt a "black-box" approach, which evaluates the set of classifiers based only on their input and output behavior, not their internal structure. Conversely, a posteriori pruning, or post-training pruning, denotes the evaluation and pruning of constituent base classifiers after a complete meta-classifier has been constructed.

Parallel Data Mining Agent (PADMA). PADMA is an agent-based architecture for parallel/distributed data mining (Kargupta-HS 1997). The PADMA system attempts to develop a flexible system that will exploit data mining agents from a special application. Although PADMA is not specialized for any particular kind of data mining domain, the current implementation uses agents specializing in unstructured text document classification. The main structural components of PADMA are:

(1) data mining agents,
(2) facilitator for coordinating the agents, and
(3) Web- based user interface.

Data mining agents are responsible for accessing data and extracting higher level useful information from the data. A data mining agent specializes in performing some activity in the domain of interest. In the current implementation, data mining agents specialize in text classification. Agents work in parallel and share their information through the facilitator. The facilitator module coordinates the agents, presents information to the user interface, and provides feedback to the agents from the user.

The PADMA has a graphical, Web-based, interface for presenting information extracted by the agents for the user. The facilitator accepts queries from the user interface in standard SQL (Structured Query Language) format; and the queries are broadcast to the agents. Agents come up with the extracted information relevant to the query. The facilitator collects the information and presents it to the user.

The PADMA model has demonstrated that agent-based data mining tools are suitable for exploiting the benefits of parallel computing. The PADMA model presents some distinct characteristics as follows:

(1) parallel query processing and data accessing,
(2) parallel data analysis, and
(3) interactive data/cluster visualization.

Collective Data Mining (CDM). Collective data mining offers a framework for distributed data modeling and knowledge discovery (Kargupta-HSPW 2000). It draws its motivations from theories of communication and blends them with our existing understanding of statistics and machine learning. This merger has evolved into an interdisciplinary framework for designing and implementing efficient algorithms that generate models from heterogeneous and distributed data with guaranteed global correctness of the model.

The CDM model makes use of an appropriate set of *orthonormal* basis functions, and computes the basis coefficients to generate a global model of the data. Basis functions are chosen to be orthonormal, since the orthonormality property can be exploited for generating correct, unambiguous local basis coefficients. Computing the basis coefficients requires computation of the basis functions of the different domain features. The CDM model distributes the task of approximate computation of the basis coefficient among different sites, using the decomposition outlined below.

1. It generates the coefficients that can be computed, using only the locally available feature data.
2. It computes the coefficients, corresponding to the basis functions that require features from different sites, using the locally generated basis coefficients and a small dataset collected from different sites.

The main steps of the CDM are:

1. generate approximate orthonormal basis coefficients at each local site;
2. move an appropriately chosen sample of the datasets from each site to a single site, and generate the approximate basis coefficients corresponding to nonlinear cross terms; and
3. combine the local models, transforming the model into the user-described canonical representation, and then output the model.

The development of different CDM-based, and other distributed data analysis algorithms, are listed below:

(a) collective decision rule learning using Fourier analysis;
(b) collective hierarchical clustering;
(c) collective multivariate regression using wavelets; and
(d) collective principal component analysis.

For example, given distributed heterogeneous data sites, we show how to approximate the results of the global Principal Component Analysis (PCA), namely, a certain number of dominant eigenvalues/eigenvectors with minimal data communication, as follows.

1. Centralized PCA from distributed heterogeneous datasets typically involves moving all the data to one single site and computing the eigenvalues and eigenvectors of the covariance matrix of the combined dataset.
2. Collective PCA analyzes each data partition at a site and decomposes it as the sum of the product of a certain number of score vectors and the transpose of corresponding loading vectors. The number of the

score/loading vectors is an empirical value that could be changed for different accuracy requirements. This decomposition can also be presented as the product of a score matrix (whose column vectors are score vectors) and the transpose of a loading matrix (whose column vectors are loading vectors). Then, the score matrix is sampled. That is, a certain number of rows are randomly chosen from it. The chosen rows, and the complete loading matrix, comprise the data which need to be moved, and the size of these data is far less than that of the whole data partition.

3. Once the loading matrices and sampled score matrices of all local sites are generated, they are moved to one single site, and the approximated global covariance matrix is constructed. PCA is then applied to this matrix to obtain the approximate PCA results.

2.5.3 Application-dependent Database Selection

For multi-database mining, Yao and Liu have proposed an approach to search for interesting knowledge in multiple databases, according to a user's query (Yao-Liu 1997). This process involves selecting all interesting information from many databases by retrieval. Mining only works on the selected data. Liu et al.have also proposed a mining technique that identifies relevant databases. Their work has been focused on the first step of multi-database mining, which is to identify databases that are most likely relevant to an application (Liu-Lu-Yao 1998). Thus, a relevance measure was proposed to identify relevant databases for mining tasks, with the objective of finding patterns, or regularities, in certain attributes. We briefly recall the work below. For more detail, please see (Liu-Lu-Yao 1998, Yao-Liu 1997).

A *relop* C is called a *selector*, where A is an attribute name that is not referenced by the query predicate Q, $relop \in \{=, <, >, \leq, \geq, \neq\}$, and C is a constant value in the domain of A. The *relevance factor* of selector s with respect to Q is

$$RF(s, Q) = Pr(s|Q)Pr(Q)\log\frac{Pr(s|Q)}{Pr(s)},$$

where $Pr(Q)$ and $Pr(s)$ are prior probabilities and are estimated by the ratios of how frequently they appear in a database; and $Pr(s|Q)$ is the posterior of the frequency ratio of s appearing, given that Q occurs. The rationale of defining relevance is as follows.

$Pr(s|Q)/Pr(s)$ shows the degree of deviation of the posterior from the prior. This ratio tells us the following different relationships between $Pr(s|Q)$ and $Pr(s)$.

Case 1 If $\frac{Pr(s|Q)}{Pr(s)}$ is close to 1 (i.e., $Pr(s|Q) \approx Pr(s)$), s is independent of Q;

Case 2 If $\frac{Pr(s|Q)}{Pr(s)}$ is close to 0 (i.e., $Pr(s|Q)$ is almost 0), s rarely occurs given Q;

Case 3 If $\frac{Pr(s|Q)}{Pr(s)}$ is less than 1, s is not frequent enough when using $Pr(Q)$
as a reference;

Case 4 If $\frac{Pr(s|Q)}{Pr(s)}$ is greater than 1, then s occurs more often given Q than
without Q. Hence, s and Q are correlated.

With the above definition for the relevance factor of selectors, we can have
a definition of the relevance of databases as follows:

- a selector s is relevant to Q if $RF(s,Q) > \delta$, where δ (> 0) is the given
  threshold;
- a table is relevant to Q if there exists at least one selector s_j ($A_i\ relop\ C$),
  where s_j is relevant to Q.

With the relevance factor RF, we can determine whether a database is
relevant to an application (such as for a query predicate) before applying data
mining algorithms. To compute $RF(s,Q)$, we need only to count three values,
$Pr(Q)$, $Pr(s)$, and $Pr(s \wedge Q)$. To determine whether a database is relevant
to Q, we need to test all selectors, which can be done by scanning the table
once. Let us assume that there are $m+1$ attributes, A_0, ..., A_m. Attribute A_0
is referenced by Q. For each of the other attribute, A_i ($1 \le i \le m$), a table
S_i is maintained to keep track of selectors and related counters. An entry
of S_i is a triple of ($S_{value}, S_{counter}, SQ_{counter}$), where S_{value} is the value of
the selector, $S_{counter}$ records the number of tuples for which $A_i = S_{value}$
is true, and $SQ_{counter}$ records the number of tuples for which both Q and
$A_i = S_{value}$ are true. With the S_i table, we can determine the relevance of
a database by scanning it once. This process has specific parts: (1) reading
each record in the database; and (2) searching for the entry of selectors and
updating the counters for each attribute in the record. The cost of part (1) is
proportional to the number of records in the database. As for part (2), with a
proper data structure, for example, using a hashing function for the selector
tables, the search for selector entries can be kept constant, regardless of the
number of selectors of an attribute. Therefore, the run-time for the overall
calculation is $O(NM)$, where V is the number of records in the database and
M is the number of attributes.

Identifying relevant databases is typically *application-dependent*. It has
to be carried out multiple times to identify relevant databases for two or
more real-world applications. It should be noted that, when users need to
mine their multi-databases without reference to any specific application, the
technique does not work well.

2.5.4 Peculiarity-oriented Multi-database Mining

Zhong et al. have proposed a way of mining peculiarity rules from multiple
statistical and transaction databases (Zhong-Yao-Ohsuga 1999). A peculiarity rule is discovered from peculiar data by searching for the relevance among

those data. Roughly speaking, data are peculiar if they represent a peculiar case described by a relatively small number of objects and are very different from other objects in a dataset. Although it looks like an exception rule, because it describes a relatively small number of objects, the peculiarity rule represents a well-known common-sense fact, which is a feature of the general rule. To find peculiar data, an attribute-oriented method was proposed as follows.

Let $X = \{x_1, x_2, ..., x_n\}$ be a dataset related to an attribute in a relation, where n is the number of different values in the attribute. The peculiarity of x_i can be evaluated by the *Peculiarity Factor $PF(x_i)$*,

$$PF(x_i) = \sum_{j=1}^{n} \sqrt{N(x_i, x_j)}.$$

It evaluates whether x_i occurs as a relatively small number and is very different from the other data x_j by calculating the sum of the square root of the conceptual distance between x_i and x_j. The reason why the square root is used in the peculiarity factor is that we prefer to evaluate closer distances for relatively large amounts of data so that peculiar data can be found from relatively small amounts of data.

The major merits of the method are: (1) it can handle both continuous and symbolic attributes based on a unified semantic interpretation, and (2) background knowledge represented by binary neighborhoods can be used to evaluate the peculiarity if such background knowledge is provided by a user.

If X is the dataset of a continuous attribute, and no background knowledge is available, then

$$N(x_i, x_j) = |x_i - x_j|.$$

On the other hand, if X is a data set of a symbolic attribute, and/or the background knowledge for representing the conceptual distances between x_i and x_j is provided by a user, the peculiarity factor is calculated by the conceptual distances, $N(x_i, x_j)$.

After evaluation for peculiarity, the peculiar data are elicited by using a threshold value

$$threshold = \text{mean of } PF(x_i) + \alpha \times \text{ variance of } PF(x_i),$$

where α can be specified by a user. That is, if $PF(x_i)$ is over the threshold value, x_i is peculiar data.

Because a peculiarity rule is discovered from the peculiar data by searching for the relevance among those data, a measurement for relevant databases is also proposed as follows.

Let $X(x)$ and $Y(y)$ be the peculiar data found in two attributes X and Y, respectively. We deal with the following two cases.

– If $X(x)$ and $Y(y)$ are found in a relation, the relevance between $X(x)$ and $Y(y)$ is evaluated in the following formula,

$$R_1 = P_1(X(x)|Y(y))P_2(Y(y)|X(x)).$$

That is, the larger the product of the probabilities of P_1 and P_2, the stronger the relevance between $X(x)$ and $Y(y)$.

– If $X(x)$ and $Y(y)$ are in two different relations, we need to use a value (or its granule) in a key (or foreign key/link) as the relevance factor, $K(k)$, to find the relevance between $X(x)$ and $Y(y)$. Thus, the relevance between $X(x)$ and $Y(y)$ is evaluated in the following formula,

$$R_2 = P_1(K(k)|X(x))P_2(K(k)|Y(y)).$$

Furthermore, the above two formulae are suitable for handling more than two lots of peculiar data, found in more than two attributes, if $X(x)$ (or $Y(y)$) is a granule of the peculiar data.

Although this work can identify new kinds of patterns in multi-databases, it still utilizes techniques already used in mono-database mining.

From the above efforts on multi-database mining, we can see that existing techniques are limited by mono-database mining techniques. Thus, as we mentioned in Chapter 1, there are still some limitations in traditional multi-database mining methods.

2.6 Summary

Due to the increasingly large number of multi-database systems, multi-database mining has become very important. Although, theoretically, any multi-relational database can be transformed into a single universal relation, in fact this can lead to many extra problems, such as universal relations of unmanageable size, infiltration of uninteresting attributes, the loss of useful relation names, unnecessary join operations, and the inconvenience for distributed processing (Zhong-Yao-Ohsuga 1999). Also, some concepts, such as regularity, causal relationships, and rules cannot be discovered if we simply search a single database, since the basic knowledge can be hidden in multiple databases. Thus, dual-level applications present more challenges than those faced by mono-database mining.

As an introduction to this book, we have described KDD techniques, existing research into multi-database mining and necessary basic concepts. From Chapter 3 on, we present techniques in multi-database mining.

3. Local Pattern Analysis

It is clear that local pattern analysis provides a new way to deal with multi-database mining problems. The local pattern analysis in this book is inspired by competition in sports. For the convenience of the reader, the terms of local instance, local pattern, global pattern, and local pattern analysis are formally defined in this chapter. We then go on to develop techniques for identifying novel patterns (high-vote patterns) in multi-databases by analyzing local patterns.

In individual branches of a large company, for example, a high-vote pattern generally contains a great deal of information that describes the uncertainty of patterns occurring individually in those branches. In this case, there can be altogether too much information for users to comprehend. Thus, it is very difficult for users to apply a pattern when making decisions. With this in mind, we also present a method for analyzing high-vote patterns so that they can be easily understood and applied. High-vote pattern analysis is essential for users.

3.1 Introduction

As previously argued, traditional multi-database mining techniques have difficulty in meeting the requirements of dual-level applications. This is because putting all the data from a certain class of databases into a single dataset can destroy the distribution of patterns. This distribution could be useful when a company is making global decisions. Using patterns mined at branches, and forwarding the patterns (rather than the original raw data) to the central company headquarters, provides a feasible way of dealing with multi-database mining problems.

However, the number of patterns forwarded may be so large that browsing the pattern set, and finding interesting patterns from it, could be rather difficult for company headquarters. In particular, it might be difficult to identify which of the forwarded patterns are really useful to a company's applications. This chapter develops a technique to search for high-vote patterns from *local patterns* within the branches of an interstate company. *This approach is particularly useful in dual-level applications.*

In the case of a large company, a high-vote pattern is often created by votes from many branches. Consequently, there is a great deal of information used to describe the uncertainty of the pattern within the branches. For example, a high-vote association rule may have different supports and confidences in branches that vote for the rule. The information is thus too diverse to be understood by users. Thus, it can become rather difficult to apply the pattern in decision-making. Therefore, this chapter also presents a technique to cluster high-vote patterns.

The chapter is organized as follows. We begin with discussing previous multi-database mining techniques in Section 3.2. Section 3.3 illustrates local patterns. In Section 3.4, we design a local pattern analysis inspired by competition in sports. In Section 3.5, we demonstrate the structure of patterns in multi-databases. In Section 3.6, an example is used for displaying the effectiveness of local instance analysis. Finally, the work in this chapter is summarized in Section 3.7.

3.2 Previous Multi-database Mining Techniques

We now outline four well-established multi-database mining techniques.

Pattern discovery based on database selection adopted mono-database mining techniques (Liu-Lu-Yao 1998, Yao-Liu 1997). The main contribution of this work is the database classification, which is an efficient data-preparation technique for multi-database mining.

Peculiarity discovery also adopted mono-database mining techniques (Zhong-Yao-Ohsuga 1999). The work is important because it offers a model for identifying exceptions from multi-database mining.

Meta-learning is a technique that seeks to compute higher-level classifiers (or classification models), referred to as meta-classifiers, that integrate in some principled fashion multiple classifiers computed separately over different databases (Prodromidis-Stolfo 1998, Prodromidis-Chan-Stolfo 2000). Meta-learning starts with a distributed database, or a set of data subsets of an original database, concurrently running a learning algorithm (or different learning algorithms) on each of the subsets. Using an integration rule, it can combine the predictions from classifiers learned from these subsets by recursively learning combiner and arbiter models in a bottom-up tree manner. This is not a local-patterns-based model, but differs from mono-database mining techniques.

The collective data mining (CDM) model makes use of an appropriate set of orthonormal basis functions and computes the basis coefficients to generate a global model of the data (Kargupta-HSPW 2000). A global model is generated to approximately fit a group of local patterns using Fourier transformation. This work is based on local patterns.

The strategy for mining geographically distributed data, which leaves the data in place, identifies local patterns, and combines the patterns at a central site, is referred to as the *in-place strategy*. And the strategy for mining geographically distributed data, which amasses all the data to a central site and identifies global patterns there, is referred to as the *centralized strategy* (Grossman-BRMT 2000, Turinsky-Grossman 2001). The former strategy is the quickest, but often the least accurate, whereas the latter strategy is more accurate but generally quite expensive in terms of the time required. Therefore, Grossman et al. have established an *intermediate strategy*, known as Papyrus, for distributed data mining (Grossman-BRMT 2000, Turinsky-Grossman 2001). In the intermediate strategy, some of the data is amassed and some of the data are left in place, analyzed locally, and the resulting patterns are moved and combined.

All of the existing strategies can only identify traditional patterns in the same way as in mono-database mining, using frequent itemsets, association rules, trends, and classification rules. However, there are also a great many other potentially useful patterns in multi-databases due to essential differences from mono-databases. For example, the distribution of local patterns is different from the traditional patterns of mono-database mining. The distribution of local patterns is referred to as a *global learning model*. The global learning model assists in global decision-making within an interstate company.

Unlike the mining strategies in meta-learning, collective mining, and Papyrus, this book designs a new *local pattern analysis* for producing global learning models in multi-databases.

3.3 Local Patterns

Local pattern analysis is a strategy for identifying laws, rules, and useful patterns from a set of local patterns in multi-databases. This section presents the definition of *local pattern*.

Strictly speaking, a pattern is a *local pattern* that has been identified in the local database of a branch. A local pattern may be a frequent itemset, an association rule, causal rule, dependency, or some other expression. For description purposes, this book sometimes takes frequent itemsets, sometimes association rules, and sometimes both frequent itemsets and association rules, as local patterns. Example 3.1 illustrates local patterns.

Example 3.1 *Consider a company that has five branches with five databases D_1, D_2, ..., D_5 as follows,*

$$D_1 = \{(A, B, C, D); (B, C); (A, B, C); (A, C)\},$$
$$D_2 = \{(A, B); (A, C); (A, B, C); (B, C); (A, B, D); (A, C, D)\},$$
$$D_3 = \{(B, C, D); (A, B, D); (B, C); (A, B, D); (A, B)\},$$

$$D_4 = \{(A, C, D); (A, B, C); (A, C); (A, D); (D, C)\},$$
$$D_5 = \{(A, B, C); (A, B); (A, C); (A, D)\},$$

where each database has several transactions, separated by a semicolon; and each transaction contains several items, separated by a comma.

When $minsupp = 0.5$, local frequent itemsets in D_1, D_2, D_3, D_4, D_5 are listed in Tables 3.1, 3.2, 3.3, 3.4, and 3.5, respectively.

Table 3.1 *Local frequent itemsets in database D_1*

Itemsets	support	$\geq minsupp$
A	0.75	y
B	0.75	y
C	1.0	y
AB	0.5	y
AC	0.75	y
BC	0.75	y
ABC	0.5	y

Table 3.2 *Local frequent itemsets in database D_2*

Itemsets	support	$\geq minsupp$
A	0.833	y
B	0.667	y
C	0.667	y
AB	0.5	y
AC	0.5	y

Table 3.3 *Local frequent itemsets in database D_3*

Itemsets	support	$\geq minsupp$
A	0.6	y
B	1.0	y
D	0.6	y
AB	0.6	y
BD	0.6	y

Table 3.4 *Local frequent itemsets in database D_4*

Itemsets	support	$\geq minsupp$
A	0.8	y
C	0.8	y
D	0.6	y
AC	0.6	y

Table 3.5 *Local frequent itemsets in database D_5*

Itemsets	support	$\geq minsupp$
A	1.0	y
B	0.5	y
C	0.5	y
AB	0.5	y
AC	0.5	y

In Tables 3.1- 3.5, XY stands for the conjunction of X and Y. All of the local frequent itemsets discovered in D_1, D_2, ..., D_5 refer to local patterns from the five branches. All association rules generated from the local frequent itemsets are also referred to as local patterns.

3.4 Local Instance Analysis Inspired by Competition in Sports

The local pattern analysis strategy in this book is inspired by competition in sports. However, first we should remember, using the company model, that there are generally dual-level applications (local and global decisions) involved. Local patterns are used for local applications in branches of a company. For global applications, the data must be analyzed in the multi-database. Patterns discovered from global applications are referred to as *global patterns*. The goal of local pattern analysis is to identify global patterns from local pattern sets in order to make global decisions. The analysis searches for patterns such as high-vote patterns (see Chapter 7), suggested patterns (see Chapter 7), exceptional patterns (see Chapter 8), and synthesizing patterns (see Chapter 9). This local pattern analysis strategy is now elucidated by using a competing model in sports.

To generate winners, many competitive sports have their competing rule sets. For example, for a 3-set match of tennis, if a player wins 2 out of 3 sets, that player wins the match. For example, assume that player A wins the first set by 7:6 and the third set by 7:6, player B wins the second set by 6:0, where 7:6 means that player A won 7 games and player B won 6 games. According to the competing rules, player A scores 2, player B scores 1, and player A wins the game. The scores of the match in two levels are depicted in Figure 3.1.

Figure 3.1 illustrates a dual-level structure of results for the match. Area "II" demonstrates the local-level results. There are three sets: "set1", "set2" and "set3". Both "set1" and "set3" indicate that the parts of circles allocated to player A are slightly bigger than those allocated to player B. And "set2" indicates that player B is allocated a whole circle. Area 'I' shows the global-level results. Here there are also three sets: "set1", "set2" and "set3". Both "set1" and "set3" indicate that player A gained the two circles, while "set2" indicates that player B got the circle. Figure 3.1 also displays a one-to-one mapping between areas "I" and "II".

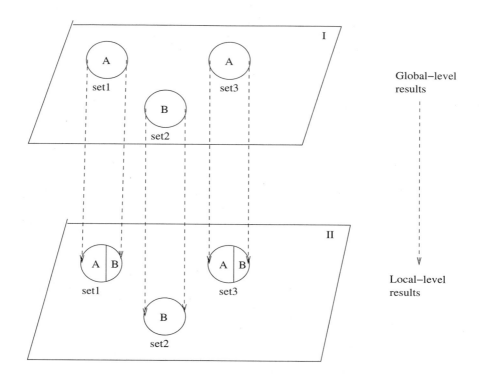

Fig. 3.1. Results in two-level decisions of a tennis match

However, from the game scores (local data) of the match depicted in Figure 3.1, player B, who won 18 games in total, scores better than player A, who won 14 games in total. This says that player B should be the winner of the match and could be used as a new way of determining the results of tennis matches. This mode is similar to traditional multi-database mining which puts all the data from one class of databases into a single dataset for discovery. In fact, it reflects one aspect of the data in multi-databases. This is the traditional method used for multi-database mining.

Using the competing model of a tennis match, we find player A is the winner of the match because she won two sets of the match. In other words, global decisions on tennis matches depend upon local patterns (set scores) rather than local data (game scores). This model provides inspiration for us to analyze local patterns from branches when identifying patterns for making global decisions within our interstate company model.

These observations have shown that a winner in sports can be generated based on a competing rule set. Let the set of the competing rules for tennis be X and the set of the rules for the second strategy (using game scores) be Y. Thus, we can say that player A won the match under X and player B won the match under Y.

Certainly, there are many other rule sets that can be used for tennis matches. For example, height, weight, and gender of people could be considered in constructing competing rules for tennis. In that case, it might be impossible to make a rule set for tennis such that the set is always reasonable. As a tradeoff model, if a rule set for tennis is reasonable in most cases, it can be accepted as an international competing rule set.

These familiar examples have encouraged us to identify global patterns directly from local patterns. This is because data mining (in particular, multi-database mining) is confronted by essentially the same problems as those met by competitive games.

For example, let $minsupp = 0.5$, itemset R_1 have supports 0.5, 0, and 0.6 in three local databases from three branches of a company, and itemset R_2 have supports 0.8, 0.49, and 0.47, respectively, in the three databases. This means that R_1 is a frequent itemset (local pattern) in two local databases, and R_2 is a frequent itemset in one local database. From the local pattern analysis in this book, R_1 can be extracted as a valid global pattern because it is supported (voted for) by most branches. And R_2 cannot be extracted as a valid pattern because it is supported by only one branch.

However, assume that each local database has 100 transactions. When we put all data from the three databases into a single dataset, R_1 cannot be extracted as a valid pattern because its support is less than $minsupp$. And R_2 can be extracted as a valid pattern because its support is greater than $minsupp$.

This example has shown the similarity between multi-database mining and the generation of champions in sports. For multi-database mining, using the company model, we can also consider the frequency, weight, and amount purchased of an item to determine whether the item is of interest. To meet dual-level applications, this book focuses on analyzing local patterns for identifying global patterns.

The above observations have also shown that patterns represent different granularity: local patterns are uncertain at a local level and certain at a global level. For example, player A defeated player B by 7:6 at a local level, while at a global level, player A scored 1 and player B scored 0. For a set (at local level), the game scores of the form $a : b$ can be one of 6:0, 6:1, ..., 6:7. This means that the game score is multi-valued at the local level. For a match (at global level), the game score of a set represents whether a player wins the set. This means that the game score is 2-valued at a global level.

This is the same as occurs in multi-database mining. For example, for an interstate company, heads of branches need to consider original raw data when identifying local patterns. However, the company's headquarters are generally interested in local patterns rather than original raw data. This is because branch heads and their company headquarters work at two different application levels. In a branch (local level), a pattern has support and confidence, which is multi-valued. In the company (global level), the pattern is 2-valued: 1 for a branch, if the branch's local pattern set contains the pattern, otherwise 0 for the branch. Thus a local pattern can be uncertain at a local level, but certain at a global level.

The granularity of patterns facilitates multi-database mining. So, for global applications, we can search for high-vote patterns, exceptional patterns, and suggested patterns from local patterns without reference to the uncertainty of the patterns. Detailed presentations follow in this chapter and in Chapter 5.

The uncertainty of a pattern, and the weight of a branch, are two important factors also to be decided. Therefore, in Chapter 6, we advocate a model for synthesizing local patterns by weighting.

3.5 The Structure of Patterns in Multi-database Environments

To recognize patterns in multi-databases, we demonstrate, in a simple way, the structure of a pattern.

In a multi-database environment, a pattern has the attributes: name of pattern, rate voted for by branches (local pattern sets), and supports (confidences for a rule) in the branches that vote for the pattern. Therefore, a pattern is a *super-point* of the form

$$P(name, vote, vsupp, vconf) \tag{3.1}$$

where

$name$ is the dimension of the name of the pattern;
$vote$ is the dimension of the voted rate of the pattern;
$vsupp$ is a vector that indicates the m dimensions of supports in m branches (local pattern sets), referred to as the support dimensions; and
$vconf$ is a vector that indicates the m dimensions of confidences in m branches (local pattern sets), referred to as the confidence dimensions.

Without loss of generality, patterns are taken as itemsets here. Consequently, a pattern is of the form $P(name, vote, vsupp)$, which is the projection of $P(name, vote, vsupp, vconf)$ on $name$, $vote$, and $vsupp$. Patterns in multidimensional space are depicted in Figure 3.2.

Figure 3.2 illustrates the properties of a pattern in multi-dimension space, where *Pattern* stands for the dimension of *name*; *Vote* stands for the dimension of the voting rate of a pattern; and *Branch*$_i$ $(1 \leq i \leq m)$ stands for the m dimensions of supports in m local pattern sets. For a global pattern P_1, there is a super-point describing the pattern, where the projection of the super-point on the *Pattern-Vote* plane is X, indicating the voting rate v; the projection of the super-point on the *Pattern-Branch*$_1$ plane is X_1, indicating the support $supp_1$ in the first branch; the projection of the super-point on the *Pattern-Branch*$_2$ plane is X_2, indicating the support $supp_2$ in the second branch; ...; and the projection of the super-point on the *Pattern-Branch*$_m$ plane is X_m, indicating the support $supp_m$ in the mth branch.

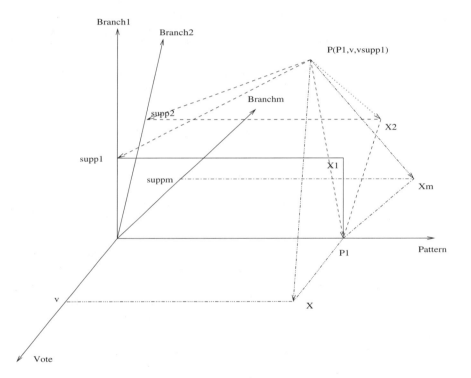

Fig. 3.2. Representation of patterns in multidimensional space

For Example 3.1, patterns A, B, C, D, and AB are represented as follows,

$$P(A, 1.0, (0.75, 0.833, 0.6, 0.8, 1.0)),$$

$$P(B, 0.8, (0.75, 0.667, 1.0, 0.2, 0.5)),$$

$$P(C, 0.8, (1.0, 0.667, 0.4, 0.8, 0.5)),$$

$$P(D, 0.4, (0.25, 0.333, 0.6, 0.6, 0.25)),$$

$$P(AB, 0.8, (0.5, 0.5, 0.6, 0.2, 0.5)).$$

From local pattern analysis, patterns A, B, C, D, and AB are actually represented as

$$P(A, 1.0, (0.75, 0.833, 0.6, 0.8, 1.0)),$$

$$P(B, 0.8, (0.75, 0.667, 1.0, 0.0, 0.5)),$$

$$P(C, 0.8, (1.0, 0.667, 0.0, 0.8, 0.5)),$$

$$P(D, 0.4, (0.0, 0.0, 0.6, 0.6, 0.0)),$$

$$P(AB, 0.8, (0.5, 0.5, 0.6, 0.0, 0.5)).$$

That is, the ith support of a pattern is 0.0, if the ith branch does not vote for the pattern.

An *ideal pattern* (interesting pattern) is of the form $P(A, v_1, vsupp_1, vconf_1)$ that satisfies

(1) $LPI(A) \geq miniVR$ (for $LPI(A)$ and $miniVR$, please see Chapter 7);
(2) for each element *supp* in the vector $vsupp_1$, either $supp = 0$ or $supp \geq minsupp$; and
(3) for each element *conf* in the vector $vconf_1$, either $conf = 0$ or $conf \geq minconf$, if the confidence dimensions exist.

However, many applications may require nonideal patterns. Decisions made by individual branches, need exceptional patterns. Therefore, we develop techniques for identifying high-vote, suggested patterns, exceptional patterns, and synthesizing patterns from local patterns. High-vote patterns are referred to as *weak ideal patterns*. Synthesizing patterns are referred to as *strong ideal patterns*.

To identify high-vote and suggested patterns from local patterns, the projection of $P(name, vote, vsupp, vconf)$ on *name* and *vote* is considered in Chapter 7. That is, the projection

$$P(name, vote) \tag{3.2}$$

is used to search for high-vote and suggested patterns of interest.

To identify exceptional patterns, the projection of $P(name, vote, vsupp, vconf)$ on *name*, *vote*, and *vsupp* is considered. Therefore, the projection

$$P(name, vote, vsupp) \tag{3.3}$$

is used to search for exceptional patterns in Chapter 8.

Synthesizing patterns by local pattern analysis,

$$P(name, vote, vsupp, vconf) \qquad (3.4)$$

is considered in Chapter 9.

3.6 Effectiveness of Local Pattern Analysis

To show the effectiveness of local pattern analysis, we use Example 3.1. Let us examine existing techniques to check whether they can identify high-vote patterns in multi-databases.

1. The first strategy (*mono-database mining*) is to put all the data from the five databases into the single database $TD = D_1 \cup D_2 \cup \cdots \cup D_5$, which has 24 transactions. When data in the five databases are put into the mono-database TD, the distribution of local patterns is destroyed. So mono-database mining techniques cannot identify high-vote patterns.
2. The second strategy is to also put all the data from the five databases into the single database TD (see (Liu-Lu-Yao 1998)). This depends upon mono-database mining techniques being used, and thus this strategy cannot yet identify high-vote patterns.

Note that both strategies are identical in the way they identify patterns.

Unlike traditional multi-database mining, the technique developed in this chapter can identify high-vote patterns. These patterns are useful for dual-level applications. This is regarded as a new strategy and is described below.

3. The third strategy is to identify high-vote patterns by analyzing local patterns. The approach works as follows. First, it searches for the high-vote patterns in local pattern sets. Second, it analyzes the high-vote patterns. Finally, it represents the high-vote patterns in operable forms.

Table 3.6 illustrates the high-vote patterns from the five branches as shown in Example 3.1.

Table 3.6 *Information of local frequent itemsets in database* TD_1

Itemsets	vote	$\geq miniVR$
A	1.0	y
B	0.8	y
C	0.8	y
D	0.4	n
AB	0.8	y
AC	0.8	y
BC	0.2	n
BD	0.2	n
ABC	0.2	n

From these observations, both the first and second strategies cannot find high-vote patterns because they pool all data from the five databases into a single database TD. (Other limitations of existing mining techniques for multi-databases were discussed in Chapter 1.) The third strategy presented in this book is significantly effective in searching for high-vote patterns from local patterns.

3.7 Summary

Multi-database mining must confront dual-level applications. At the local level, local databases have been searched for local applications. Putting all data together from (a class of) multi-databases into a single database for discovery leads to (1) a re-analysis of all data and (2), in particular, the destruction of some information that reflects the distribution of local patterns.

In this chapter, moving on from traditional multi-database mining that depends upon mono-database mining techniques, we have presented a new and effective mining strategy — a local pattern analysis, inspired by competing models in sports.

Using the local pattern analysis strategy, we can identify three kinds of potentially useful patterns: high-vote patterns, exceptional patterns, and global patterns in multiple databases. The principal achievements of this chapter are as follows.

(1) A local pattern analysis strategy was presented, inspired by competing models in sports.
(2) The structure of patterns in a multi-database environment was illustrated.

4. Identifying Quality Knowledge

With the advance of Web techniques, individuals and organizations can make use of low-cost information and knowledge on the Internet when carrying out data mining for applications. However, information from different data-sources is often untrustworthy, contradictory, fraudulent, and even potentially dangerous to applications. Therefore, the discovery of reliable knowledge from different data-sources (databases or datasets) has become a critical task in multi-database mining research. In this chapter, a data-source is taken as a knowledge base (From our local pattern analysis, this assumption is reasonable.). A framework is thus presented for identifying quality knowledge from different data-sources.

4.1 Introduction

The vast amount of relevant information available on the World Wide Web has great potential to improve the quality of decision-making, by enhancing results mined from databases (Lesser 1998, 2000). That is, if a company has a dataset D to be mined, high-profit pressures generate an urgent need for collecting information from data-sources D_1, D_2, ..., D_n, when mining D. Therefore, knowledge discovery from different data-sources (multi-database) is now being recognized as an important research topic in the KDD community. The dataset D is referred to as an internal data-source, whereas D_1, D_2, ..., D_n are the external data-sources. And the knowledge from D is referred to as internal knowledge, whereas the knowledge from D_1, D_2, ..., D_n is the external knowledge, which, as we have already pointed out, can be unreliable.

Traditional data mining techniques for knowledge discovery from different data-sources are carried out in data collection steps. Data collection obtains necessary data from various internal/external data-sources and pools all the data into a huge homogeneous dataset. This can disguise potentially useful patterns. Also, privacy is a very sensitive issue, and protecting privacy in a data-source is of extreme importance (Wu-Zhang 2003). Most of those who create data-sources take privacy very seriously, and allow for some protection facilities. Sharing knowledge is a feasible way to achieve source-sharing in real-world applications. This is because (1) certain data, such as commercial data, are secret for competitive reasons; (2) reanalyzing data is costly; and (3) inexperienced decision-makers don't know how to deal with huge amounts of data. Hence, sharing knowledge (rather than the original raw data) presents a feasible way of dealing with different data-source problems.

In this chapter, then, we move beyond the traditional data mining framework that deals with different data-sources, and take a data-source as a knowledge base to design a framework for identifying quality knowledge from different data-sources.

The rest of this chapter is organized as follows. In the next section, we state specific problems and review some basic concepts of modal logic. In Section 4.3 we first present the relationship between internal knowledge and external knowledge, and then define a logic and its semantics for multi-database mining. Section 4.4 constructs the proof theory of the proposed logic. Section 4.5 enriches our logic with the explicit mention of what a data-source has collected. In Section 4.6, we illustrate how the proposed logical framework is used to identify quality knowledge from different data-sources. We summarize in the last section.

4.2 Problem Statement

We now formulate the problems presently inherent in mining multiple data-sources, outline our approach, and recall some basic concepts.

4.2.1 Problems Faced by Traditional Multi-database Mining

The input to traditional mining algorithms assumes that the data in multi-databases are nicely distributed, containing no missing, inconsistent, or incorrect values. Therefore, traditional data mining algorithms borrow data directly from external data-sources to create a huge dataset deemed suitable for a given mining task. Thus, internal data (in the dataset given) and external data (collected from external sources) can play equally important roles in the mining task. The process of traditional KDD, using external data, is depicted in Figure 4.1.

In Figure 4.1, 'InternalDS' is a set of internal data that will be mined; 'ExternalDSi' is the ith data-source collected; 'Datacollection' is the data collection procedure; 'Hugedataset' is the set of all data in internal and external data-sources after joining; and 'Ruleset' is the set of rules (patterns) that are discovered from 'Hugedataset'. To the left of the curved line 'L' is data collection. To the right of 'L' is the rest of the process of KDD.

While Web technologies such as HTTP and HTML have dramatically changed enterprise information management, a corporation can benefit from intranets and the Internet to gather, manage, distribute, and share data, inside and outside the corporation. Many clever and successful decision-makers are already good at analyzing and utilizing available information when making competitive decisions. Therefore, ways of employing external data in applications is a challenging research topic.

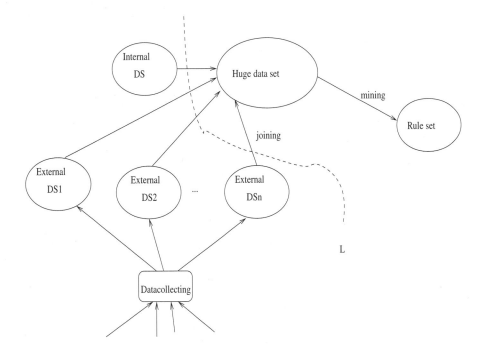

Fig. 4.1. Data collection for a mining task

Using techniques described in Figure 4.1, we join data from internal and external data-sources to form a single dataset for a mining task. This, however, has three main limitations.

1. Poor quality (including noisy, erroneous, ambiguous, untrustworthy, and fraudulent) data can disguise really useful patterns.
2. It is not clear which of the collected data-sources are relevant to a given mining task. In other words, data in irrelevant data-sources play an equally important role in the mining task.
3. There is no confirmation as to which of the collected data-sources are really useful to the specific mining task.

Because of noise and related issues, external data can be impure. Also, collected data may be fraudulent, while really useful patterns can be disguised.

Fraudulent data can also cause applications to fail. For example, a stock investor needs to collect information from other data-sources for an investment decision. If the investor gathers fraudulent information, and the information is directly applied to investment decisions, he may suffer financially. Hence, it is very important that only quality external data are selected.

The above observations clearly indicate that new techniques for discovering suitable knowledge from multiple data-sources are necessary.

As stated previously, companies can only share their knowledge but not their data with each other in real-world applications. In this chapter, we construct a logical framework for identifying quality knowledge from different data-sources by the introspection and the veridicality of data-sources.

4.2.2 Effectiveness of Identifying Quality Data

An example is used below to show the effectiveness of identifying quality data. Without loss of generality, we often refer to a data-source as a database, or a relation.

Consider an internal database (data-source) $ID = \{(A, B, C); (A, C)\}$ and six external (collected) databases (data-sources) D_1, D_2, ..., D_6, as follows.

$$D_1 = \{(A, B, C, D); (B, C); (A, B, C); (A, C)\},$$
$$D_2 = \{(A, B); (A, C); (A, B, C); (B, C); (A, B, D)\},$$
$$D_3 = \{(B, C, D); (A, B, C); (B, C); (A, D)\},$$
$$D_4 = \{(A, F, G, H, I, J); (E, F, H); (F, H)\},$$
$$D_5 = \{(B, E, F, H, J); (F, H); (F, H, J); (E, J)\},$$
$$D_6 = \{(C, F, H, I, J); (E, H, J); (E, F, H); (E, I)\}.$$

Here, each database has several transactions, separated by semicolons; each transaction contains several items, separated by commas.

Let $minsupp = 0.5$. We can search local frequent itemsets in D_1 as follows: A, B, C, AB, AC, BC, and ABC, where XY indicates the conjunction of X and Y. Local frequent itemsets in D_2 are searched for as follows: A, B, C, and AB. Local frequent itemsets in D_3 are searched for as follows: A, B, C, and BC. Local frequent itemsets in D_4 are searched as follows: F, H, and FH. Local frequent itemsets in D_5 are searched for as follows: E, F, H, J, EJ, FH, FJ, and FHJ. And local frequent itemsets in D_6 are searched for as follows: E, F, H, I, J, EH, FH, and HJ.

Local frequent itemsets in internal database ID are searched for as follows: A, B, C, AB, AC, BC, and ABC.

Let's examine existing techniques and check whether some can serve the purpose of selection, pretending no knowledge of which database contains interesting information. We call this the first solution.

1. The first solution (the traditional data collection technique) is to put all data together from the given database and the six collected databases to create a single database $TD = ID \cup D_1 \cup D_2 \cup \cdots \cup D_6$, which has 26 transactions. We now search the local frequent itemsets in TD above, as listed in Table 4.1.

Table 4.1 *Information of local frequent itemsets in the database TD*

Itemsets	Frequency	$\geq minsupp$
A	12	n
B	12	n
C	13	y
AB	7	n
AC	8	n
BC	9	n
ABC	5	n
E	6	n
F	8	n
H	9	n
I	3	n
J	6	n
EH	4	n
EJ	3	n
FH	8	n
HJ	5	n
FHJ	4	n

There is only one frequent itemset C when $minsupp = 0.5$. To discover the database TD, we need another minimum support as specified by users or experts. For example, $minsupp = 0.115$. Then, all the above itemsets listed in Table 4.1 are frequent itemsets, and itemsets such as AD, BD, and EF are also frequent itemsets in TD.

Actually, in the above six external databases, only the former three databases are likely to be relevant to the internal database. The latter three databases are unlikely to be relevant to the internal database. The technique developed in this chapter can meet the requirements of the above application.

The second solution is now described.

2. The second solution is the quality data model presented in this book. The approach works as follows. First, it selects believable databases: $class_1 = \{D_1, D_2, D_3\}$. Second, the databases and internal database are put into a single database TD_1. TD_1 has 13 transactions. Finally, it explores TD_1. In this way, we get a better effect from the quality data model. Table 4.2 illustrates the effectiveness of identifying quality data in TD_1.

Table 4.2 *Information of local frequent itemsets in the database* TD_1

Itemsets	Frequency	$\geq minsupp$
A	11	y
B	11	y
C	12	y
AB	7	n
AC	8	y
BC	9	y
ABC	5	n

By $minsupp = 0.5$, A, B, C, AC, and BC are frequent itemsets in TD_1.

From the above, commonly used techniques can not only increase search costs, but also disguise useful patterns due to the fact that huge amounts of irrelevant data are included. Our quality data model is significantly more effective. The following sections explore basic techniques for identifying quality data.

4.2.3 Needed Concepts

Our logical framework for identifying quality knowledge is based on the work in (Su-LWZZC 2001), and we now recall some necessary concepts.

As argued previously, data sharing is often impossible. Assume that a data-source is taken as a knowledge base and a company is viewed as a data-source.[1] Then, we interchange the terms "internal knowledge" and "known knowledge". In the description of our logical framework, we don't deal with support and confidence of a rule yet. That is, a rule has two values in a data-source: true (the data-source supports the rule) and false (otherwise). This means, if an association rule is identified from a data-source, then the rule is true in the data-source.

To identify quality knowledge from data-sources, we advocate a formal framework that pursues the following principle.

> If a data-source i believes that another data-source j is *veridical*, that is, in terms of standard multi-modal language $K_i(K_j\alpha \Rightarrow \alpha)$ for all formulas α, then data-source i inherits and accepts the knowledge in data-source j. Otherwise, the knowledge in the data-source j must be pre-processed before it is applied.

In the above stipulation, the knowledge in the data-source i is referred to as internal knowledge and the knowledge in the data-source j is referred to as external knowledge.

---

[1] For convenience, we also call a company a data-source in a knowledge sharing environment. This is because a company is taken as a data-source when the company's knowledge is also shared by other companies.

For example, let D_1 be a data-source with a rule set $\{a_1 \rightarrow b_1\}$, D_2 be an external data-source with a rule set $\{a_2 \rightarrow b_2, a_3 \rightarrow b_3\}$, and data-source D_1 denotes that the external data-source D_2 is *veridical*. Then the data-source D_1 inherits and accepts the knowledge in D_2. This means D_1 has a rule set $\{a_1 \rightarrow b_1, a_2 \rightarrow b_2, a_3 \rightarrow b_3\}$, after collecting knowledge from D_2.

Our framework is focused on the following epistemic properties.

- *Veridicality.* Knowledge is true.
- *Introspection.* A data-source is aware of what it supports and of what it does not support.
- *Consistency.* A data-source's knowledge is noncontradictory.

The well-known modal logics **S5**, **K**, **T**, **K45**, and **KD45** have been constructed on different combinations among the above properties. In this chapter we build a new modal logic for multi-database mining, in which the veridicality and the introspection of knowledge are taken into account.[2] We allow the explicit mention of the introspection and the veridicality of a data-resource on its knowledge so that the formulae in our language indicate which one of K, T, S5, or K45 can be used by the data-resource.

We now recall some basic concepts and notations related to the modal logics for multi-database mining, which are used throughout this chapter.

The language of such logics is a propositional logic augmented by the modal operators $K_1, K_2, ..., K_n$, where $K_i\phi$ is read as *data-source i supports* ϕ.

We denote this language by $\mathcal{L}_n$. For convenience, we define *true* as an abbreviation for a fixed valid propositional formula, say $p \vee \neg p$, where p is primitive proposition. We abbreviate $\neg true$ by *false*.

According to (Halpern-Moses 1992), the semantics of these formulae can be given by means of the *Kripke structure* (Kripke 1963), which formalizes the intuition behind possible worlds. A Kripke structure is a tuple $(W, \pi, \mathcal{K}_1, ..., \mathcal{K}_n)$, where W is a set of *worlds*, π associates a truth assignment with the primitive propositions with each world, so that $\pi(w)(p) \in \{\textbf{true}, \textbf{false}\}$ for each world w, and primitive proposition p, and $\mathcal{K}_1, ..., \mathcal{K}_n$ are binary accessibility relations. By convention, $\mathcal{K}_i^M$ and π^M are used to refer to the $\mathcal{K}_i$ relation and the π function in the Kripke structure M, respectively. We omit the superscript M if it is clear from the context. Finally, we define

$$\mathcal{K}_i(w) = \{w' \mid \forall \phi \in w'(\mathcal{K}_i\phi)\}.$$

That is, $\mathcal{K}_i(w)$ is the set of worlds that data-source i considers possible in the world w.

A *situation* is a pair (M, w) consisting of a Kripke structure M and a world w in M. By using situations, we can inductively give semantics to formulae as follows: for primitive propositions p,

---

[2] The consistency is dealt with in Chapter 6. Therefore, we assume that the knowledge in data-sources is consistent for the time being.

$(M, w) \models p$ iff $\pi^M(w)(p) = $ **true**.

Conjunctions and negations are dealt with in the standard way. Finally,

$(M, w) \models \mathcal{K}_i \alpha$ iff for all $w' \in \mathcal{K}_i^M(w)$, $(M, w') \models \alpha$.

Thus, a data-source i supports α if α is true in all situations that the data-source considers possible.

Note that the Kripke structure M is fixed in the above inductive interpretation. However, as we show in the next section, our interpretation is different from the above case.

4.3 Nonstandard Interpretation

This section presents the semantical framework for our logic.

The language we define in this section is $\mathcal{L}_n$, augmented by two classes of special proposition constants: $\mathbf{I}_i$ and $\mathbf{V}_i$ $(1 \leq i \leq n)$, denoted by $\mathcal{L}_n(\mathbf{VI})$, where $\mathbf{I}_i$ and $\mathbf{V}_i$ $(1 \leq i \leq n)$ correspond to the epistemic properties, introspection and veridicality, respectively. The formula $\mathbf{I}_i$ means that data-source i is able to respect its knowledge, and the formula $\mathbf{V}_i$ means that data-source i supports true knowledge only.

The language $\mathcal{L}_n(\mathbf{VI})$ is tailored to represent and tackle the relationship between the internal and external knowledge encountered by data-sources. The most important advantage of this logic is that it distinguishes internal knowledge from external knowledge for a data-source, and allows us to identify quality knowledge from external data-sources.

Before interpreting the formulae of the language $\mathcal{L}_n(\mathbf{VI})$, we make some informal remarks concerning relationships. Generally, external knowledge may be subject to noise, and thus, if a data-source wants to gather reliable knowledge, it needs to have the ability to refine external knowledge. For these refining processes, we focus on the following three cases that are relevant to this chapter:

- If data-source i is veridical, then the data-source must have the refining process that deletes false pieces of external knowledge. Thus, even if data-source i has collected some fact p, data-source i does not necessarily support p whenever p is false and data-source i is veridical.
- For each data-source, there are usually certain special pieces of knowledge that concern the data-source itself. That is, the knowledge is immediately recognizable and accessible without having to be, considered together with its own or other data-sources, epistemic properties. Data-sources believe or refute such pieces of knowledge firmly, no matter what has been collected for them. The introspection property here is considered as such knowledge. That is, if data-source i is able to introspect, then data-source i must support it, no matter what has been collected for it.

- If data-source i is introspective, then the data-source has the refining process of introspection. This process is surprisingly dependent on the veridicality of data-source i, which leads to a somewhat subtle relationship between the external knowledge and the data-source's knowledge. In the absence of veridicality, the introspection of data-source i means that if it has collected some knowledge, then the data-source must support what has been collected. In the presence of veridicality, data-source i pays attention only to true knowledge. The introspection of data-source i thus indicates that (a) if data-source i has collected a proposition p which is true, then the data-source supports it, and (b) if a proposition p is false, then data-source i doesn't support p. Therefore, the meaning of introspection we use here is consistent with that in the literature.

We now present the interpretation of $\mathcal{L}_n(\mathbf{VI})$. By way of description, we use standard Kripke structures and situations in a nonstandard way. The key point is that the accessibility relation $\mathcal{K}_i$ in the Kripke structure is no longer related to data-source i's knowledge. In each situation (M, w), the syntactic counterpart of the situation, (M, w'), where $w' \in \mathcal{K}_i(w)$, is what data-source i has collected rather than its knowledge. Nonetheless, the relation $\mathcal{K}_i$, together with the actual world w, uniquely determines data-source i's knowledge in some implicit way.

Let $\models_N$ be the satisfaction relation we are going to define. The most subtle case is certainly that of dealing with the formulae of form $K_i\alpha$. One might tend to let

$$(M, w) \models_N K_i\alpha \text{ iff for all } w' \in \mathcal{K}_i(w), (M, w') \models_N \alpha.$$

This would be completely true if the (M, w')'s ($w' \in \mathcal{K}_i(w)$) were exactly those situations that are thought possible from the standpoint of data-source i's knowledge. Unfortunately, these (M, w')'s are thought possible only from the standpoint of what data-source i has collected. Indeed, if we did it in this way, we would get nothing but the well-known modal logic K_n. Thus, it is crucial to ask what situations data-source i might think possible from the standpoint of what it actually supports after checking and cogitating on the external knowledge. Therefore, let $\mathcal{S}_i(M, w)$ be the set of all such possible situations for the given situation (M, w). Then we interpret formulae of the form $K_i\alpha$ as

$$(M, w) \models_N K_i\alpha \text{ iff for all } (M', w') \in \mathcal{S}_i(M, w), (M', w') \models_N \alpha.$$

We now figure out what $\mathcal{S}_i(M, w)$ should be. There are four cases according to the logical style of data-source i in the situation (M, w).

1. If the logical style is $\mathbf{K}$, that is, the value of $\pi(w)$ is **false** at both $\mathbf{I}_i$ and $\mathbf{V}_i$, then data-source i is unable to distinguish its knowledge from what has been collected, and hence the situations in $\mathcal{S}_i(M, w)$ are exactly the same as in (M, w')'s, where $w' \in \mathcal{K}_i(w)$.

2. Assume the logical style is **T**, that is,

$$\pi(w)(\mathbf{I}_i) = \textbf{false} \text{ and } \pi(w)(\mathbf{V}_i) = \textbf{true};$$

then we get $\mathcal{S}_i(M, w)$ by adding the actual world w to each (M, w'), where $w' \in \mathcal{K}_i(w)$. This enables data-source i to delete the false piece of the collected knowledge.

3. Suppose the logical style is **K45**, that is,

$$\pi(w)(\mathbf{I}_i) = \textbf{true} \text{ and } \pi(w)(\mathbf{V}_i) = \textbf{false}.$$

Assuming data-source i thinks situations (M', w') possible based on its internal knowledge, we have, by the introspection of data-source i, that data-source i's external knowledge in each of those situations (M', w') is exactly the same as that in the actual situation (M, w), which is semantically represented as

$$\mathcal{K}_i^{M'}(w') = \mathcal{K}_i^{M}(w).$$

On the other hand, as we mentioned above, the introspection property $\mathbf{I}_i$ is such knowledge that, if it holds, then data-source i must support it, no matter what data-source i has collected. Thus, in each of those situations (M', w'), $\mathbf{I}_i$ must hold. Hence,

$$\pi^{M'}(w')(\mathbf{I}_i) = \textbf{true}.$$

Based on the above discussions, we define $\mathcal{S}_i(M, w)$ as the set of those situations (M', w'), where $w' \in \mathcal{K}_i^{M}(w)$ and M' coincides with M, but,

$$\mathcal{K}_i^{M'}(w') = \mathcal{K}_i^{M}(w) \text{ and } \pi^{M'}(w')(\mathbf{I}_i) = \textbf{true}.$$

For convenience, we denote the above M' Kripke structures by

$$M\left[\frac{\mathcal{K}_i(w')}{\mathcal{K}_i(w)}; \frac{\pi(w')(\mathbf{I}_i)}{\textbf{true}}\right].$$

4. Let the logical style be **S5**. Then, by considering the veridicality, we should put the actual world w into the set $\mathcal{K}_i^{M}(w)$, and assume that $\mathcal{K}_i^{M}(w) \cup \{w\}$ is the set of worlds possible from the standpoint of data-source i's external knowledge. By considering the introspection, we define $\mathcal{S}_i(M, w)$ in the same way as in the case of **K45**. Nevertheless, $\mathcal{K}_i^{M}(w)$, the set of worlds possible from the standpoint of data-source i's external knowledge, is replaced by $\mathcal{K}_i^{M}(w) \cup \{w\}$. In other words, we define $\mathcal{S}_i(M, w)$ as the set of those situations (M', w'), where $w' \in \mathcal{K}_i^{M}(w) \cup \{w\}$, and M' coincides with M, but

$$\mathcal{K}_i^{M'}(w') = \mathcal{K}_i^{M}(w) \cup \{w\} \text{ and } \pi^{M'}(w')(\mathbf{I}_i) = \textbf{true}.$$

For convenience, we denote the M' Kripke structures by

$$M \left[\frac{\mathcal{K}_i(w')}{\mathcal{K}_i(w) \cup \{w\}} ; \frac{\pi(w')(\mathbf{I}_i)}{\textbf{true}} \right].$$

As we have seen, $\mathcal{S}_i(M, w)$ is equal to

1. $\{(M, w') \mid w' \in \mathcal{K}_i^M(w)\}$,

    if $\pi(w)(\mathbf{I}_i) = \textbf{false}$ and $\pi(w)(\mathbf{V}_i) = \textbf{false}$;

2. $\{(M, w') \mid w' \in \mathcal{K}_i^M(w)\} \cup \{(M, w)\}$,

    if $\pi(w)(\mathbf{I}_i) = \textbf{false}$ and $\pi(w)(\mathbf{V}_i) = \textbf{true}$;

3. $\{(M[\frac{\mathcal{K}_i(w')}{\mathcal{K}_i(w)}; \frac{\pi(w')(\mathbf{I}_i)}{\textbf{true}}], w') \mid w' \in \mathcal{K}_i^M(w)\}$,

    if $\pi(w)(\mathbf{I}_i) = \textbf{true}$ and $\pi(w)(\mathbf{V}_i) = \textbf{false}$;

4. $\{(M[\frac{\mathcal{K}_i(w')}{\mathcal{K}_i(w) \cup \{w\}}; \frac{\pi(w')(\mathbf{I}_i)}{\textbf{true}}], w') \mid w' \in \mathcal{K}_i^M(w) \cup \{w\}\}$,

    if $\pi(w)(\mathbf{I}_i) = \textbf{true}$ and $\pi(w)(\mathbf{V}_i) = \textbf{true}$.

From the above discussion, we can obtain the following properties of $\mathcal{S}_i$.

Proposition 4.1 *For all situations (M, w):*

(1) if $\pi^M(w)(\mathbf{V}_i) = \textbf{true}$ and $\pi^M(w)(\mathbf{I}_i) = \textbf{false}$,
    then $(M, w) \in \mathcal{S}_i(M, w)$;

(2) if $\pi^M(w)(\mathbf{V}_i) = \textbf{true}$ and $\pi^M(w)(\mathbf{I}_i) = \textbf{true}$,
    then $\left(M \left[\frac{\mathcal{K}_i(w)}{\mathcal{K}_i(w) \cup \{w\}} \right], w \right) \in \mathcal{S}_i(M, w)$;

(3) if $\pi^M(w)(\mathbf{I}_i) = \textbf{true}$,
    then, for all situations (M', w') in $\mathcal{S}_i(M, w)$,

$$\pi^{M'}(w')(\mathbf{I}_i) = \textbf{true} \text{ and } \mathcal{S}_i(M', w') = \mathcal{S}_i(M, w)$$

The properties can be directly proven by the above definitions and discussion.

We now formally present our semantics framework by defining inductively the satisfaction relation $\models_N$ between a situation and a formula, as follows.

(1) $(M, w) \models_N p$ iff $\pi(w)(p) = \textbf{true}$, for primitive propositions p.
(2) $(M, w) \models_N \neg\alpha$ iff not $(M, w) \models_N \alpha$, and $(M, w) \models_N \alpha \wedge \beta$ iff $(M, w) \models_N \alpha$
    and $(M, w) \models_N \beta$.
(3) $(M, w) \models_N K_i\alpha$ iff $(M', w') \models_N \alpha$ for all $(M', w') \in \mathcal{S}_i(M, w)$.

We remark that according to this semantics, a veridical data-source takes the knowledge that has been collected and adds the current world to the set of possibilities to obtain its knowledge. However, it seems difficult to construct such a knowledge-sharing environment for data-sources because a data-source typically does not support what is in the current world, and it is impossible for it to perform this operation of adding the current world. Nevertheless, this does not imply this semantics is counter intuitive and suspectable. There might be no veridical data-source in the real world, but there are data-sources that do have the veridicality properties from the viewpoint of some other data-sources. For example, if data-source j thinks that data-source i is veridical, then, from data-source j's viewpoint, data-source i does not yet support the current world, but data-source j supports (or believes) that the current world is one of data-source j's possible worlds. Thus, if data-source j supposes that the current world is w and data-source i's set of possible worlds (corresponding to its external knowledge) is W, then data-source j thinks that data-source i's knowledge is determined by the set W adding the supposed current world w.

We end this section by presenting the following propositions, which are helpful for proving the validity of axioms in the next section.

Proposition 4.2 *For all formulae ϕ, if*

$$\pi^M(w)(\mathbf{V}_i) = \mathbf{true} \ \text{and} \ \pi^M(w)(\mathbf{I}_i) = \mathbf{true}$$

then, for each world w',

$$\left(M\left[\frac{\mathcal{K}_i(w)}{\mathcal{K}_i(w) \cup \{w\}}\right], w' \right) \models_N \phi \ \text{iff} \ (M, w') \models_N \phi.$$

Proof. The proof of this proposition is arrived at by somewhat tedious induction on the structure of ϕ. More precisely, assuming, for all subformulae of ϕ, that this claim holds for all M, i, w, and w', we show that it holds also for ϕ. Suppose

$$\pi^M(w)(\mathbf{V}_i) = \mathbf{true} \ \text{and} \ \pi^M(w)(\mathbf{I}_i) = \mathbf{true}.$$

If ϕ is a primitive proposition p, it is immediately derived from the facts that assignment function π is the same in both the Kripke structures M and $M[\frac{\mathcal{K}_i(w)}{\mathcal{K}_i(w) \cup \{w\}}]$. Cases, where ϕ is a conjunction or a negation, follow from the definition of $\models_N$ above.

If ϕ is of the form $K_i\psi$, then, in the case of $w = w'$, the claim holds since it is easy to check that

$$\mathcal{S}_i(M, w) = \mathcal{S}_i\left(M\left[\frac{\mathcal{K}_i(w')}{\mathcal{K}_i(w) \cup \{w\}}\right], w \right)$$

Thus, we can assume $w \neq w'$. There are four subcases as follows:

1. $\pi^M(w')(\mathbf{V}_i) = \mathbf{false}$ and $\pi^M(w')(\mathbf{I}_i) = \mathbf{false}$;
2. $\pi^M(w')(\mathbf{V}_i) = \mathbf{true}$ and $\pi^M(w')(\mathbf{I}_i) = \mathbf{false}$;
3. $\pi^M(w')(\mathbf{V}_i) = \mathbf{false}$ and $\pi^M(w')(\mathbf{I}_i) = \mathbf{true}$;
4. $\pi^M(w')(\mathbf{V}_i) = \mathbf{true}$ and $\pi^M(w')(\mathbf{I}_i) = \mathbf{true}$.

Subcases 1 and 2 are followed immediately through the definition of $\models_N$ and the inductive assumption. For subcase 3, we first note that, by $w \neq w'$,

$$\mathcal{K}_i^M(w') = \mathcal{K}_i^{M\left[\frac{\mathcal{K}_i(w)}{\mathcal{K}_i(w) \cup \{w\}}\right]}(w').$$

Accordingly, by definition of $\models_N$, it suffices to show, for each $w'' \in \mathcal{K}_i^M(w')$, that

$$\left(M\left[\frac{\mathcal{K}_i(w)}{\mathcal{K}_i(w) \cup \{w\}}\right]\left[\frac{\mathcal{K}_i(w'')}{\mathcal{K}_i(w')}; \frac{\pi(w'')(\mathbf{I}_i)}{\mathbf{true}}\right], w''\right) \models_N \psi$$

iff

$$\left(M\left[\frac{\mathcal{K}_i(w'')}{\mathcal{K}_i(w')}; \frac{\pi(w'')(\mathbf{I}_i)}{\mathbf{true}}\right], w''\right) \models_N \psi.$$

Note that the assertion above holds if $w'' = w$, because

$$M\left[\frac{\mathcal{K}_i(w)}{\mathcal{K}_i(w) \cup \{w\}}\right]\left[\frac{\mathcal{K}_i(w)}{\mathcal{K}_i(w')}; \frac{\pi(w)(\mathbf{I}_i)}{\mathbf{true}}\right]$$

equals

$$M\left[\frac{\mathcal{K}_i(w)}{\mathcal{K}_i(w')}; \frac{\pi(w)(\mathbf{I}_i)}{\mathbf{true}}\right].$$

And, if $w'' \neq w$, then this assertion holds also by the inductive assumption. Subcase 4 can also be proved in the same way.

Finally, suppose that ϕ is of the form $K_j\psi$ for $j \neq i$. This case is also divided into four subcases depending upon the values of $\pi^M(w)$ at $\mathbf{V}_j$ and $\mathbf{I}_j$. We prove the claim only in the case where data-source i's logical style is **S5**, that is,

$$\pi^M(w')(\mathbf{V}_i) = \mathbf{true} \text{ and } \pi^M(w')(\mathbf{I}_i) = \mathbf{true},$$

since other cases are simpler, or can be handled in the same way. In this subcase, by the definition of $\models_N$, it suffices to show, for every $w'' \in \mathcal{K}_j(w') \cup \{w'\}$, that

$$\left(M\left[\frac{\mathcal{K}_i(w)}{\mathcal{K}_i(w) \cup \{w\}}\right]\left[\frac{\mathcal{K}_i(w'')}{\mathcal{K}_i(w') \cup w'}; \frac{\pi(w'')(\mathbf{I}_i)}{\mathbf{true}}\right], w''\right) \models_N \psi$$

iff

$$\left(M\left[\frac{\mathcal{K}_i(w'')}{\mathcal{K}_i(w') \cup \{w'\}}; \frac{\pi(w'')(\mathbf{I}_i)}{\mathbf{true}}\right], w''\right) \models_N \psi.$$

But this can be obtained in a straightforward way by the inductive assumption because, even if $w'' = w$, in the Kripke structure

$$M \left[\frac{\mathcal{K}_i(w'')}{\mathcal{K}_i(w') \cup \{w'\}} ; \frac{\pi(w'')(\mathbf{I}_i)}{\mathbf{true}} \right] ,$$

data-source i's logical style in world w remains **S5**, that is,

$$\pi^M(w')(\mathbf{V}_i) = \mathbf{true} \text{ and } \pi^M(w')(\mathbf{I}_i) = \mathbf{true}.$$

Hence, the inductive assumption can be applied.   ◇

The following proposition reflects some of the formal properties of $\models_N$.

Proposition 4.3 *For all formulae α, $\beta \in \mathcal{L}_n(\mathbf{VI})$, and situations (M, w):*

(1) $(M, w) \models_N (K_i\alpha \wedge K_i(\alpha \Rightarrow \beta)) \Rightarrow K_i\beta$;
(2) $(M, w) \models_N \mathbf{V}_i \Rightarrow (K_i\alpha \Rightarrow \alpha)$;
(3) $(M, w) \models_N \mathbf{I}_i \Rightarrow (K_i\mathbf{I}_i \wedge (K_i\alpha \Rightarrow K_iK_i\alpha) \wedge (\neg K_i\alpha \Rightarrow K_i\neg K_i\alpha))$.

Proof. To prove part (1), assuming $(M, w) \models_N K_i\alpha \wedge K_i(\alpha \Rightarrow \beta)$, we must show $(M, w) \models_N \beta$. But by the assumption, we have, for each $(M', w') \in \mathcal{S}_i(M, w)$, $(M', w') \models_N \alpha$ and $(M', w') \models_N \alpha \Rightarrow \beta$. It follows that $(M', w') \models_N \beta$ for all such (M', w') and, therefore, $(M, w) \models_N \beta$. Parts (2) and (3) can immediately be obtained from Proposition 4.1(1) and Proposition 4.1(2), respectively.   ◇

4.4 Proof Theory

With respect to the semantic framework in the previous section, we present a sound and complete proof theory below. For any data-source i:

P. All instances of axioms of propositional logic,
K. $(K_i\alpha \wedge K_i(\alpha \Rightarrow \beta)) \Rightarrow K_i\beta$,
T. $\mathbf{V}_i \Rightarrow (K_i\alpha \Rightarrow \alpha)$,
K45. $\mathbf{I}_i \Rightarrow (K_i\mathbf{I}_i \wedge (K_i\alpha \Rightarrow K_iK_i\alpha) \wedge (\neg K_i\alpha \Rightarrow K_i\neg K_i\alpha))$,

and rules of inference:

R1. From α and $\alpha \Rightarrow \beta$ infer β
R2. From α infer $K_i\alpha$.

Axioms **P** and **K**, and the inference rules **R1** and **R2**, consist of the well-known modal logical system K_n. Axioms **T** and **K45** capture the aforementioned meanings of the constants $\mathbf{I}_i$s and $\mathbf{V}_i$, respectively. We denote this system by $K_n^{\mathbf{VI}}$, for convenience. Two main results of our logic are the soundness and completeness of the proof system $K_n^{\mathbf{VI}}$. The soundness is easy to check; nevertheless, we need Proposition 4.2 to prove the validity of Axiom **T**, as shown in the proof of Proposition 4.3. Completeness is proved by the standard techniques originally due to Kaplan (Kaplan 1966) that show the close correspondence between the axioms and a particular Kripke structure called the *canonical structure*.

Theorem 4.1 *For the language* $\mathcal{L}_n(\mathbf{VI})$, *the system* $K_n^{\mathbf{VI}}$ *is a sound and complete axiomatization with respect to the semantics presented in the previous section.*

Proof. *The soundness part:* The validity of axiom **P** and rule **R1** follows immediately from the fact that the interpretation of $\wedge$ and $\neg$ in the definition of $\models_N$ is the same in the propositional calculus. The validity of axioms **K**, **T**, and **45** are just from Proposition 4.3. For rule **R2**, if $(M, w) \models_N \alpha$ for all situations (M, w), then for any fixed situation (M', w'), it follows that $(M, w) \models_N \alpha$ for all situations $(M, w) \in \mathcal{S}_i(M', w')$. Thus, $(M', w') \models_N K_i\alpha$ for all situations (M', w').

The completeness part: It suffices to prove that every consistent formula is satisfied by some situation. We construct a special Kripke structure M^c, called a canonical Kripke structure, as follows. Given a set w of formulae, define $w/K_i = \{\phi : K_i\phi \in V\}$. Let $M^c(W, \pi, \mathcal{K}_1, ..., \mathcal{K}_n)$, where

$$
\begin{aligned}
W &= \{w : w \text{ is a maximal consistent set}\} \\
\pi(w)(p) &= \begin{cases} \mathbf{true} & \text{if } p \in w \\ \mathbf{false} & \text{if } p \notin w \end{cases} \\
\mathcal{K}_i &= \{(w, w') : w/K_i \subseteq w'\}.
\end{aligned}
$$

We first show that for each $w \in W$, $\mathcal{S}_i(M^c, w) = \{(M^c, w') : w' \in \mathcal{K}_i(w)\}$, we have

$$(M^c, w) \models_N K_i\phi \text{ iff } (M^c, w') \models_N \phi \text{ for all } w' \in \mathcal{K}_i(w), \qquad (*)$$

which is referred to as fact $(*)$.

First, if the logical style of data-source i is K, that is,

$$\pi(w)(\mathbf{I}_i) = \mathbf{false} \text{ and } \pi(w)(\mathbf{V}_i) = \mathbf{false},$$

then, by the definition of $\mathcal{S}_i$, this claim is trivially true.

Second, if the logical style of data-source i is T, that is,

$$\pi(w)(\mathbf{I}_i) = \mathbf{false} \text{ and } \pi(w)(\mathbf{V}_i) = \mathbf{true},$$

then, by the definition,

$$\mathcal{S}_i(M^c, w) = \{(M^c, w') : w' \in \mathcal{K}_i(w)\} \cup \{(M^c, w)\}.$$

But by Axiom **T**, and maximality of w, we have that $w/K_i \subseteq w$. It follows then that $w \in \mathcal{K}_i(w)$, and hence

$$\mathcal{S}_i(M^c, w) = \{(M^c, w') : w' \in \mathcal{K}_i(w)\}$$

Third, suppose that the logical style of data-source i is K45, or

$$\pi(w)(\mathbf{I}_i) = \mathbf{true} \text{ and } \pi(w)(\mathbf{V}_i) = \mathbf{false}.$$

By the definition, it suffices to show that

$$\forall w' \in \mathcal{K}_i(w), (M^c[\frac{\mathcal{K}_i(w')}{\mathcal{K}_i(w)}; \frac{\pi(w')(\mathbf{I}_i)}{\mathbf{true}}], w') = (M^c, w'),$$

that is, $\mathcal{K}_i(w') = \mathcal{K}_i(w)$ and $\pi(w')(\mathbf{I}_i) = \mathbf{true}$. By Axiom **45** and the fact $\pi(w)(\mathbf{I}_i) = \mathbf{true}$, that is, $\mathbf{I}_i \in w$, we have $K_i \mathbf{I}_i \in w$, and hence $\mathbf{I}_i \in w'$, that is, $\pi(w')(\mathbf{I}_i) = \mathbf{true}$. To show $\mathcal{K}_i(w') = \mathcal{K}_i(w)$, given an arbitrary $w'' \in W$, we must prove that $w/K_i \subseteq w''$ iff $w'/K_i \subseteq w'$. Assuming $w/K_i \subseteq w''$ and $\phi \in w'/K_i$, we want to show $\phi \in w''$. If not, then $K_i \phi \notin w$, and hence $\neg K_i \phi \in w$. Thus, by Axiom **45**, we would have $K_i \neg K_i \phi \in w$ whence $\neg K_i \phi \in w'$, contradicting the assumption $\phi \in w'/K_i$.

On the other hand, assuming $w'/K_i \subseteq w''$ and $\phi \in w/K_i$, we have that $K_i \phi \in w$, and hence by Axiom **45**, $K_i K_i \phi \in w$. Thus

$$K_i \phi \in w' (\text{by } w/K_i \subseteq w')$$

and

$$\phi \in w'' (w'/K_i \subseteq w'')$$

Finally, for the case where the logical style of data-source i is S5, that is, $\pi(w)(\mathbf{I}_i) = \mathbf{true}$ and $\pi(w)(\mathbf{V}_i) = \mathbf{true}$, by the same argument above, it suffices to show that $w \in \mathcal{K}_i(w)$, $\mathcal{K}_i(w') = \mathcal{K}_i(w)$, and $\pi(w')(\mathbf{I}_i) = \mathbf{true}$. But, as we have shown, the first follows from $\pi(w)(\mathbf{V}_i) = \mathbf{true}$ and Axiom **T**, and the last two from $\pi(w)(\mathbf{I}_i) = \mathbf{true}$ and Axiom **45**.

We now show, by induction on the structure of ϕ, that for all w we have that

$$(M^c, w) \models_N \phi \text{ iff } \phi \in w. \qquad (**)$$

More exactly, assuming that the claim holds for all subformulae of ϕ, we also show that it holds for ϕ. If ϕ is a primitive proposition p, this comes immediately from the definition of $\pi(w)$ above. The case where ϕ is a conjunction of a negation follows easily from the definition of $\models_N$, and some of the basic properties of a maximally consistent set of formulae.

Finally, suppose that ϕ is of the form $K_i \psi$ and that $\psi \in w$; then $\psi \in w/K_i$. Thus, by definition of K_i, for all $w' \in \mathcal{K}_i(w)$, $\psi \in w'$, and hence, by the inductive hypothesis, $(M^c, w') \models_N \psi$. Thus, by the fact $(*)$, it follows that $(M^c, w) \models_N K_i \psi$.

For the other direction, assuming $(M^c, w) \models_N K_i \psi$, we must prove $K_i \psi \in w$. We first show that $w/K_i \cup \{\psi\}$ is inconsistent. Suppose not; then, it would have a maximal consistent extension w', and, by construction, we would have that $w' \in \mathcal{K}_i(w)$. By the inductive hypothesis, we would have $(M^c, w') \models_N \neg \psi$, and so $(M^c, w) \not\models_N K_i \psi$ by the fact $(*)$, contradicting our previous assumption.

Since $w/K_i \cup \{\psi\}$ is inconsistent, some finite subset, say, $\{\phi_1, ..., \phi_k, \neg \psi\}$, must be also inconsistent. Thus, by propositional reasoning, we have

$$\vdash \phi_1 \Rightarrow (\phi_2 \Rightarrow (\cdots (\phi_k \Rightarrow \psi) \cdots)).$$

By **R2**, we have

$$K_i \vdash \phi_1 \Rightarrow (\phi_2 \Rightarrow (\cdots (\phi_k \Rightarrow \psi) \cdots)).$$

Therefore, by iterated applications of Axiom **K** and propositional reasoning, we get

$$K_i\phi_1, K_i\phi_2, \cdots K_i\phi_k \vdash K_i\psi.$$

Since ϕ_1, ..., $\phi_k \in w/K_i$, we must have $K_i\phi_1$, ..., $K_i\phi_k \in w$. Since w is a maximally consistent set of formulae, it must be closed under $\vdash$. Therefore, $K_i\psi \in w$. $\diamond$

4.5 Adding External Knowledge

We now present a more explicit analysis of the relationship between external knowledge and internal knowledge. As mentioned earlier, this issue is thought surprisingly subtle whenever more than one data-source is in an environment.

To clarify some of subtleties involved in this issue, we formally define the language $\mathcal{L}_n^T(\mathbf{VI})$ to be the result of extending $\mathcal{L}_n(\mathbf{VI})$ by adding new operators T_1, ..., T_n. Thus, if ϕ is a formula, then so is $T_i\phi$, which is read as *data-source i has collected ϕ*.

For data-source i, the external or objective state, means what has been collected from other data-sources and what holds in the actual world excluding the introspection property of data-source i. Formulae that describe data-source i's external state are called *i-objective*. More precisely, i-objective formulae are Boolean combinations of primitive propositions (excluding $\mathbf{I}_i$) and formulae of the form $T_j\phi$, $j \neq i$. Similarly, i-subjective formulae are those that describe data-source i's subject state, that is, what data-source i has collected.

We formally interpret the language $\mathcal{L}_n^T(\mathbf{VI})$ by using the semantics presented in Section 4.3. We need only deal with formulae of the form $T_i\phi$. As we mentioned earlier, in our semantics, what accessibility relation $\mathcal{K}_i$ in Kripke structure directly models is simply the knowledge that data-source i has collected (rather than data-source i's knowledge). Thus, given a situation (M, w), we define

$$(M, w) \models_N T_i\phi \text{ iff } (M, w') \models_N \phi \ \forall w' \in \mathcal{K}_i(w).$$

According to the above definition, modality T_is need not satisfy veridicality axioms and introspection axioms. Intuitively, the reason for non-introspection is clear; we can certainly tell, or not tell, you something without telling you that we have collected or not collected it. Assuming that data-source i's external state remains unchanged since collection occurred, it seems that the veridicality depends only upon the honesty of the teller. We, however, argue that, even if the teller is honest, the veridicality of modality T_is is not necessarily true for i-subjective sentences, since data-source i's subjective state described by i-subjective sentences can be changed after data-source i has collected something. For example, once data-source i has collected "p is true but you do not support it," this sentence does not hold any longer, because the fact that data-source i has already collected changes data-source i's subjective state.

Let $K_n(T)$ be the well-known system K_n for the modalities T_i, instead of K_i. Clearly, the axioms **P** and **K**, and the inference rules in the system $K_n(T)$, are valid with respect to the semantics presented above. In addition, in the absence of K_i, the system $K_n(T)$ is complete also. Furthermore, we capture the following important properties of the relationship between external knowledge and internal knowledge.

Theorem 4.2 *Let ϕ and φ be arbitrary formulae of $\mathcal{L}_n^T(\mathbf{VI})$, and ψ be i-objective. Then the following formulae are valid, that is, satisfied in all situations (M, w):*

$(K_i\phi \wedge K_i(\phi \Rightarrow \varphi)) \Rightarrow K_i\varphi$;

$(\neg\mathbf{I}_i \wedge \neg\mathbf{V}_i) \Rightarrow (K_i\phi \Leftrightarrow T_i\phi)$;

$(\neg\mathbf{I}_i \wedge \mathbf{V}_i) \Rightarrow (K_i\phi \Leftrightarrow (T_i\phi \wedge \phi))$;

$\mathbf{I}_i \Rightarrow K_i\mathbf{I}_i$;

$(\mathbf{I}_i \wedge \neg\mathbf{V}_i) \Rightarrow (K_i\psi \Leftrightarrow T_i\psi)$;

$(\mathbf{I}_i \wedge \mathbf{V}_i) \Rightarrow (K_i\psi \Leftrightarrow T_i\psi \wedge \psi)$;

$(\mathbf{I}_i \wedge \neg\mathbf{V}_i) \Rightarrow ((T_i\phi \Rightarrow K_iT_i\phi) \wedge \\ (\neg T_i\phi \Rightarrow K_i\neg T_i\phi))$;

$(\mathbf{I}_i \wedge \mathbf{V}_i) \Rightarrow (((T_i\phi \wedge \phi) \Rightarrow K_iT_i\phi) \wedge$

$((\neg T_i\phi \vee \neg\phi) \Rightarrow K_i\neg T_i\phi)))$.

These results of the theorem are easy to check by using a routine method; we omit their proofs here. Let $TK_n^{\mathbf{VI}}$ be the system that results from adding the above valid formulae for each i to the axioms for the system $K_n(T)$. For convenience, we use TK_j, for $1 \leq j \leq 8$, to refer to the jth formulae in the theorem above. By $\vdash_{TK} \varphi$ we mean that φ is a theorem in $TK_n^{\mathbf{VI}}$.

Theorem 4.3 *For each formula ϕ in $\mathcal{L}_n^T(\mathbf{VI})$, there is a formula ϕ' such that, in the system $TK_n^{\mathbf{VI}}$, the two formulae are provably equivalent, but the latter does not have any appearance of K_is.*

Proof. Note that each formula with an appearance of K_i must have a sub-formula of the form $K_i\phi$, where ϕ has no appearance of K_i. Thus, it suffices to show that the formula $K_i\phi$ is provably equivalent to some formula without any appearance of K_i. We prove this assertion by induction on the length of ϕ, and assume that the assertion holds for all formulae with a length less than that of ϕ.

There are three cases. First, if ϕ is objective, then, by Axioms TK_2, TK_3, TK_5, and TK_6, it follows that

$$\vdash_{TK} K_i\phi \Leftrightarrow (((\neg\mathbf{I}_i \wedge \neg\mathbf{V}_i) \wedge T_i\phi)$$
$$\vee ((\neg\mathbf{I}_i \wedge \mathbf{V}_i) \wedge (T_i\phi \wedge \phi))$$
$$\vee ((\mathbf{I}_i \wedge \neg\mathbf{V}_i) \wedge T_i\phi)$$
$$\vee ((\mathbf{I}_i \wedge \mathbf{V}_i) \wedge (T_i\phi \wedge \phi))).$$

Second, if ϕ is of the form $\phi_1 \wedge \phi_2$, then, by axiom TK_1, we have that

$$\vdash_{TK} K_i\phi \Leftrightarrow K_i\phi_1 \wedge K_i\phi_2.$$

Our assertion holds by the inductive assumption.

Finally, suppose ϕ is of the form $\neg\varphi$; then we further assume φ is of the form $\varphi_1 \wedge \varphi_2$, since the case when φ itself is the negation of a formula is trivial. As ϕ is not objective, without loss of generality, we suppose φ_1 to be one of the following forms (i) I_i, (ii) $\neg I_i$, (iii) $T_i\alpha$, and (iv) $\neg T_i\alpha$.

In case (i), by Axiom TK_4, we have that $\vdash_{TK} I_i \Rightarrow (K_i\phi \Leftrightarrow K_i\neg\varphi_2)$. Thus, we have

$$\vdash_{TK} K_i\phi \Leftrightarrow (((\neg\mathbf{I}_i \wedge \neg\mathbf{V}_i) \wedge T_i\phi)$$
$$\vee ((\neg\mathbf{I}_i \wedge \mathbf{V}_i) \wedge (T_i\phi \wedge \phi))$$
$$\vee (\mathbf{I}_i \wedge K_i\neg\varphi_2)).$$

The assertion holds by the inductive assumption.

In case (ii), by Axiom TK_4, we have that $\vdash_{TK} I_i \Rightarrow K_i\phi$. Hence

$$\vdash_{TK} K_i\phi \Leftrightarrow (((\neg\mathbf{I}_i \wedge \neg\mathbf{V}_i) \wedge T_i\phi)$$
$$\vee ((\neg\mathbf{I}_i \wedge \mathbf{V}_i) \wedge (T_i\phi \wedge \phi))$$
$$\vee \mathbf{I}_i).$$

The assertion thus holds.

Before considering cases (iii) and (iv), we give, by axioms TK_7 and TK_8, that

$$\vdash_{TK} I_i \Rightarrow (K_i T_i\alpha \vee K_i\neg T_i\alpha).$$

Thus,

$$\vdash_{TK} I_i \Rightarrow (K_i(\beta \vee \gamma) \Leftrightarrow (K_i\beta \vee K_i\gamma)).$$

So, in case (iii), we get that

$$\vdash_{TK} K_i\phi \Leftrightarrow (((\neg\mathbf{I}_i \wedge \neg\mathbf{V}_i) \wedge T_i\phi)$$
$$\vee ((\neg\mathbf{I}_i \wedge \mathbf{V}_i) \wedge (T_i\phi \wedge \phi))$$
$$\vee ((\mathbf{I}_i \wedge \neg\mathbf{V}_i) \wedge (\neg T_i\alpha \vee K_i\neg\varphi_2))$$
$$\vee ((\mathbf{I}_i \wedge \mathbf{V}_i) \wedge ((\neg T_i\alpha \vee \neg\alpha)$$
$$\vee K_i\neg\varphi_2))),$$

and in case (iv),

$$\vdash_{TK} K_i\phi \Leftrightarrow (((\neg\mathbf{I}_i \wedge \neg\mathbf{V}_i) \wedge T_i\phi)$$
$$\vee ((\neg\mathbf{I}_i \wedge \mathbf{V}_i) \wedge (T_i\phi \wedge \phi))$$
$$\vee ((\mathbf{I}_i \wedge \neg\mathbf{V}_i) \wedge (T_i\alpha \vee K_i\neg\varphi_2))$$
$$\vee ((\mathbf{I}_i \wedge \mathbf{V}_i) \wedge ((T_i\alpha \wedge \alpha) \vee K_i\neg\varphi_2))).$$

The assertion then holds by the inductive assumption.   ◇

For convenience, for an arbitrary formula φ and ϕ in $\mathcal{L}_n^T(\mathbf{VI})$, by $\overline{\varphi}$ we denote a formula that is provably equivalent to φ and has no appearance of K_is. By the above result, the following theorem follows immediately.

Theorem 4.4 (Soundness and completeness) *For the formulae in $\mathcal{L}_n^T(\mathbf{VI})$, the system $TK_n^{\mathbf{VI}}$ is a sound and complete axiomatization with respect to the semantics above.*

Proof. The proof of the soundness is easy; axioms TK_1 ... TK_8 are valid by Theorem 2, and other axioms and inference rules are trivially true. As for the completeness, assume that Γ is an arbitrary set of consistent formulae. We must prove that Γ is satisfied by some Kripke structure. Let the formula set $\Gamma' = \{\overline{\varphi} \mid \varphi \in \Gamma\}$. By Theorem 3, Γ is provably equivalent to Γ', and it suffices to show Γ' is satisfied by some Kripke structure. But it is well known that $K_n(T)$ is complete with respect to general Kripke structures. We therefore conclude that Γ' is satisfied by a Kripke structure.   ◇

We end this section by pointing out that

$$(\mathbf{I}_i \wedge \mathbf{V}_i) \Rightarrow (K_i\neg T_i\phi \Leftrightarrow (\neg T_i\phi \vee \neg\phi))$$

is valid and thus the formula $K_i\neg T_ip$ doesn't necessarily imply $\neg T_ip$, even under the condition $(\mathbf{I}_i \wedge \mathbf{V}_i)$. It follows that Axiom **T** doesn't hold for our extended language, which makes this system novel compared to the usual combinations of two classes of modalities (or modal logics).

This also sheds some light on the appropriateness of S5 as a logic of knowledge. The introspection axiom of S5 has been attacked at some length in the literature of philosophy and artificial intelligence (see, e.g., (Lamarre-Shoham 1994)). Our research indicates that, for veridical and introspective data-sources, logic $S5_n$ is an appropriate logic of knowledge; and the introspection axiom reasonably stands, even if there are other interactive modalities in the picture. Nevertheless, the veridicality axiom, which was not attacked before, does not necessarily hold in the presence of other modalities with respect to our semantics.

4.6 The Use of the Framework

As we have seen, the above framework provides a formal description for considering external knowledge under two epistemic properties: introspection and veridicality. It can be taken as a basis for K3D. This section illustrates the use of the logical framework by way of examples.

Let $DS_1 = \{a_1 \rightarrow b_1\}$ be an internal data source, and let $DS_2 = \{a_2 \rightarrow b_2, a_3 \rightarrow b_3, a_4 \rightarrow b_4\}$ and $DS_3 = \{a_2 \rightarrow b_2, a_5 \rightarrow b_4\}$ be two external data sources. Then DS_1 can form its own knowledge set $Ruleset1$ by collecting quality knowledge from DS_2 and DS_3 as follows.

1. When $\mathbf{I}_1$, DS_1 has the ability to select true rules in $DS_2 \cup DS_3$ and add them to $Ruleset1$. When $not(\mathbf{I}_1)$, $Ruleset1$ is formed dependent on $K_1(\mathbf{I}_2)$, $K_1(\mathbf{I}_3)$, $K_1(\mathbf{V}_2)$, and $K_1(\mathbf{V}_3)$.
2. When $not(\mathbf{V}_1)$, $Ruleset1 = \emptyset$. When $\mathbf{V}_1$, $Ruleset1$ is formed dependent on $K_1(\mathbf{I}_2)$, $K_1(\mathbf{I}_3)$, $K_1(\mathbf{V}_2)$, and $K_1(\mathbf{V}_3)$.
3. When $K_1(\mathbf{I}_2)$, $Ruleset1 = DS_1 \cup DS_2$. When $K_1(\mathbf{I}_3)$, $Ruleset1 = DS_1 \cup DS_3$. When $K_1(\mathbf{I}_2)$ and $K_1(\mathbf{I}_3)$, $Ruleset1 = DS_1 \cup DS_2 \cup DS_3$.
4. When $K_1(\mathbf{V}_2)$, true rules in DS_2 are added to $Ruleset1$. When $K_1(\mathbf{V}_3)$, true rules in DS_3 are added to $Ruleset1$.
5. When $K_1(\mathbf{V}_2)$ and $K_1(\mathbf{V}_3)$, true rules in $DS_2 \cup DS_3$ are added to $Ruleset1$. When $K_1(\mathbf{V}_2)$ or $K_1(\mathbf{V}_3)$, if the rule $a_2 \rightarrow b_2$ in $DS_2 \cap DS_3$ is true, $a_2 \rightarrow b_2$ are added to $Ruleset1$.

In the above examples, $K_1(\mathbf{I}_i)$ means that data-source DS_1 believes that data-source DS_i has introspection ability, while $K_1(\mathbf{V}_i)$ means that data-source DS_1 believes that data-source DS_i is veridical.

The values of $\mathbf{I}_1$ and $\mathbf{V}_1$ are determined by the domain knowledge in DS_1, whereas the values of $K_1(\mathbf{I}_2)$, $K_1(\mathbf{I}_3)$, $K_1(\mathbf{V}_2)$, and $K_1(\mathbf{V}_3)$ are determined by both domain knowledge and the experienced knowledge in DS_1. Domain knowledge can be a set of constraints. For example, the salary of a regular employee is not over $1000.00 per week. Experienced knowledge can be a set of rules extracted from historical data in data-sources. For example, customers think that the supermarket Safeway is credible.

4.6.1 Applying to Real-world Applications

We now show how to apply the proposed framework to a real-world application by example.

Consider a scenario as follows. An investor intends to buy a small company. He would like to consult his advisors about the purchase. After the two advisors analyze their information, both inform the investor that "if you buy the company you will get at least 5% each year on your investment." That advice may be weakened by unexpected competition, and thus it would prove to be unbelievable. But past experience of the investor indicates that, at every moment, at least one of advisors is believable. The investor therefore thinks one, at least, has *veridical* knowledge and concludes that he can buy the company and will profit by the purchase.

To model this simple example, we first introduce the operator $\text{Inform}_{i,j}$. Here $\text{Inform}_{i,j}\varphi$ means "data-source i tells data-source j φ" (or data-source j collects φ from data-source i). Suppose that the data-sources are honest, and our first constraint on this operator is:

$$\text{Inform}_{i,j}\varphi \Rightarrow K_i\varphi.$$

For $\text{Inform}_{i,j}\varphi \Rightarrow K_j\varphi$, we propose a constraint as follows,

$$\text{Inform}_{i,j}\varphi \Rightarrow T_j(K_i\varphi).$$

Note that, if φ is an objective formula, the above constraint leads, by the system $TK_n\mathbf{VI}$, to

$$\text{Inform}_{i,j}\varphi \wedge K_j\mathbf{V}_i \Rightarrow K_j\varphi.$$

This seems reasonable. Accordingly, we define the operator $\text{Inform}_{i,j}$ as follows,

$$\text{Inform}_{i,j}\varphi \Leftrightarrow (K_i\varphi \wedge T_j(K_i\varphi)).$$

Now name the investor as data-source 1, and the two advisors as data-source 2 and data-source 3. In addition, by the primitive proposition p, we denote the sentence "*if you buy the company you will get at least 5% each year on your investment.*" We thus get the following.

R1 $K_1(\mathbf{V}_2 \vee \mathbf{V}_3)$
R2 $\text{Inform}_{2,1}p \wedge \text{Inform}_{3,1}p.$

Thus, we get, by the system $TK_n\mathbf{VI}$, that K_1p. Therefore, the investor can get a reward of at least 5% each year from buying the company. Therefore, the investor can buy the company according to the above judgement.

In the above observation, our framework can match human intelligence. The investor uses personal experience to identify quality knowledge, R1 and R2, from data-sources for the purpose of problem solving before investment.

4.6.2 Evaluating Veridicality

To use the framework, we need to determine which data-sources are veridical with historical data, concerning data-sources. Using the veridicality, we can rank all data-sources by their veridical degrees decreasingly, and select the first 10%, or more, as veridical data-sources for applications.

The purpose of ranking is to pre-process the collected knowledge by determining veridical degrees of data-sources. With increasing information about data-sources, the reference list becomes more and more accurate, and data-sources will solely rely on it to share their data.

Consider data-sources $DS1$ through $DS4$ for 10 real-world applications as follows.

Table 4.3 *Historical data of using data-sources*

	DS1	DS2	DS3	DS4	result
a_1		1	1	1	yes
a_2	1	1	1	1	yes
a_3	1	1			no
a_4	1		1		no
a_5	1		1		no
a_6	1			1	yes
a_7		1	1	1	yes
a_8	1	1	1		yes
a_9	1	1			no
a_{10}	1	1	1	1	yes

Here, DSi stands for the ith data-source; a_i indicates the ith applications, and 1 stands for that the knowledge in a data-source is applied to an application. We use $DSi = 1$ to indicate that the ith data-source is applied to an application; *result* measures the success of the applications; *result* = *yes* means that an application is successful, and *result* = *no* means that an application has failed. For application a_1, three data-sources $DS2$, $DS3$, and $DS4$ have been applied.

After analyzing the past data, we can learn which data-sources are veridical. The data in the above table show

$$R1 : DS4 = 1 \rightarrow result = yes,$$
$$R2 : (DS1 = 1) \wedge (DS2 = 1) \wedge (DS3 = 1) \wedge (DS4 = 1)$$
$$\rightarrow result = yes,$$
$$R3 : (DS1 - 1) \wedge (DS2 - 1) \rightarrow result = no,$$
$$R4 : (DS1 = 1) \wedge (DS3 = 1) \rightarrow result = no,$$
$$R5 : (DS1 = 1) \wedge (DS2 = 1) \wedge (DS3 = 1) \rightarrow result = yes,$$
$$R6 : (DS1 = 1) \wedge (DS4 = 1) \rightarrow result = yes, and$$
$$R7 : (DS2 = 1) \wedge (DS3 = 1) \wedge (DS4 = 1) \rightarrow result = yes,$$

where $R1$ means that applications are successful when the knowledge in data-source $DS4$ is used in the applications; $R2$ means that applications are successful when $DS1$ through $DS4$ are all applied to the applications; and so on.

The above seven rules are considered when we determine the veridicality of data-sources. For example, the rules show that data-source $DS4$ is veridical in past applications.

Also, we can check whether an external pattern is trustworthy according to its historical data. Let $P1$, $P2$, ..., $P6$ be six patterns. The historical data for applying the patterns is listed in Table 4.4 as follows,

Table 4.4 *Historical data of applying patterns*

	P1	P2	P3	P4	P5	P6	result
a_1	1	1	1	1			yes
a_2	1	1			1	1	yes
a_3		1		1		1	no
a_4			1	1	1		no
a_5		1	1			1	no
a_6	1	1			1	1	yes
a_7	1	1	1	1			yes
a_8	1	1	1		1	1	yes
a_9		1	1		1	1	no
a_{10}			1	1	1	1	yes

where, Pi stands for the ith patterns, 1 says that a pattern is applied to an application (we use $Pi = 1$ to indicate that the ith pattern is applied to an application), and a_i and *result* are the same as in Table 4.3. For application a_1, the first four patterns, $P1$ through $P4$, have been applied.

From the data in Table 4.4, we can obtain

$$PR1: \ P1 = 1 \rightarrow result = yes,$$
$$PR2: \ (P1 = 1) \wedge (P2 = 1) \rightarrow result = yes,$$
$$PR3: \ (P1 = 1) \wedge (P5 = 1) \rightarrow result = yes,$$
$$PR4: \ (P1 = 1) \wedge (P6 = 1) \rightarrow result = yes,$$
$$PR5: \ (P1 = 1) \wedge (P2 = 1) \wedge (P5 = 1) \rightarrow result = yes,$$
$$PR6: \ (P1 = 1) \wedge (P2 = 1) \wedge (P6 = 1) \rightarrow result = yes,$$
$$PR7: \ (P1 = 1) \wedge (P5 = 1) \wedge (P6 = 1) \rightarrow result = yes,$$
$$PR8: \ (P1 = 1) \wedge (P2 = 1) \wedge (P5 = 1) \wedge (P6 = 1) \rightarrow result = yes,$$
$$PR9: \ (P1 = 1) \wedge (P3 = 1) \rightarrow result = yes,$$
$$PR10: (P1 = 1) \wedge (P2 = 1) \wedge (P3 = 1) \rightarrow result = yes,$$
$$PR11: (P1 = 1) \wedge (P4 = 1) \rightarrow result = yes,$$
$$PR12: (P1 = 1) \wedge (P2 = 1) \wedge (P4 = 1) \rightarrow result = yes,$$
$$PR13: (P1 = 1) \wedge (P3 = 1) \wedge (P4 = 1) \rightarrow result = yes,$$
$$PR14: (P1 = 1) \wedge (P2 = 1) \wedge (P3 = 1) \wedge (P4 = 1) \rightarrow result = yes,$$
$$PR15: (P3 = 1) \wedge (P4 = 1) \wedge (P5 = 1) \wedge (P6 = 1) \rightarrow result = yes, and$$
$$PR16: (P4 = 1) \wedge (P5 = 1) \wedge (P6 = 1) \rightarrow result = yes.$$

where $PR1$ means that applications are successful when the pattern $P1$ is used in those applications, $PR2$ means that applications are successful when both $P1$ and $P2$ are applied to the applications, and so on.

The above 16 rules are useful for determining which patterns can be used in future applications.

We now evaluate the veridicality of data-sources. In Table 4.4, the cases for applying the four data-sources, $DS1$ through $DS4$, are listed in Table 4.5 as follows.

Table 4.5 *The cases applying the four data-sources DS1, DS2, DS3, DS4*

	frequency	success	fail	success-ratio
DS1	8	4	4	0.5
DS2	7	5	2	0.714
DS3	7	5	2	0.714
DS4	4	4	0	1

Here, $frequency$ is the number of applications that use a data-source; $success$ is the successful times of application when a data-source was applied; $fail$ is the failure times of applications when a data-source was applied, success-ratio is $success/frequency$.

From the above table, $DS1$ was applied 8 times, with success-ratio 0.5; $DS2$ was applied 7 times, with success-ratio 0.714; $DS3$ was applied 7 times with success-ratio 0.714; and $DS4$ was applied 4 times with success-ratio 1.

Certainly, we can use the success-ratios to determine the veridical degrees of the data-sources. One way is to normalize the success-ratios of the veridical degrees of the data-sources as shown below.

$$vd_{DS1} = \frac{0.5}{0.5 + 0.714 + 0.714 + 1} = 0.167,$$

$$vd_{DS2} = \frac{0.714}{0.5 + 0.714 + 0.714 + 1} = 0.238,$$

$$vd_{DS3} = \frac{0.714}{0.5 + 0.714 + 0.714 + 1} = 0.238,$$

$$vd_{DS4} = \frac{1}{0.5 + 0.714 + 0.714 + 1} = 0.357,$$

where vd_{DSi} stands for the veridical degree of the ith data-source ($i = 1, 2, 3, 4$).

We have seen that data-source $DS4$ has the highest success-ratio and that it has the highest veridical degree. On the other hand, $DS1$ has the lowest success-ratio and it has the lowest veridical degree.

Furthermore, the the veridical degree of DS_i ($i = 1, 2, ..., n$) can be defined as follows.

$$vd_{DS_i} = \frac{\text{success-ratio of } DS_i}{\sum_{j=1}^{n} \text{success-ratio of } DS_j}. \tag{4.1}$$

However, for highlighting the data-sources with high success-ratios, we can construct many formulae to assign veridical degrees to data-sources. The simplest way is defined as

$$vd_{DS_i} = \frac{(\text{success-ratio of } DS_i)^2}{\sum_{j=1}^{n} (\text{success-ratio of } DS_j)^2}. \tag{4.2}$$

We now check the effectiveness using the above data.

$$vd_{DS1} = \frac{0.5^2}{0.5^2 + 0.714^2 + 0.714^2 + 1^2} = 0.11,$$

$$vd_{DS2} = \frac{0.714^2}{0.5^2 + 0.714^2 + 0.714^2 + 1^2} = 0.225,$$

$$vd_{DS3} = \frac{0.714^2}{0.5^2 + 0.714^2 + 0.714^2 + 1^2} = 0.225,$$

$$vd_{DS4} = \frac{1^2}{0.5^2 + 0.714^2 + 0.714^2 + 1^2} = 0.44.$$

In these formulae, data-source $DS4$ has the highest success-ratio and its veridical degree has been increased while $DS1$ has the lowest success-ratio and its veridical degree has been decreased. In other words, the data-sources with high success-ratios are highlighted. Accordingly, they are ranked as $DS4$, $DS2$, $DS3$, and $DS1$.

In our approach, we only focus on the veridicality when data-sources are ranked. Other factors are similar to the above. If there are multiple factors, we can synthesize them using the weighting techniques in (Good 1950).

4.7 Summary

Knowledge discovery in large-scale databases has received much attention recently (Agrawal-Imielinski-Swami 1993, Srikant-Agrawal 1996, Provost-Kolluri 1999). However, existing techniques may not always be helpful in identifying patterns from different data-sources. This is because knowledge from external data-sources may be untrustworthy, even fraudulent, and it can disguise certain real patterns useful to the application. For this reason, we have presented a framework for multi-database mining, aimed at identifying quality knowledge in high-veridical data-sources. As we have shown, the evaluation shows that our approach has improved the performance of utilizing external data-sources.

Our approach differs from traditional data mining techniques because (1) we distinguish internal knowledge from external knowledge; (2) our operating objects are different data-sources; and (3) untrustworthy and fraudulent knowledge is eliminated by veridicality analysis.

5. Database Clustering

In the past, identifying relevant databases has been typically *application-dependent*. The process had to be carried out multiple times to identify relevant databases for two or more real-world applications. This chapter advocates an efficient and effective application-independent database classification for mining multi-databases.

5.1 Introduction

In order to deal with the size of multi-databases, Liu et al. have developed an approach for identifying relevant databases (Liu-Lu-Yao 1998). The approach is effective in reducing search costs for mining applications. This can be taken as a first step in multi-database mining.

Because the database classification of Liu et al. selects the databases that are likely to be relevant to an application, their database classification is referred to as *database selection*. Database selection has to be carried out multiple times to identify relevant databases for two or more real-world applications. It should be noted that, when a mining task is without reference to any specific application, the database selection strategy does not work satisfactorily.

In this chapter we present an application-independent database classification strategy for multi-database mining. This classification is appropriate for general-purpose mining applications. The experimental results show that our proposed approach is effective and promising.

The rest of this chapter is organized as follows. In Section 5.2, the effectiveness of the classification is illustrated in a simple way. In Section 5.3, an approach is presented for classifying databases by similarity. In Section 5.4, we design an algorithm for searching for a good classification for given databases. In Section 5.5, we analyze the algorithm designed. In Section 5.6 the proposed approach is evaluated. The chapter is then summarized in the last section.

(Note: We take each database as a relation or a table, in this chapter and in the following chapters.)

5.2 Effectiveness of Classifying

If an interstate company, for example, is a comprehensive organization whose databases belong to different types of business and have different meta-data structures, the databases would have to be classified before the data are analyzed. Therefore, if a company such as Coles-Myer has 25 branches, including 5 supermarkets for food, 7 supermarkets for clothing, and 13 supermarkets for general commodities, they cannot simply apply mining techniques to discover patterns from the 25 databases in the 25 branches. The databases would first have to be classified into three classes according to specific business types. To show the effectiveness of classifying, an example is outlined below. Consider six databases D_1, D_2, ..., D_6, where

$$D_1 = \{(A, B, C, D); (B, C); (A, B, C); (A, C)\},$$
$$D_2 = \{(A, B); (A, C); (A, B, C); (B, C); (A, B, D)\},$$
$$D_3 = \{(B, C, D); (A, B, C); (B, C); (A, D)\},$$
$$D_4 = \{(F, G, H, I, J); (E, F, H); (F, H)\},$$
$$D_5 = \{(E, F, H, J); (F, H); (F, H, J); (E, J)\},$$
$$D_6 = \{(F, H, I, J); (E, H, J); (E, F, H); (E, I)\},$$

and each database has several transactions, separated by a semicolon, and each transaction contains several items, separated by a comma.

Let $minsupp = 0.5$. We can obtain frequent itemsets in each database as follows:

D_1 : A, B, C, AB, AC, BC, ABC;

D_2 : A, B, C, AB;

D_3 : A, B, C, BC;

D_4 : F, H, FH;

D_5 : $E, F, H, J, EJ, FH, FJ, FHJ$;

D_6 : $E, F, H, I, J, EH, FH, HJ$.

Let us examine the existing techniques to check whether some can serve the purpose of selection, pretending no knowledge as to which database contains interesting information (Liu-Lu-Yao 1998).

1. The first strategy (*technique for mono-database mining*) is to put all data together from the six databases to create a single database $TD = D_1 \cup D_2 \cup \cdots \cup D_6$ with 24 transactions. Each of the frequent itemsets from each database is listed in Table 5.1, where $minsupp = 0.5$.

Table 5.1 *Information of local frequent itemsets in the database* TD

Itemsets	Frequency	$\geq minsupp$
A	9	n
B	10	n
C	10	n
AB	6	n
AC	6	n
BC	8	n
ABC	4	n
E	6	n
F	8	n
H	9	n
I	3	n
J	6	n
EH	4	n
EJ	3	n
FH	8	n
HJ	5	n
FHJ	4	n

From Table 5.1, we can see there is no frequent itemset in TD when $minsupp = 0.5$. For applications, we need to specify another minimum support by users or experts. For example, $minsupp = 0.125$. Then all the above itemsets listed in Table 5.1 are frequent itemsets. And itemsets such as AD, BD, and EF are also frequent itemsets in TD.

If each database is large, and the number of databases is greater than six, then the number of frequent itemsets from each database may be so large that browsing them and finding interesting association rules can be rather difficult. Therefore, it is hard to identify which of the frequent itemsets from individual databases are useful.

There are also other problems in this strategy. (See (Liu-Lu-Yao 1998))

2. The second strategy is to use the application-dependent database selection in (Liu-Lu-Yao 1998) to select the databases that are likely to be relevant to an application. However, this mining task is without reference to any specific application. In this case, the strategy cannot work well.

In fact, the above six databases belong to two classes of applications. The first class is relevant to items A, B, C, and D; and the second is relevant to items E, F, G, H, I, and J. The technique developed in this chapter meets the requirements of the above application. It is regarded as the third strategy, and is described below.

3. The third strategy is a application-independent database classification. The approach works as follows. First, it classifies the databases into two

classes: $class_1 = \{D_1, D_2, D_3\}$ and $class_2 = \{D_4, D_5, D_6\}$. Second, the databases in $class_1$ are put into a single database TD_1, which has 13 transactions. And the databases in $class_2$ are put into a single database TD_2, which has 11 transactions. Finally, TD_1 and TD_2 are mined individually. In this way, we are able to receive a more effective result from the application-independent database classification. Tables 5.2 and 5.3 illustrate the effectiveness of classifying the databases into TD_1 and TD_2.

Table 5.2 *Information of local frequent itemsets in the database* TD_1

Itemsets	Frequency	$\geq minsupp$
A	9	y
B	10	y
C	10	y
AB	6	n
AC	6	n
BC	8	y
ABC	4	n

Table 5.3 *The information of local frequent itemsets in the database* TD_2

Itemsets	Frequency	$\geq minsupp$
E	6	y
F	8	y
H	9	y
I	3	n
J	6	y
EH	4	n
EJ	3	n
FH	8	y
HJ	5	n
FHJ	4	n

By $minsupp = 0.5$, A, B, C, and BC are frequent itemsets in TD_1; and E, F, H, J, and FH are frequent itemsets in TD_2.

From the above, we have seen that the technique for mono-database mining can disguise useful patterns because huge amounts of irrelevant data are included. Database selection is typically application-dependent. It cannot work well for the multi-database problem. (Further limitations of previous mining techniques for multi-databases were discussed in Chapter 2.) The application-independent database classification presents significant effectiveness.

The following sections aim at attacking certain key problems in database classification. They are (i) how to effectively measure the relevance of database-independent applications and (ii) how to effectively search for the best classification. These problems are difficult to solve, but are very important in the development of general-purpose multi-database mining systems.

5.3 Classifying Databases

In this section, we present a classification scheme by similarity between different databases, and also construct a criterion for evaluating different classifications.

5.3.1 Features in Databases

To classify multiple databases, we need to check what is used to evaluate the relevance between different databases. Indexing databases by features is a common technique. Therefore, we can measure the relevance between two databases by comparing their features.

There are different types of databases. They can be roughly divided into relational databases, transaction databases, and document sets from data structures. For convenience, the features for indexing the three kinds of databases are discussed briefly below.

1. A relational database is a set of relations. A relation is sometimes referred to as a database for convenience. A relational database (relation) scheme is a set of definite-size attributes. A relational database consists of definite-size records, where each record is an entity and each attribute of the entity is assigned a value in its domain.

   For different applications, we can use one each of a key set, attribute set, and record set as basis units of a database to represent that database.

2. A transaction database consists of indefinite-size transactions, where each transaction is a set of items. For different applications, we can use a transaction set, or item set, as basic units of a database to represent the database.

3. A document set is a set of documents, where a "document" typically consists of strings of characters. For an application, we can use single words (keywords), or phrases, or texts as the basic units of a document set to represent that set.

For simplicity, this chapter focuses on transaction databases. All items in a transaction database are taken as basic features for indexing the database.

If two databases share a significant number of common items, the two databases are relevant to each other. Classification is based on the items in each database. If a large transaction database has been mined for association rules, we can also use the discovered rules, or all items that occur in those rules, to represent the database.

Selecting features in a database is not easy when the items in the database are not given. Because databases in real-world applications are often very large, it is costly to search all features in multiple databases. In this case, we can use sampling techniques to sample each large database (Liu-Motoda 2001).

5.3.2 Similarity Measurement

"Metric databases" are databases where a metric similarity function is defined for pairs of database objects. Similarity between database objects is expressed by the closeness function such that a high closeness corresponds to a high degree of similarity, whereas two database objects with a very low closeness are considered to be rather dissimilar.

Assume that the database objects are drawn from a set *Databases* of multiple databases, and that *sim* is a metric closeness function for pairs of database objects, that is,

$$sim : Database \times Databases \rightarrow [0, 1].$$

A technique is presented to construct functions for similarity, *sim*, below.

Let $D_1, D_2, ..., D_m$ be m databases from the branches of an interstate company; $Item(D_i)$ the set of items in D_i; and S_i the set of association rules from D_i ($i = 1, 2, ..., m$). Databases in $DB = \{D_1, D_2, ..., D_m\}$ need to be classified. That is, DB is classified into K classes (subsets) such that any two databases in a class are relative, and any two databases in two different classes are not relative, under a measurement.

If we do not have any other information about these databases, the items from the databases can be used to measure the closeness of a pair of database objects. We call the measure sim_1, and define it as

1. The similarity between the items of two databases D_i and D_j is defined as follows,

$$sim_1(D_i, D_j) = \frac{|Item(D_i) \cap Item(D_j)|}{|Item(D_i) \cup Item(D_j)|} \tag{5.1}$$

where $\cap$ denotes set intersection, $\cup$ denotes set union, and $|Item(D_i) \cap Item(D_j)|$' is the number of elements in set $Item(D_i) \cap Item(D_j)$.

In the above definition of similarity, $sim_1 : DB \times DB \rightarrow [0, 1]$, the size of the intersection of a pair of database objects, is used to measure the closeness of the two databases. That is, a large intersection corresponds to a high degree of similarity, whereas two database objects with a small intersection are considered to be rather dissimilar.

Traditional similarity between database objects is expressed by the distance function, in which a low distance corresponds to a high degree of similarity, whereas two database objects with a large distance are considered to be rather dissimilar.

To capture the properties of the distance function, we can take $1 - sim_1$ as the distance of two database objects. For the purpose of description in this chapter, similarity is still measured by the size of the intersection of the two database objects.

The use of the above similarity is now illustrated by an example.

Example 5.1 *Let* $Item(D_1) = \{a_1, a_2, a_3\}$ *and* $Item(D_2) = \{a_2, a_3, b_1, b_2\}$ *be two sets of items of two databases* D_1 *and* D_2*, respectively. The similarity between* D_1 *and* D_2 *is as follows.*

$$
\begin{aligned}
sim_1(D_1, D_2) &= \frac{|Item(D_1) \cap Item(D_2)|}{|Item(D_1) \cup Item(D_2)|} \\
&= \frac{2}{5} \\
&= 0.4.
\end{aligned}
$$

If $sim_1(D_i, D_j) = 1$, it means only that $Item(D_i) = Item(D_j)$ or that D_i and D_j can belong entirely to the same class under the measurement sim_1. It does not mean that $D_i = D_j$, when $sim_1(D_i, D_j) = 1$.

The sim_1 measure is useful to estimate the similarity between two large transaction databases, because getting more information from the databases (such as the amount of items purchased by customers) is often expensive.

As we know, in the first instance, association rules for the database of each branch of an interstate company can be useful for the branch. And so association analysis at each branch is important and useful. In this way, we can get interesting information for the databases we deal with, using association rules of interest from each branch. If an item occurs at least once in a rule, we can take the item as an interesting one. To demonstrate how to construct a measure for similarity, another function is presented below using items of interest.

Meanwhile, the similarity between the two databases D_i and D_j can be approximated by the intersection of their two interesting items, where, for a database D_k, the interesting items are the items that occur in the rule set S_k from D_k $(k = 1, 2, ..., m)$.

2. We can construct the similarity sim_2 by using the interesting items in $S_1, S_2, ..., S_m$ as follows.

$$
sim_2(D_i, D_j) = \frac{|Item(S_i) \cap Item(S_j)|}{|Item(S_i) \cup Item(S_j)|}, \tag{5.2}
$$

where $Item(S_k)$ stands for the set of all items that occur in the association rules of S_k.

Let $S = \{S_1, S_2, ..., S_m\}$; then similarity sim_2 is the function $sim_2 : S \times S \to [0, 1]$. The size of the intersection of the interesting items of a pair of database objects is used to measure the closeness of the two databases. The use of similarity sim_2 is demonstrated by the following example.

Example 5.2 *Let* $S_1 = \{i_1 \wedge i_3 \to i_2, i_2 \to i_4, i_3 \to i_5\}$ *and* $S_2 = \{i_1 \wedge i_3 \to i_4, i_3 \to i_5, i_6 \to i_7\}$ *be two sets of association rules of two databases* D_1 *and* D_2, *respectively. Then* $Item(S_1) = \{i_1, i_2, i_3, i_4, i_5\}$ *and* $Item(S_2) = \{i_1, i_3, i_4, i_5, i_6, i_7\}$ *are the sets of interesting items of the databases* D_1 *and* D_2, *respectively. The similarity between* D_1 *and* D_2 *on the interesting items is as follows.*

$$sim_2(D_1, D_2) = \frac{|Item(S_1) \cap Item(S_2)|}{|Item(S_1) \cup Item(S_2)|}$$
$$= \frac{4}{7}$$
$$= 0.571.$$

In the above example, if $Item(D_1) = Item(D_2) = \{i_1, i_2, ..., i_8\}$, then $sim_1(D_1, D_2) = 1$, although $sim_2(D_1, D_2) = 0.571$. In fact, sim_2 measures the degree of interest. And, if D_1 and D_2 are the databases of two supermarkets in different places, then sim_2 can measure whether customers in the two places have the same purchasing behavior. This is useful for the decision-making of a company.

Actually, we can also define the function of similarity between two databases D_i and D_j directly by using the association rules.

3. We construct similarity sim_3 by $S_1, S_2, ..., S_m$ as follows:

$$sim_3(D_i, D_j) = \frac{|S_i \cap S_j|}{|S_i \cup S_j|}. \tag{5.3}$$

Similarity sim_3 is a function $sim_3 : S \times S \to [0, 1]$. The size of the intersection of the association rules of a pair of database objects is used to measure the closeness of the two databases. We illustrate the use of similarity sim_3 by the example below.

Example 5.3 *Consider the data in Example 5.2. The similarity between* D_1 *and* D_2 *is as follows.*

$$sim_3(D_1, D_2) = \frac{|S_1 \cap S_2|}{|S_1 \cup S_2|}$$
$$= \frac{1}{5}$$
$$= 0.2.$$

Note that, because $|S_i|$ may be far larger than $Item(D_i)$, similarity sim_3 may cause low efficiency.

Also, if D_1 and D_2 are the databases of two supermarkets in different places, then sim_3 can measure whether the customers in the two places have the same purchasing behavior. This is useful when predicting possible selling quantities for new products.

In the similarity function sim_2, all interesting items are equally important without respect to the frequency of items in the association rules. Actually, some items have high frequencies occurring in the association rules from a database while some items have low frequencies. It is commonsense that high-frequency items are more important than low-frequency ones. To reflect this property, we can assign a large weight to a high-frequency item and a small weight to a low-frequency item when we evaluate the similarity of pairs of database objects. This metric is referred to as a "weighting function".

The weighting function of similarity between two databases D_i and D_j is defined by the frequencies of interesting items. For D_k, interesting items are those that occur in the rules in S_k, denoted as $Item(S_i)$, where $k = 1, 2, ..., m$. And for each item I, in $Item(S_i)$, the item has a frequency that is the number of its occurrences in the association rules of S_i, written as $frequency(I_{S_i})$.

4. We can also construct the similarity sim_4 using the occurrences of items in $S_1, S_2, ..., S_m$ as follows.

$$sim_4(D_i, D_j)$$
$$= \frac{\sum\limits_{X \in Item(S_i), Y \in Item(S_j)} g(frequency(X_{S_i}), frequency(Y_{S_j}))}{\sqrt{\sum\limits_{X \in Item(S_i)} frequency(X_{S_i})^2 * \sum\limits_{Y \in Item(S_j)} frequency(Y_{S_j})^2}}.$$

where
$g(frequency(X_{S_i}), frequency(Y_{S_j})) = frequency(X_{S_i}) * frequency(Y_{S_j})$
when $X = Y$, $g(frequency(X_{S_i}), frequency(Y_{S_j})) = 0$ when $X \neq Y$.

Similarity sim_4 is a function $sim_4 : S \times S \to [0, 1]$. The size of the weighted correlation of the interesting items of a pair of database objects is used to measure the closeness of the two databases, where the frequency of each item indicates how important the item is. We illustrate the use of similarity sim_4 below.

Example 5.4 *Consider Example 5.3 where i_1, i_2, i_3, i_4, i_5 in $Item(S_1)$ have frequencies 1, 2, 2, 1, 1, respectively, and $i_1, i_3, i_4, i_5, i_6, i_7$ in $Item(S_2)$ have frequencies 1, 2, 1, 1, 1, 1, respectively. The similarity between D_1 and D_2 is as follows.*

$$sim_4(D_1, D_2)$$

$$= \frac{\displaystyle\sum_{X \in Item(S_1), Y \in Item(S_2)} g(frequency(X_{S_1}), frequency(Y_{S_2}))}{\sqrt{\displaystyle\sum_{X \in Item(S_1)} frequency(X_{S_1})^2 * \sum_{Y \in Item(S_2)} frequency(Y_{S_2})^2}}$$

$$= \frac{1 + 2*0 + 2*2 + 1 + 1 + 0*1 + 0*1}{\sqrt{(1+4+4+1+1)(1+4+1+1+1+1)}}$$

$$= \frac{7}{\sqrt{99}}$$

$$\approx 0.7.$$

Here, sim_4 is more accurate than sim_2 and sim_3 for measuring customer purchasing behavior. In this metric, high-frequency items are certainly highlighted.

Four simple, and understandable, functions have been proposed for measuring the similarity between pairs of database objects. Certainly, we can construct more functions for similarity by using such data as the weights of items and the amounts of items purchased by customers. The work in this chapter advocates only how to construct measures for similarity. The four measure functions have properties as follows.

Property 5.1 *The similarity functions $sim_k(D_i, D_j)$ ($k = 1, 2, 3, 4$) satisfy that*

(1) $0 \le sim_k(D_i, D_j) \le 1$;
(2) $sim_k(D_i, D_j) = sim_k(D_j, D_i)$;
(3) $sim_k(D_i, D_i) = 1$.

Proof: For (1), because

$$0 = |\emptyset| \le |Item(D_i) \cap Item(D_j)| \le |Item(D_i) \cup Item(D_j)|$$

$$0 \le |Item(D_i) \cap Item(D_j)| / |Item(D_i) \cap Item(D_j)| \le 1$$

and

$$0 \le sim_1(D_i, D_j) \le 1$$

Also, we have

$$0 \le sim_2(D_i, D_j) \le 1$$

$$0 \le sim_3(D_i, D_j) \le 1$$

We now consider $sim_4(D_i, D_j)$. Because

$$0 \leq \sum_{X \in Item(S_i), Y \in Item(S_i)} g(frequency(X_{S_i}), frequency(Y_{S_j})),$$

This can be obtained directly from the definitions.

The properties (2) and (3) can be obtained directly from their definitions above.

$$\diamondsuit$$

It can be seen from the above four measurements that each one reflects one aspect of commonness in a pair of databases. Thus, sim_1 serves us well when we do not have any information about a pair of databases. For two-level applications in multi-databases, local databases have been mined. So database classification can directly work on local pattern sets. There is a direct and low-cost method of measuring the closeness of a pair of databases by comparing their local patterns. It is the sim_3 function. However, $|S_i|$ may be far larger than $Item(D_i)$, and similarity sim_3 may cause low efficiency. In addition, sim_2 uses interesting items that occur in local patterns to determine the similarity of a pair of databases. Certainly, sim_2 is highly efficient although it is cost relative to sim_3. For measuring the closeness of a pair of databases, sim_2 also presents as more accurate than sim_3. However, sim_4 works better than sim_2 for measuring the similarity of a pair of databases. In real-world applications, we select one from the four measures, or even construct a new measure, according to demand. For application-independent database classification we should select sim_1 because of our ignorance of the databases.

5.3.3 Relevance of Databases and Classification

For description purposes, the similarity function used in the following sections is sim_1, except when specified. Using this similarity, the relevance of databases is defined below.

Definition 5.1 *A database D_i is α-relevant to D_j under measure sim_1 if $sim_1(D_i, D_j) > \alpha$, where α (> 0) is the given threshold.*

For example, let $\alpha = 0.4$. Consider the data in Example 5.2. Because $sim_1(D_1, D_2) = 0.571 > \alpha = 0.4$, the database D_1 is 0.4-relevant to D_2.

Definition 5.2 *Let D be a set of m databases $D_1, D_2, ..., D_m$. The similarity of a database D_i, under measure sim_1, denoted as $D.similarity(D_i, sim_1, \alpha)$, is a subset of D as follows,*

$$D.similarity(D_i, sim_1, \alpha) = \{d \in D | sim_1(d, D_i) \geq \alpha\}.$$

For example, consider the six databases in Section 5.2. Let D be a set of 6 databases $D_1, D_2, ..., D_6$. Then we have

$$D.similarity(D_1, sim_1, 0.5) = \{D_2, D_3\},$$

$$D.similarity(D_2, sim_1, 0.5) = \{D_1, D_3\},$$

$$D.similarity(D_3, sim_1, 0.5) = \{D_1, D_2\},$$

$$D.similarity(D_4, sim_1, 0.5) = \{D_5, D_6\},$$

$$D.similarity(D_5, sim_1, 0.5) = \{D_4, D_6\},$$

$$D.similarity(D_6, sim_1, 0.5) = \{D_4, D_5\}.$$

The similarity in this example provides a good classification of the six databases, independent of specific applications. As mentioned before, the classification of multi-databases in (Liu-Lu-Yao 1998, 2001, Yao-Liu 1997) is constructed for each specific application. This is called database selection. It can be viewed as a special example of the approach in this chapter.

Now, the classification of a set of given databases is defined as follows.

Definition 5.3 Let D be the set of m databases $D_1, D_2, ..., D_m$. The class $class^\alpha$ of D under measure sim_1 is defined as

$$class^\alpha = \{d \in D | \forall d' \in class^\alpha (sim_1(d, d') \geq \alpha)\}. \tag{5.4}$$

The definition of a class clarifies that any two database objects in that class are α-relevant to each other.

Definition 5.4 Let D be a set of m databases $D_1, D_2, ..., D_m$, and

$$class(D, sim, \alpha) = \{class_1^\alpha, class_2^\alpha, ..., class_n^\alpha\} \tag{5.5}$$

be a classification of $D_1, D_2, ..., D_m$ under measure sim_1 if

(1) $class_1^\alpha \cup class_2^\alpha \cup \cdots \cup class_n^\alpha = D$;
(2)   for any two databases D_i and D_j in $class_k$, $sim(D_i, D_j) \geq \alpha$.

This definition shows what a classification of D is, for given multiple databases. The definition also allows a database to belong to more than one class. However, we often expect to find a good classification for more than one application when we mine multiple databases. This is discussed in the next section. We now demonstrate a classification for given multiple databases by example.

Example 5.5 *Let $S_1, S_2, ..., S_{10}$ be a set of association rules of 10 databases*

$$D_1, \ D_2, \ ..., \ D_{10},$$

respectively, where
$$Item(S_i) = \{a_1, a_2, a_3, a_4, b_i\}$$

for $i = 1, 2, 3, 4$,
$$Item(S_{4+j}) = \{b_1, b_2, b_3, b_4, c_j\}$$

for $j = 1, 2, 3, 4$,
$$Item(S_{8+k}) = \{c_1, c_2, c_3, c_4, d_k\}$$

for $k = 1, 2$, and $\alpha = 0.4$. Then

$$class_1^{0.4} = \{D_1, D_2, D_3, D_4\},$$
$$class_2^{0.4} = \{D_5, D_6, D_7, D_8\},$$
$$class_3^{0.4} = \{D_9, D_{10}\},$$

form a classification of $D_1, D_2, ..., D_{10}$.

5.3.4 Ideal Classification and Goodness Measurement

As we have seen, we can get many different classifications by changing α. However, how many classes are appropriate for a set of databases in an application? For some special applications, we need to consider their requirements so as to select an appropriate classification. Generally, a good classification would be determined by the structure and distribution of data in given databases. Therefore, two definitions for ideal classification and goodness measurement are presented.

Definition 5.5 *Let $class(D, sim_1, \alpha) = \{class_1^\alpha, class_2^\alpha, ..., class_n^\alpha\}$ be a classification of m databases $D_1, D_2, ..., D_m$ under measure sim_1. The class is* ideal *if*

(1)   for any two classes $class_i^\alpha$ and $class_j^\alpha$ in class, $class_i^\alpha \cap class_j^\alpha = \emptyset$ when $i \neq j$;

(2)   for any two databases D_i in $class_l^\alpha$ and D_j in $class_h^\alpha$, $sim_1(D_i, D_j) \leq \alpha$ when $l \neq h$.

Certainly, for $\alpha = 1$, we can obtain an ideal classification for a set of given databases. Also, for $\alpha = 0$, we can obtain an ideal classification for a set of given databases. These two classifications are referred to as "trivial classifications".

For general applications, these databases can be divided into classes that belong to a nontrivial ideal classification. However, for some special applications, there is no nontrivial ideal classification in these databases. This argument is illustrated by an example as follows.

Example 5.6 *Let* $Item_1 = \{A, B, C\}$, $Item_2 = \{B, C, D\}$, $Item_3 = \{C, D, E\}$, *and* $Item_4 = \{D, E, F\}$ *be four sets of items of two data sources* D_1, D_2, D_3, *and* D_4, *respectively.*

The similarity between D_1 *and* D_2 *is as follows.*

$$sim_1(D_1, D_2) = \frac{Item_1 \cap Item_2}{Item_1 \cup Item_2} = \frac{2}{4} = 0.5,$$

$$sim_1(D_1, D_3) = \frac{Item_1 \cap Item_3}{Item_1 \cup Item_3} = \frac{1}{5} = 0.2,$$

$$sim_1(D_1, D_4) = \frac{Item_1 \cap Item_4}{Item_1 \cup Item_4} = \frac{0}{6} = 0.$$

However, because

$$sim_1(D_2, D_3) = \frac{Item_2 \cap Item_3}{Item_2 \cup Item_3} = \frac{2}{4} = 0.5,$$

$$sim_1(D_2, D_4) = \frac{Item_2 \cap Item_4}{Item_2 \cup Item_4} = \frac{1}{5} = 0.2,$$

$$sim_1(D_3, D_4) = \frac{Item_3 \cap Item_4}{Item_3 \cup Item_4} = \frac{2}{4} = 0.5.$$

there is no nontrivial ideal classification for the four databases.

From the above definitions, we can obtain several theorems.

Theorem 5.1 *If a classification*

$$class(D, sim_1, \alpha) = \{class_1^\alpha, \ class_2^\alpha, \ ..., \ class_n^\alpha\}$$

of m *databases* $D_1, D_2, ..., D_m$ *under measure* sim_1 *is ideal, then if* $sim_1(D_i, D_j) \geq \alpha$ *and* $sim_1(D_j, D_l) \geq \alpha$,

$$sim_1(D_i, D_l) \geq \alpha.$$

Proof: By the definitions of similarity, D_i and D_j belong to a class, $class_l^\alpha$, and D_j and D_k belong to a class $class_k^\alpha$.

Again, the classification $class(D, sim_1, \alpha)$ is ideal. So, if $l \neq k$, then $class_l^\alpha \cap class_k^\alpha = \emptyset$. However, $D_j \in class_l^\alpha$ and $D_j \in class_k^\alpha$. This means $class_l^\alpha \cap class_k^\alpha \neq \emptyset$. Hence, $l = k$. And

$$sim_1(D_i, D_l) \geq \alpha$$

$\diamond$

Theorem 5.2 *If a classification*

$$class(D, sim_1, \alpha) = \{class_1^\alpha, class_2^\alpha, ..., class_n^\alpha\}$$

of m *databases* $D_1, D_2, ..., D_m$ *under measure* sim_1 *is ideal then, for any two databases* D_i *and* D_j, $sim_1(D_i, D_j) \geq \alpha$ *if, and only if, there is a* $class_k$ *such that* $class_k$ *contains both* D_i *and* D_j.

Proof: (1) $\Rightarrow$: if $sim(D_i, D_j) \geq \alpha$, then there is a $class_k$ such that $class_k$ contains both D_i and D_j.

This can be directly obtained from the definitions of similarity and ideal classification.

(2) $\Leftarrow$: if a $class_k$ contains both D_i and D_j, then $sim_1(D_i, D_j) \geq \alpha$.

This can be directly proven from the definition of ideal classification.

$$\diamondsuit$$

To evaluate an ideal classification we must define a goodness value: *Goodness*. The goodness of an ideal classification is estimated by all the sums of distances of pairs of the databases within the classes of classification. Thus, the sum of the distances of pairs of databases in a class is defined first.

Definition 5.6 *Let $class^\alpha$ be a class of given multiple databases. The sum of the distances of pairs of databases in $class^\alpha$ under measure sim_1 is defined as follows.*

$$Value(class^\alpha) = \sum_{\substack{D_i, D_j \in class^\alpha}}^{i \neq j} (1 - sim_1(D_i, D_j)). \tag{5.6}$$

As stated, $1 - sim_1(D_i, D_j)$ is the distance between two databases D_i and D_j. Thus, we have the following property.

Property 5.2 *For a class $class^\alpha$ of given multiple databases, we have*

$$0 \leq Value(class^\alpha) \leq |class^\alpha|^2 - |class^\alpha|,$$

where $|class^\alpha|$ indicates the number of elements in the class $class^\alpha$ under measure sim_1.

Proof: Because $0 \leq sim_1(D_i, D_j) \leq 1$, so $0 \leq 1 - sim_1(D_i, D_j) \leq 1$, and $Value(class^\alpha) \geq 0$.

Again, there are $|class^\alpha|^2$ distance values for the class $class^\alpha$. Thus, the distances between D_i and D_j are 0 when $i = j$. And other $|class^\alpha|^2 - |class^\alpha|$ distances for the class may not be 0. Hence, the $|class^\alpha|^2 - |class^\alpha|$ distances need to be added together. By $1 - sim_1(D_i, D_j) \leq 1$, we have,

$$Value(class^\alpha) \leq |class^\alpha|^2 - |class^\alpha|.$$

$$\diamondsuit$$

Using all the sums of distances of pairs of databases in classes, we can define the goodness of a classification as follows.

Definition 5.7 *Let $class(D, sim, \alpha) = \{class_1^\alpha, class_2^\alpha, ..., class_n^\alpha\}$ be a classification of m databases $D_1, D_2, ..., D_m$ under measure sim_1. The goodness of the class is defined as follows.*

$$Goodness(class, \alpha) = \sum_{i=1}^{n} Value(class_i^{\alpha}). \qquad (5.7)$$

Therefore, we have the following property.

Property 5.3 *Let $Goodness(class, \alpha)$ be the goodness of an ideal classification $class(D, sim, \alpha)$, which is $\{class_1^{\alpha}, class_2^{\alpha}, ..., class_n^{\alpha}\}$ for m databases under measure sim_1. Then*

$$0 \leq Goodness(class, \alpha) \leq m^2 - m.$$

Proof: Because $Value(class^{\alpha}) \geq 0$, thus $Goodness(class, \alpha) \geq 0$. According to Property 5.2,

$$\begin{aligned}
Goodness(class, \alpha) &\leq (|class_1^{\alpha}|^2 - |class_1^{\alpha}|) + (|class_2^{\alpha}|^2 - |class_2^{\alpha}|) \\
&\quad + \cdots + (|class_n^{\alpha}|^2 - |class_n^{\alpha}|) \\
&= |class_1^{\alpha}|^2 + |class_2^{\alpha}|^2 + \cdots + |class_n^{\alpha}|^2 \\
&\quad - (|class_1^{\alpha}| + |class_2^{\alpha}| + \cdots + |class_n^{\alpha}|).
\end{aligned}$$

Again, because $class(D, sim_1, \alpha)$ is an ideal classification,

$$m = |class_1^{\alpha}| + |class_2^{\alpha}| + \cdots + |class_n^{\alpha}|.$$

On the other hand,

$$m^2 \geq |class_1^{\alpha}|^2 + |class_2^{\alpha}|^2 + \cdots + |class_n^{\alpha}|^2.$$

Then we have,

$$\begin{aligned}
m^2 - m &\geq |class_1^{\alpha}|^2 + |class_2^{\alpha}|^2 + \cdots + |class_n^{\alpha}|^2 \\
&\quad - (|class_1^{\alpha}| + |class_2^{\alpha}| + \cdots + |class_n^{\alpha}|).
\end{aligned}$$

Hence,

$$Goodness(class, \alpha) \leq m^2 - m.$$

$\diamond$

As we have depicted, the number ($|class|$) of elements in a classification *class* is also related to α. To elucidate relationships between $|class|$, $Goodness$, and α, an example is outlined below.

Example 5.7 *Consider six databases D_1, D_2, ..., D_6, where*

$Item(D_1) = \{A, B, C, D, E\},$

$Item(D_2) = \{A, B, C\},$

$Item(D_3) = \{A, B, D\},$

$Item(D_4) = \{F, G, H, I, J\},$

$Item(D_5) = \{F, G, H\},$ and

$Item(D_6) = \{F, G, I\}$

For simplicity, only the similarity function sim_1 is used to show changes in the number of classes and the Goodness when α is changed. The similarity between pairs of six database objects is illustrated in Table 5.4.

Table 5.4 Similarity between pairs of six database objects

sim_1	D_1	D_2	D_3	D_4	D_5	D_6
D_1	1	0.6	0.6	0	0	0
D_2	0.6	1	0.5	0	0	0
D_3	0.6	0.5	1	0	0	0
D_4	0	0	0	1	0.6	0.6
D_5	0	0	0	0.6	1	0.5
D_6	0	0	0	0.6	0.5	1

(1)   When $\alpha = 0$, $n = 1$ with

$$class = \{\{D_1, D_2, ..., D_6\}\}$$

$$Goodness(class, 0) = 2(4(1 - 0.6) + 2(1 - 0.5) + 9) = 23.2.$$

(2)   When $0 < \alpha \leq 0.5$, $n = 2$ with

$$class = \{\{D_1, D_2, D_3\}; \{D_4, D_5, D_6\}\}$$

$$Goodness(class, 0) = 4(2(1 - 0.6) + (1 - 0.5)) = 5.2.$$

(3)   When $0.5 < \alpha \leq 0.6$, there is no nontrivial ideal classification. This interval is different from $0.6 < \alpha \leq 1$.

(4)   When $0.6 < \alpha \leq 1$, $n = 6$ with

$$class = \{\{D_1\}; \{D_2\}; \{D_3\}; \{D_4\}; \{D_5\}; \{D_6\}\}$$

$$Goodness(class, 0) = 6(1 - 1) = 0$$

This example illustrates the fact that we can obtain a good classification when the distance between n and Goodness obtains the smallest value for $\alpha \in [0, 1]$. A new function is now defined for judging the goodness of a classification.

Definition 5.8 *Let* $class(D, sim, \alpha) = \{class_1^\alpha, class_2^\alpha, ..., class_n^\alpha\}$ *be a classification of m databases* D_1, D_2, *...,* D_m *under measure* sim_1. *The absoluteness of the difference between the Goodness and* $|class|$ *is written as* $distance_{Goodness}^f$ *for* $\alpha \in [0, 1]$. *It is defined as*

$$distance_{Goodness}^f(class, \alpha) = |Goodness(class, \alpha) - f(\alpha)|. \tag{5.8}$$

For $|class|$ and *Goodness* with respect to different α, we can obtain different $distance_{Goodness}^f$ from ideal classifications for given multiple databases. The use of $distance_{Goodness}^f$ is now illustrated in an example.

Example 5.8 *Consider the six databases in Example 5.7.*

(1)   When $\alpha = 0$,

$$class = \{\{D_1, D_2, ..., D_6\}\},$$
$$distance_{Goodness}^f(class, 0) = |23.2 - 1| = 22.2.$$

(2)   When $0 < \alpha \leq 0.5$,

$$class = \{\{D_1, D_2, D_3\}; \{D_4, D_5, D_6\}\};$$
$$distance_{Goodness}^f(class, \alpha) = |5.2 - 2| = 3.2.$$

(3)   When $0.5 < \alpha \leq 0.6$, *there is no nontrivial ideal classification. This interval is different from* $0.6 < \alpha \leq 1$.

(4)   When $0.6 < \alpha \leq 1$,

$$class = \{\{D_1\}; \{D_2\}; \{D_3\}; \{D_4\}; \{D_5\}; \{D_6\}\},$$
$$distance_{Goodness}^f(class, \alpha) = |0 - 6| = 6.$$

As we have seen, $distance_{Goodness}^f$ has a polar-point for a set of given database objects. In this example, $distance_{Goodness}^f = 3.2$ is the minimal value for $\alpha \in (0, 0.5]$ corresponding to the best classification. This chapter aims to search for the best classification for given multiple databases under $distance_{Goodness}^f$.

Note that $distance_{Goodness}^f$ locates no value because there is no nontrivial ideal classification when $\alpha \in (0.5, 0.6]$.

5.4 Searching for a Good Classification

To search for a good classification from given multiple databases, a two-step approach is advocated in this section. The first step is to design a procedure that generates a classification for an α. The second is to develop an algorithm that can search for a good classification by $distance_{Goodness}^f$. A searching algorithm is now designed.

5.4.1 The First Step: Generating a Classification

For given m databases D_1, D_2, ..., D_m, we can select a measure of similarity, such as sim_1, to build a relation table of similarity among the databases in Table 5.5.

Table 5.5 *Relation table of similarity*

sim_1	D_1	D_2	...	D_m
D_1	$sim_1(D_1, D_1)$	$sim_1(D_1, D_2)$	...	$sim_1(D_1, D_m)$
D_2	$sim_1(D_2, D_1)$	$sim_1(D_2, D_2)$	...	$sim_1(D_2, D_m)$
$\vdots$	$\vdots$	$\vdots$	$\vdots$	$\vdots$
D_m	$sim_1(D_m, D_1)$	$sim_1(D_m, D_2)$	...	$sim_1(D_m, D_m)$

While α is assigned a definite value, we can generate a corresponding classification *class* for the databases according to the relation table of similarity. The procedure *GreedyClass* for generating classification is designed as follows.

Procedure 5.1 *GreedyClass*
begin
Input: D_i $(1 \leq i \leq m)$: *databases, α: threshold value;*
Output: *$Class^\alpha$: set of classes consisting of α-relevant databases;*
(1)   **construct** the relation table of similarity by sim_1;
(2)   **let** $Class^\alpha \leftarrow \{\}$;
(3)   **for** $i := 1$ **to** m **do**
    begin
    (3.1)   **let** $flag \leftarrow .false.$;
    (3.2)   **for** any class c in $Class^\alpha$ **do**
            begin
            let $b \leftarrow .true.$;
            if $\neg flag$ **then**
                for any database d in c **do**
                    if b and $(sim_1(D_i, d) < \alpha)$ **then**
                        let $b \leftarrow .false.$;
            if b **then**
                begin
                    let $c \leftarrow c \cup \{D_i\}$;
                    let $flag \leftarrow .true.$;
                end
            end
    (3.3)   **if** $\neg flag$ **then**
            begin
                create a new class $\{D_i\}$;
                let $Class^\alpha \leftarrow Class^\alpha \cup \{D_i\}$;

end

    end

(4)   **output** the classification $Class^\alpha$;

end;

The procedure *GreedyClass* generates a classification $Class^\alpha$ for given multiple databases D_i ($1 \leq i \leq m$), under similarity sim_1, when the threshold α is assigned. Steps (1) and (2) comprise initialization of the procedure, where Step (1) constructs the relation table of similarity, and Step (2) assigns an empty set to $Class^\alpha$.

Step (3) is a three-step subprocedure, used to place database D_i in a class. Step (3.1) designs a logical variable $flag$, and assigns it *.false.* for representing that D_i does not belong to any class. Step (3.2) checks whether D_i can be placed in an existing class c. If $sim_1(D_i, d) \geq \alpha$ for any database d in c, D_i is placed in class c. And $flag$ is also assigned *.true.* to represent that D_i has been placed in a class of $Class^\alpha$. Step (3.3) is to generate a class for D_i, if D_i is not placed in any class of $Class^\alpha$. And the new class is also appended to $Class^\alpha$.

Step (4) outputs the classification $Class^\alpha$.

The performance of the procedure was illustrated in Example 5.7. The relation table of similarity among the six databases was first constructed as Table 5.4, letting $\alpha = 0.4$.

When $i = 1$ in the loop of Step (3) there is no class in $Class^{0.4}$. Therefore, class $\{D_1\}$ is generated and appended to $Class^{0.4}$. When $i = 2$ in the loop of Step (3) it checks if D_2 belongs to any class in $Class^{0.4}$. Because $sim_1(D_2, D_1) > 0.4$ for the unique class with a unique element D_1, D_2 is placed in the class. When $i = 3$ in the loop of Step (3) it checks whether D_3 belongs to any class in $Class^{0.4}$. Because $sim_1(D_3, D_1) > 0.4$ and $sim_1(D_3, D_2) > 0.4$ for the unique class with two elements D_1 and D_2, D_3 is placed in the class.

When $i = 4$ in the loop of Step (3), it checks whether D_4 belongs to any class in $Class^{0.4}$. However, because $sim_1(D_4, D_1) < 0.4$, D_4 cannot be placed in the class, a new class $\{D_4\}$ is generated and appended to $Class^{0.4}$.

When $i = 5$ in the loop of Step (3), it checks if D_5 belongs to the first class in $Class^{0.4}$. Because $sim_1(D_5, D_1) < 0.4$, D_5 cannot be placed in the class. It checks whether D_5 belongs to the second class in $Class^{0.4}$. Because $sim_1(D_5, D_4) > 0.4$ for the second class with a unique element D_4, D_5 is placed in the class.

When $i = 6$ in the loop of Step (3), it checks whether D_6 belongs to the first class in $Class^{0.4}$. Because $sim_1(D_6, D_1) < 0.4$, D_6 cannot be placed in the class. It then checks whether D_6 belongs to the second class in $Class^{0.4}$. Because $sim_1(D_6, D_4) > 0.4$ and $sim_1(D_6, D_5) > 0.4$ for the second class with D_4 and D_5, D_6 is placed in the class.

When $i = 6$ in the loop of Step (3), the loop is stopped. The result

$$Class^{0.4} = \{\{D_1, D_2, D_3\}; \{D_4, D_5, D_6\}\}$$

is output in Step (4), and the procedure is ended.

The procedure has generated an ideal classification $Class^{0.4}$ for $\alpha = 0.4$. However, when $\alpha = 0.52$, the procedure will generate a classification

$$Class^{0.52} = \{\{D_1, D_2\}; \{D_3\}; \{D_4, D_5\}; \{D_6\}\},$$

which is not an ideal classification.

5.4.2 The Second Step: Searching for a Good Classification

As we have seen, $|class| = n = f(\alpha)$ is an incremental function for ideal classifications. That is, for $\alpha_1 < \alpha_2$ in $[0, 1]$, we have, $f(\alpha_1) \leq f(\alpha_2)$. And $Goodness(class, \alpha)$ is a decreasing function for ideal classifications. That is, for $\alpha_1 < \alpha_2$ in $[0, 1]$, we have,

$$Goodness(class, \alpha_1) \geq Goodness(class, \alpha_2).$$

However, the absoluteness of the difference between the $Goodness$ and $|class|$

$$distance^f_{Goodness}(class, \alpha) = |Goodness(class, \alpha) - f(\alpha)|$$

is a function for ideal classifications, which has a unique polar-point: minimum $distance^f_{Goodness}(class, \alpha_0)$. That is, for $\alpha_1 \in [0, 1]$, we have

$$distance^f_{Goodness}(class, \alpha_0) \leq distance^f_{Goodness}(class, \alpha_1).$$

Again, $distance^f_{Goodness}$ is a jumping function. There is a neighborhood of α_0: $[a, b] \subset [0, 1]$ such that

$$distance^f_{Goodness}(class, \alpha_1) = distance^f_{Goodness}(class, \alpha_0)$$

for $\forall \alpha_1 \in [a, b]$.

Accordingly, $distance^f_{Goodness}$ is a decreasing function in $[0, a]$. That is, for $\alpha_1 < \alpha_2$ in $[0, a]$, we have

$$distance^f_{Goodness}(class, \alpha_1) \geq distance^f_{Goodness}(class, \alpha_2)$$

and $distance^f_{Goodness}$ is an incremental function in $[b, 1]$. That is, for $\alpha_1 < \alpha_2$ in $[b, 1]$, we have

$$distance^f_{Goodness}(class, \alpha_1) \leq distance^f_{Goodness}(class, \alpha_2).$$

Using the above properties of $distance^f_{Goodness}(class, \alpha)$ for ideal classifications, an algorithm is designed below to search for a good classification from given multiple databases: D_i $(1 \leq i \leq m)$.

Algorithm 5.1 *GoodClass*
begin
Input: D_i *($1 \leq i \leq m$)*: *databases*; λ: *the size of step of* α;
Output: *Class*: *set of classes consisting of* α-*relevant databases*;
(1) **let** $\alpha_1 \leftarrow 1$;
(2) **call** the procedure *GreedyClass* for α_1;
     let $x_1 \leftarrow temp \leftarrow distance_{Goodness}^{f}(Class, \alpha_1)$;
     let $class \leftarrow Class^{\alpha_1}$;
(3) **let** $\alpha_2 \leftarrow \alpha_1 - \lambda$;
(4) **call** the procedure *GreedyClass* for α_2;
     let $x_2 \leftarrow distance_{Goodness}^{f}(Class, \alpha_2)$;
     if $Class^{\alpha_2}$ is not an ideal classification **then**
       begin
         let $\alpha_2 \leftarrow Max\{sim_1(D_i, D_j)|sim_1(D_i, D_j) < \alpha_2\}$;
         go to Step (4);
       end
(5)   **if** $x_1 \geq x_2$ **then**
     begin
         let $\alpha_1 \leftarrow \alpha_2$; $x_1 \leftarrow X_2$; $\alpha_2 \leftarrow \alpha_1 - \lambda$;
         go to Step (4);
     end
(6)   **else**
     begin
     (6.1) **let** $\alpha_3 \leftarrow (\alpha_1 + \alpha_2)/2$;
     (6.2) **call** the procedure *GreedyClass* for α_3;
         if $Class^{\alpha_3}$ is an ideal classification **then**
           let $x_3 \leftarrow distance_{Goodness}^{f}(Class, \alpha_3)$;
         else if $Class^{\alpha_3}$ is not an ideal classification **then**
           begin
             let $b \leftarrow .false.$;
             let $y_1 \leftarrow \{sim_1(D_i, D_j)|\alpha_2 < sim_1(D_i, D_j) < x_3\}$;
             let $y_2 \leftarrow \{sim_1(D_i, D_j)|x_3 < sim_1(D_i, D_j) < \alpha_1\}$;
           LL: **if** $y_1 \cup y_2 = \emptyset$ **then**
              begin
                let $class \leftarrow Class^{\alpha_1}$;
                go to Step (7);
              end
            if $y_1 = \emptyset$ **then**
              begin
                let $\alpha_3 \leftarrow y_2$; **go to** Step (6.2);
              end
            if $y_2 = \emptyset$ **then**
              begin
                let $\alpha_3 \leftarrow y_1$; **go to** Step (6.2);

> **end**
> **call** the procedure *GreedyClass* for y_1 and y_2;
> **if** $Class^{y_1}$ and $Class^{y_2}$ are ideal classifications **then**
> > **begin**
> > > **let** $x_3 \leftarrow Min\{distance^f_{Goodness}(Class, y_1),$
> > > $distance^f_{Goodness}(Class, y_1)\}$;
> > > **let** $\alpha_3 \leftarrow$ one of y_1 and y_2 according to x_3;
> > **end**
> > **else**
> > > **begin**
> > > > **if** $Class^{y_1}$ is not an ideal classification **then**
> > > > **let** $y_1 \leftarrow \{sim_1(D_i, D_j) | \alpha_2 < sim_1(D_i, D_j) < y_1\}$;
> > > > **if** $Class^{y_2}$ is not an ideal classification **then**
> > > > **let** $y_2 \leftarrow \{sim_1(D_i, D_j) | y_2 < sim_1(D_i, D_j) < \alpha_1\}$;
> > > > **goto** LL;
> > > **end**
> > **end**
> (6.3) **if** $(x_1 > x_3)$ and $(x_2 > x_3)$ **then**
> > **begin**
> > > **let** $\alpha_1 \leftarrow \alpha_3$; $x_1 \leftarrow x_3$;
> > > **go to** Step (5.1);
> > **end**
> (6.4) **else if** $(x_1 \leq x_3)$ and $(x_2 \geq x_3)$ **then**
> > **begin**
> > > **let** $\alpha_2 \leftarrow \alpha_3$;
> > > **let** $x_2 \leftarrow x_3$;
> > > **go to** Step (6.1);
> > **end**
> (6.5) **else if** $(x_1 = x_3)$ and $(x_2 = x_3)$ **then**
> > **begin**
> > > **let** $class \leftarrow Class^{\alpha_3}$;
> > > **go to** Step (7);
> > **end**
> (6.6) **else**
> > **begin**
> > > **let** $class \leftarrow x_1$;
> > > **go to** Step (7);
> > **end**
> **end**
(7) **output** the classification *class*;
end;

The algorithm *GoodClass* searches for a good classification from possible classifications for given multiple databases. Step (1) is the initialization of the algorithm. The search begins by calling the procedure *GreedyClass* for $\alpha_1 = 1$ in Step (2). Step (3) selects the next threshold α_2 by α_1 and the step size λ.

Step (4) calls in the procedure *GreedyClass* for α_2. If the classification $Class^{\alpha_2}$ is not an ideal classification, we assign

$$Max\{sim_1(D_i, D_j)|sim_1(D_i, D_j) < \alpha_2\}$$

to α_2 and repeat Step (4).

If $Class^{\alpha_2}$ is an ideal classification, we compare

$$x_1 = distance^f_{Goodness}(Class, \alpha_1)$$

and

$$x_2 = distance^f_{Goodness}(Class, \alpha_2)$$

in Step (5). If $x_1 \geq x_2$, we take α_2 as α_1 to go to Step (4).

If $x_1 < x_2$, it means a good classification can be found in $[\alpha_1, \alpha_2)$; and the search in $[\alpha_1, \alpha_2)$ is carried out in Step (6). For example, the center point $(\alpha_1 + \alpha_2)/2$ is taken as a new threshold α_3 to check which of the sub-intervals of $(\alpha_2, \alpha_1]$ contain a good classification. If the classification $Class^{\alpha_2}$ is not an ideal classification, we assign a new value in $[\alpha_1, \alpha_2)$ to α_3 by considering $\{sim_1(D_i, D_j)|\alpha_2 < sim_1(D_i, D_j) < y_1\}$ and $\{sim_1(D_i, D_j)|y_2 < sim_1(D_i, D_j) < \alpha_1\}$.

Step (7) outputs the searched good classification *class*.

The performance of the algorithm is illustrated by using Example 5.7.

Let $\lambda = 0.05$.

First, $\alpha_1 = 1$ and $x_1 = distance^f_{Goodness}(Class, 1) = 6$. Because

$$distance^f_{Goodness}(Class, \alpha) = 6$$

for the points 0.95, 0.8, ..., 0.6, we get

$$\alpha_1 = 0.6, \ and$$
$$x_1 = distance^f_{Goodness}(Class, 0.6) = 6$$

after repeating Steps (4) and (5).

When $\alpha_2 = \alpha_1 - 0.05 = 0.55$, we can find that the $Class^{0.55}$ is not an ideal classification in Step (4). We need to select a proper value for α_2. For example, $\alpha_2 = \alpha_2 - 0.05 = 0.5$. And we get

$$x_2 = distance^f_{Goodness}(Class, 0.5) = 3.2.$$

Because $x_1 > x_2$, we find

$$\alpha_1 = 0.5, \ and$$

$$x_1 = distance_{Goodness}^f(Class, 0.5) = 3.2$$

Steps (4) and (5) are repeated until

$$\alpha_1 = 0.05, and$$

$$x_1 = distance_{Goodness}^f(Class, 0.05) = 3.2.$$

Now,

$$\alpha_2 = \alpha_1 - 0.05 = 0, \ and$$

$$x_2 = distance_{Goodness}^f(Class, 0) = 22.2.$$

Because $x_1 < x_2$, we search for a good classification when α is within $(0, 0.05]$. We take

$$\alpha_3 = (\alpha_1 + \alpha_2)/2 = 0.025, \ and$$

$$x_3 = distance_{Goodness}^f(Class, 0.025) = 3.2.$$

Because the condition of Step (6.4) is satisfied,

$$\alpha_2 = \alpha_3 = 0.025, \ and$$

$$x_2 = distance_{Goodness}^f(Class, 0.025) = 3.2.$$

This means that we search for a good classification when α is within $(0.025, 0.05]$. We take

$$\alpha_3 = (\alpha_1 + \alpha_2)/2 = 0.0375, \ and$$

$$x_3 = distance_{Goodness}^f(Class, 0.0375) = 3.2.$$

Because the condition of Step (6.5) is satisfied,

$$Class^{0.0375}\{\{D_1, D_2, D_3\}; \{D_4, D_5, D_6\}\}$$

is output as a good classification in step (7). Therefore, $Class^{0.0375}$ is a good classification.

5.5 Algorithm Analysis

For an understanding of the designed algorithms, this section simply analyzes the procedure *GreedyClass* and algorithm *GoodClass*.

5.5.1 Procedure *GreedyClass*

Procedure *GreedyClass* generates a classification of given multiple databases for an α. We have a theorem for the procedure as follows.

Theorem 5.3 *Procedure GreedyClass works correctly.*

Proof: Clearly, from Steps (3) and (4), a classification of databases is generated, and output for a given α. We need to show that all given databases are contained by classes of the classification $Class^{\alpha}$, and each database belongs to only one of the classes.

For any unclassified database D_i $(1 \leq i \leq m)$, if D_i is α-relevant to all databases in a class, it is added to the class in Step (3.2); or else a new class is generated for D_i in Step (3.3). This means that all given databases are contained by classes of the classification $Class^{\alpha}$.

On the other hand, in the loop in Step (3), each database is handled once and the database is classified into either an old class (in Step (3.2)), or a new class (in Step (3.3)). This means that each database belongs to only one of the classes.

$$\diamond$$

In Procedure *GreedyClass*, m databases are required to be input for simplicity. In fact, it only requires the sets of features (items) of the databases. (For databases, we can use the sampling techniques in (Liu-Motoda 2001) to obtain items.) Hence, we need

$$|Item(D_1)| + |Item(D_2)| + \cdots + |Item(D_m)|$$

units to save all items, which is less than, or equal to, n, where n is the maximum among $|Item(D_1)|$, $|Item(D_2)|$, ..., $|Item(D_m)|$. For Step (1) of *GreedyClass*, we need m^2 units to save the similarities. Consequently, the space complexity of *GreedyClass* is $O(n^2 + m^2) = O(n^2)$ for $n \geq m$ ($O(m^2)$ for $n < m$).

Obviously, the time complexity of *GreedyClass* is dominated by the loop in Steps (1) and (3). Therefore, we have the following theorem.

Theorem 5.4 *The time complexity of GreedyClass is $O(n^2m^2 + m^4)$, where n is the maximum among $|Item(D_1)|$, $|Item(D_2)|$, ..., $|Item(D_m)|$, and m is the number of databases given.*

Proof: For Step (1), there are $m^2/2$ similarities that need to be computed according to sim_1 and Property 3.1. Each similarity needs, at most, n^2 comparisons. Therefore, the time complexity of Step (1) is $O(n^2m^2)$.

For Step (3), there are m databases that need to be classified. For each database, Step (3.2) dictates the complexity by a twice-loop. No matter how the databases are distributed, at most $i-1$ comparisons are needed to classify the ith database, although Step (3.2) is a twice-loop. Each comparison is used to access the $m \times m$ relation table of similarity. Hence, the time complexity of Step (3) is $O(m^4)$.

Accordingly, the time complexity of *GreedyClass* is $O(n^2m^2 + m^4)$.

$$\diamond$$

Note that Step (1) is included in *GreedyClass* for the purpose of description. Actually, Step (1) is taken as a procedure in applications, and is only called once for generating the relation table of similarity. This means that *the time complexity of GreedyClass is really $O(m^4)$*, by taking away Step (1).

As we have seen, database classification is time consuming. It is obvious that, when m (the number of databases) is very large, the time complexity becomes severe. To face this problem, there are many mature techniques available in information retrieval and pattern analysis. A commonly used method is first to divide a large set of databases into several smaller sets and then merge classes from the smaller sets. Thus, *GreedyClass* can be optimized by resizing in information retrieval and pattern analysis when m is large.

5.5.2 Algorithm *GoodClass*

Algorithm *GoodClass* is used to search for an ideal and good classification from possible classifications for a set of given databases. We have a theorem for the algorithm as follows.

Theorem 5.5 *Algorithm GoodClass works correctly.*

Proof: Clearly, in Steps (6) and (7), an ideal and good classification is searched for, and output for a given set of databases. We need to show that if there is an ideal and good classification for the databases, the classification can be found, and if there is no ideal and good classification for the databases, a trivial ideal classification is reported.

For m given databases, there are at most $m^2/2$ different similarities according to sim_1 and Property 5.1. The similarities can divide $[0, 1]$ into $m^2/2 - 1$ subsets. For each subset, $distance^f_{Goodness}(class, \alpha)$ is a constant. This means that $distance^f_{Goodness}(class, \alpha)$ can get at most $m^2/2 - 1$ different values for $\alpha \in [0, 1]$, and there are at most $m^2/2 - 1$ different classifications for the databases. In particular, a classification for the databases is ideal and good when $distance^f_{Goodness}(class, \alpha)$ gets the minimal value among the $m^2/2 - 1$ different values.

Hence, if it is in existence, the polar-point of $distance^f_{Goodness}(class, \alpha)$ can be obtained in Step (6) by, at most, $Max\{m^2/2 - 1, Int(1/\lambda)\}$ comparisons, where $Int(1/\lambda)$ is an integer function and λ is the size of the searching step. This means that, if there is an ideal and good classification for the databases, the classification can be found by *GoodClass*.

If there is no nontrivial ideal classification, the value of *class* is not changed, and $class = Class^1$ is output in Step (7). This means that if there is no ideal and good classification for the databases, the trivial ideal classification $Class^1$ is reported by *GoodClass*. (Note that $Class^1 \leq Class^0$.)

$\diamond$

In the algorithm *GoodClass*, the procedure *GreedyClass* is called in. The space complexity of *GoodClass* is approximately equal to the space complexity of *GreedyClass*.

The time complexity of *GoodClass* is dominated by the loop from Step (3) to Step (6). The body of the loop is performed, at most, $Int(1/\lambda)$ times. And the procedure *GreedyClass* is called, at most, $Int(1/\lambda)$ times during looping. So, the time complexity of *GoodClass* is $O(hm^4)$, where $h = Int(1/\lambda)$ and $O(m^4)$ is the time complexity of *GreedyClass*, by taking away the step for generating the relation table of similarity.

5.6 Evaluation of Application-independent Database Classification

As we have seen, identifying relevant databases is application-dependent. See (Liu-Lu-Yao 1998, 2001, Yao-Liu 1997). Therefore, the classification in this chapter is application-independent, and the former can be taken as a special case of the latter. To understand the proposed approach, a detailed example is used to illustrate the behavior of defined measures $|class|$, α, *Goodness*, and $distance^f_{Goodness}$, as well as to search for a good classification of databases by $distance^f_{Goodness}$.

5.6.1 Dataset Selection

To obtain multiple possibly relevant databases, the techniques in (Liu-Lu-Yao 1998, 2001, Yao-Liu 1997) have been adopted. That is, to vertically partition a database into a number of subsets, each one must contain a certain number of attributes. It is hoped that the databases obtained are relevant to each other by way of class. In this example, multiple databases are generated by databases from the Synthetic Classification Data Sets on the Internet (http://www.kdnuggets.com/). There are four databases shown below for this example. They are generated from a Web site. The main properties of the four databases are as follows. There are $|R| = 1000$ attributes, and the average number of attributes T per row is 5, 6, 7, and 8. The number $|r|$ of rows is approximately 3000. The average size I of maximal frequent sets is 4. The databases are vertically partitioned into 3, 4, 5, and 6 subsets. Table 5.6 summarizes the parameters for the datasets.

Table 5.6 *Synthetic dataset characteristics*

Dataset Name	$|R|$	T	$|r|$	Subset
T5.I4.D100K	1000	5	2969	T5S1, T5S2, T5S3
T6.I4.D100K	1000	6	2983	T6S1,..., T6S4
T7.I4.D100K	1000	7	3024	T7S1,..., T7S5
T8.I4.D100K	1000	8	3101	T8S1,..., T8S6

5.6.2 Experimental Results

Using the above data, the relationships among the defined measures $|class|$, α, $Goodness$, and $distance^{f}_{Goodness}$ are illustrated by experiments below.

In the experiments, for a set D of given m databases, the number n (or $|class|$) of elements (classes) in $class(D, sim_1, \alpha)$ is relative to α. This can be described by point-pairs in a function $n = f(\alpha)$, where, $1 \leq n \leq m$, $\alpha \in [0,1]$. The relationship between the number of classes and α, for ideal classifications, is illustrated in Figure 5.1.

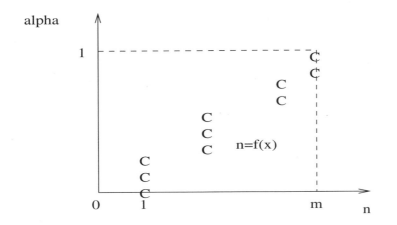

Fig. 5.1. Relationship between $|class|$ and α for ideal classifications

In Figure 5.1, a sequence of "C" is used to replace a line segment for describing $|class|$ (the number of elements in the $class$) when $a \leq \alpha \leq b$. For two trivial ideal classifications, $n = 1$ when $\alpha = 0$; and n is generally asymptotic to m when $\alpha \to 1$. The relation $n = f(\alpha)$ is a jumping function in the rectangle enclosed by the n axes and the lines: $n = 1$, $\alpha = 1$, and $n = m$.

We know $f(\alpha)$ is a jumping function because the number of elements in a $class$ is an integer.

On the other hand, for a different α, we obtain different $Goodness$ from the ideal classifications for given multiple databases. The relationship between $Goodness$ and α for ideal classifications is sketched in Figure 5.2.

In Figure 5.2, a sequence of "X" is used to replace a line segment to describe the value of $Goodness$, when α belongs to a small interval in $[0,1]$. For two trivial ideal classifications, $Goodness = 0$ when $\alpha = 1$; and $Goodness$

obtains the maximum value when $\alpha = 0$. Also, *Goodness* is a jumping function in the rectangle enclosed by the n axes, α axes, and the lines $\alpha = 1$ and $n = m^2 - m$.

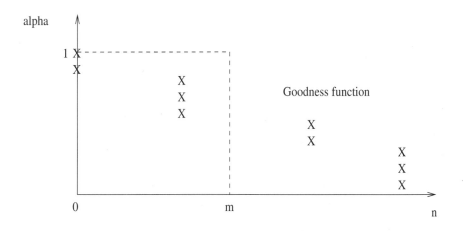

Fig. 5.2. Relationship between *Goodness* and α for ideal classifications

For the databases in Table 5.6, the results from using sim_1 to measure the similarity are as follows.

(1) $sim_1(T5S1,\ T5S2) = 0.76$, $sim_1(T5S1,\ T5S3) = 0.831$, $sim_1(T5S1,\ TiSj) = 0$ for other datasets; $sim_1(T5S2,\ T5S3) = 0.785$, $sim_1(T5S2,\ TiSj) = 0$ for other datasets; and $sim_1(T5S3,\ TiSj) = 0$ for other datasets $(i \neq 5)$.

(2) $sim_1(T6S1,\ T6S2) = 0.804$, $sim_1(T6S1,\ T6S3) = 0.783$, $sim_1(T6S1,\ T6S4) = 0.83$, $sim_1(T6S1,\ TiSj) = 0$ for other datasets; $sim_1(T6S2,\ T6S3) = 0.773$, $sim_1(T6S2,\ T6S4) = 0.693$, $sim_1(T6S2,\ TiSj) = 0$ for other datasets; $sim_1(T6S3,\ T6S4) = 0.715$, $sim_1(T6S3,\ TiSj) = 0$ for other datasets; and $sim_1(T6S4,\ TiSj) = 0$ for other datasets $(i \neq 6)$.

(3) $sim_1(T7S1,\ T7S2) = 0.701$, $sim_1(T7S1,\ T7S3) = 0.73$, $sim_1(T7S1,\ T7S4) = 0.743$, $sim_1(T7S1,\ T7S5) = 0.63$, $sim_1(T7S1,\ TiSj) = 0$ for other datasets; $sim_1(T7S2,\ T7S3) = 0.711$, $sim_1(T7S2,\ T7S4) = 0.652$, $sim_1(T7S2,\ T7S5) = 0.68$, $sim_1(T7S2,\ TiSj) = 0$ for other datasets; $sim_1(T7S3,\ T7S4) = 0.67$, $sim_1(T7S3,\ T7S5) = 0.71$, $sim_1(T7S3,\ TiSj) = 0$ for other datasets; $sim_1(T7S4,\ T7S5) = 0.75$, $sim_1(T7S4,\ TiSj) = 0$ for other datasets; and $sim_1(T7S5,\ TiSj) = 0$ for other datasets $(i \neq 7)$.

(4) $sim_1(T8S1,\ T8S2) = 0.661$, $sim_1(T8S1,\ T8S3) = 0.673$, $sim_1(T8S1,\ T8S4) = 0.802$, $sim_1(T8S1,\ T8S5) = 0.672$, $sim_1(T8S1,\ T8S6) = 0.661$,

$sim_1(T8S1, TiSj) = 0$ for other datasets; $sim_1(T8S2, T8S3) = 0.721$, $sim_1(T8S2, T8S4) = 0.706$, $sim_1(T8S2, T8S5) = 0.724$, $sim_1(T8S2, T8S6) = 0.761$, $sim_1(T8S2, TiSj) = 0$ for other datasets; $sim_1(T8S3, T8S4) = 0.715$, $sim_1(T8S3, T8S5) = 0.63$, $sim_1(T8S3, T8S6) = 0.71$, $sim_1(T8S3, TiSj) = 0$ for other datasets; $sim_1(T8S4, T8S5) = 0.686$, $sim_1(T8S4, T8S6) = 0.651$, $sim_1(T8S4, TiSj) = 0$ for other datasets; $sim_1(T8S5, T8S6) = 0.712$, $sim_1(T8S5, TiSj) = 0$ for other datasets; and $sim_1(T8S6, TiSj) = 0$ for other datasets ($i \neq 8$).

For Table 5.6, the relationship between |*class*| and α, and the relationship between the *Goodness* and α, for ideal classifications, are illustrated in Figure 5.3.

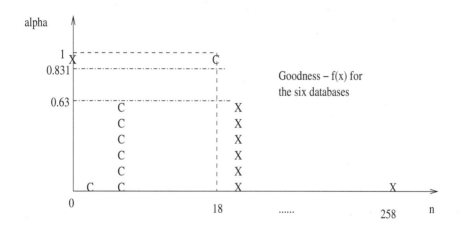

Fig. 5.3. |*class*|, *Goodness*, and α in an example for ideal classifications

In Figure 5.3, when α belongs to a small interval in $[0, 1]$, a sequence of "C" is used to replace a line segment when describing the number of elements in the *class*, and a sequence of "X" is used to replace a line segment when describing the value of *Goodness*. For two trivial ideal classifications, $n = 18$ and *Goodness* = 0, when $\alpha = 1$; and $n = 1$ and *Goodness* gets the maximum value 257.128, when $\alpha = 0$. In particular, there is no nontrivial ideal classification when $\alpha \in (0.63, 0.831]$.

This example illustrates the fact that we can obtain a good classification when the distance between n and *Goodness* obtains the smallest value for $\alpha \in [0, 1]$.

The relationship between $distance^f_{Goodness}$ and α for ideal classifications is sketched in Figure 5.4.

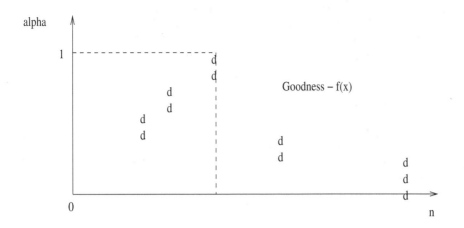

Fig. 5.4. Difference of $|class|$ and *Goodness* for ideal classifications

In Figure 5.4, a sequence of "d" is used to replace a line segment for describing the value of $distance^{f}_{Goodness}$ when α belongs to a small interval in $[0,1]$. For two trivial ideal classifications, *Goodness* $= 0$ when $\alpha = 1$; and *Goodness* gets the maximum value when $\alpha = 0$. *Goodness* is a jumping function in the rectangle enclosed by the n axes, *alpha* axes, and the lines $alpha = 1$ and $n = m^2 - m$.

For Table 5.6, the absoluteness of the difference between $|class|$ and *Goodness* by α is illustrated in Figure 5.5.

In Figure 5.5, a sequence of "d" is used to replace a line segment when describing the value of $distance^{f}_{Goodness}$ if α belongs to a small interval in $[0,1]$ for datasets in Table 5.6.

5.6.3 Analysis

Classification is a complicated procedure, but it is an efficient technique for exploring pattern analysis, grouping, decision-making, and machine-learning. Indeed, the goodness of classification is related to many factors, including selected features for an object. However, application-independent database classification works well under $distance^{f}_{Goodness}$ construction. Experiments have shown that the proposed techniques in this chapter are effective, efficient, and promising.

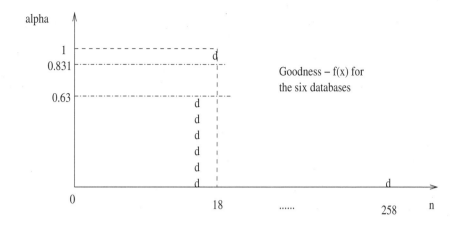

Fig. 5.5. The difference of $|class|$ and *Goodness* in the example for ideal classifications

5.7 Summary

Data mining and knowledge discovery in databases aim at the discovery of useful information from large collections of data (Cheung-Ng-Fu-Fu 1996, Han-Pei-Yin 2000, Webb 2000, Wu-Lo 1998). Recently, it has been recognized in the KDD community that multi-database mining is an important research topic (Zhong-Yao-Ohsuga 1999). Liu et al. have proposed a mining technique that identifies relevant databases (Liu-Lu-Yao 1998, 2001). We regard this as a database selection strategy that is typically application-dependent.

As discussed previously, the development of effective database classification techniques and methodologies is one of the key issues in the design of truly general-purpose, high-performance multi-database mining systems. Therefore, the research here is of great significance to multi-database mining and its applications.

The existing database classification strategy, known as database selection, identifies databases that are most likely relevant to a mining task for efficiency and accuracy. This is typically application-dependent. Database selection is inadequate in real-world applications. (see (Liu-Lu-Yao 1998, 2001)) For example, database selection must be carried out multiple times in order to identify relevant databases for two or more real-world applications. In particular, when a mining task is without reference to any specific application, application-dependent techniques are not efficient.

In this chapter we have created two database classification techniques to deal with key problems that have not been satisfactorily solved before. The first problem is how to effectively measure the relevance of databases. The second is how to effectively search for the best classification.

The new clustering strategy described in this chapter has significantly enhanced the utilization of multi-database mining systems, due to its application-independence. It has increased the ability of multi-database mining systems, due to its complete classification, and it has improved the performance of multi-database mining systems because of the reduction of search costs. Experiments have supported our proposed approach and show that it is effective and efficient.

Briefly:

1. our application-independent database classification is oriented to two or more applications, even without reference to any specific application.
2. this classification uses similarity functions to measure the relevance of databases.
3. in this classification, measures $|class|$, α, $Goodness$, and $distance^f_{Goodness}$ have been defined to search for a good classification in multi-databases. This can be taken as the basis of database classification.
4. our experiments have shown that the proposed approach is effective in classifying multiple databases.

6. Dealing with Inconsistency

Having recognized the importance, there has been some research into negative association rule mining. It generates a crucial challenge in mining multi-databases as negative association rules can cause knowledge conflicts within multi-databases. In this chapter, a database is taken as a knowledge base as, from our local pattern analysis, this assumption is reasonable. A framework is now presented for resolving conflicts within multiple databases.

6.1 Introduction

Negative association rules can catch the mutually exclusive correlations among items, and they are very important in decision-making. For example, the objective of a market surveillance team is to ensure that a fair and efficient trading environment is available to all participants by adopting an alarm system. It is negative association rules that assist in examining which alarms can be ignored. Assume that each piece of evidence A, B, C, D can sound a warning of unfair trading X and if, given rules $A \rightarrow \neg X$ and $C \rightarrow \neg X$, the team can make a decision of fair trading when A or C occurs, in other words, alarms caused by A or C can be ignored. This example gives us an insight into the importance of negative association rule mining.

However, negative association rules in a database can conflict with association rules in other databases. For local pattern analysis, we should develop techniques to resolve this conflict.

In this chapter, we take a database as a knowledge base, and design a framework for resolving the conflicts within multiple databases, based on the logic in (Konieczny-Perez 1997, Lin 1995, Tsikrika-Lalmas 2001).

The rest of this chapter is organized as follows. We begin by stating the problem, and reviewing some basic concepts of modal logic. Then, in Section 6.3 we firstly present the relationship between internal knowledge and external knowledge, and then define a logic and its semantics for K3D. Section 6.4 constructs the proof theory of the proposed logic. Section 6.5 enriches our logic, explicitly mentioning what a database has collected. In Section 6.6, we illustrate how to use the proposed logical framework to identify quality knowledge from multiple databases. We summarize our contributions in the last section.

6.2 Problem Statement

When a company has a dataset D to be mined, the pressure of high profits generates an urgent need to collect relevant information from external data sources (say D_1, D_2, ..., D_n). Therefore, knowledge discovery from multi-databases has become an important research topic in the data mining community.

Recall the concepts in Chapter 3. A local pattern is a pattern that has been identified in a database. It may be a frequent itemset, an association rule, a causal rule, or some other expression. A *local pattern set* K is a finite set of local patterns. Local pattern analysis is a strategy for identifying laws, rules, and useful patterns from a set of local pattern sets $\{K_1, K_2, ..., K_n\}$ from multiple databases.

A rule has one of two possible values in a data-source: true (the data-source supports the rule) or false (otherwise).

In our logical framework, we use the technique for computing the weights of local pattern sets as described in (Wu-Zhang 2003). Here, if a data-source supports a larger number of high-frequency rules, the weight of the data-source should also be higher.

On an abstract level, the integration of local patterns can be subsumed under the general problem of synthesizing multiple local pattern sets that may contradict each other. There appear to be two major methods for synthesizing local pattern sets, which we describe below.

The first is to compute the maximal consistent subsets of the union of these local pattern sets, and then take as the result the disjunction of all the maximal consistent subsets. Using the weight of the local pattern sets, the maximal consistent subsets are computed by taking as many local patterns as possible from the local pattern sets of higher weights. However, such an approach does not take into account the majority view (or weighted majority view) of the local pattern sets. For example, suppose three local pattern sets $L_1 = \{a\}$, $L_2 = \{a\}$, and $L_3 = \{\neg a\}$ have the same weight. Then we would like the result of the synthesis to be $\{a\}$, since the local pattern sets are of equal weight and two out of the three local pattern sets support a. But the approach yields $a \vee \neg a$, a tautology, which does not support either a or $\neg a$.

The other method is to use the weighted majority rule to synthesize multiple local pattern sets. But this can produce contradictory results. For example, let us define that a group of local pattern sets supports a local pattern α if, and only if, the combined weight of the local pattern sets that support α is greater than the combined weight of the local pattern sets that support $\neg\alpha$. Then, suppose a group consists of $L_1 = \{a\}$, $L_2 = \{b\}$, and $L_3 = \{\neg a \vee \neg b\}$, each with the same weight. It is not difficult to verify that the group supports a and B and $\neg a \vee \neg b$, which is a contradiction.

In this chapter, we assume each local pattern set to be associated with a weight representing the relative degree of importance of that local pattern set. We present a formal semantics for synthesizing multiple local pattern sets with weights. The semantics has the property of obeying the weighted majority principle in case of conflicts. For the example, $L_1 = \{a\}$, $L_2 = \{a\}$, and $L_3 = \{\neg a\}$, each with the same weights, the semantics returns a as the result of synthesizing. In addition, for synthesizing, it has desirable properties, such as syntax independence and guaranteed consistency of results.

6.3 Definitions of Formal Semantics

Suppose **L** is a propositional logic formed in the usual way from a set of atoms $\mathcal{P}$ where a local pattern is an atom, or an expression of atoms. A *possible world* is a truth assignment to the atoms in $\mathcal{P}$, that is, a mapping from $\mathcal{P}$ to $\{true, false\}$. The set of all possible worlds is denoted by $\mathcal{W}$. Logical equivalence is denoted by $\equiv$. A *model* of a local pattern ϕ is a possible world, where ϕ is true in the usual sense. The set of all models of ϕ is denoted by $\Omega(\phi)$. A *literal* is an atom or negation of an atom. For convenience, if p is a literal then we use $\neg p$ to denote the negation of the literal.

We say the local pattern set K *supports* a local pattern α if K implies α (i.e., $K \models \alpha$), and K *opposes* α, if K implies $\neg\alpha$ (i.e., $K \models \neg\alpha$). We say K *consistently supports* α if K supports α and K does not support $\neg\alpha$, that is, if K is consistent and K supports α.

Suppose $K_1, K_2, ..., K_n$ ($n \geq 1$) are the local pattern sets to be synthesized, and μ is a function that assigns each of the local pattern sets a value in $[0, 1]$ as its weight. The weight function μ is constructed according to (Wu-Zhang 2003), which captures the relative degree of importance of the local pattern sets. The higher $\mu(K_i)$ is, the more important K_i is within the group of local pattern sets.

A synthesizing operator *Synthesize* is a mapping from $\{K_1, K_2, ..., K_n\}$ and μ to a new local pattern set, or

$$Synthesize(\{K_1, K_2, ..., K_n\}, \mu)$$

Our objective in synthesizing a set of local pattern sets is to obtain a maximal amount of consistent patterns from each local pattern set. To do so, we define an order over the set of possible worlds $\mathcal{W}$ depending on the given local pattern sets; and then define the models of the synthesized pattern set to be the worlds in $\mathcal{W}$ that are minimal with respect to the order. The order can be thought of as a measure of *distance* between a world and $\{K_1, K_2, ..., K_n\}$, so that the models of the synthesized pattern set are the worlds that are closest to $\{K_1, K_2, ..., K_n\}$.

Using the method in (Lin 1995), we define the distance between a world and a local pattern set to be the minimum number of atoms on which the world differs from some model of the local pattern set. Formally, the distance between a world w, and a local pattern set K, is defined as:

$$dist(w, K) = min_{w' \in \Omega(K)} dist(w, w'),$$

where $dist(w, w')$ is the number of atoms whose valuations differ in the two possible worlds. When $\Omega(K)$ is empty (i.e., K is inconsistent), $dist(w, K) = 0$.

To take into account the weights of the local pattern sets, we define the overall distance as

$$\sum_{i=1}^{n} (dist(w, K_i) * \mu(K_i)). \tag{6.1}$$

Apparently, lower-weighted local pattern sets have less influence on the overall distance in Equation (6.1), whereas those with greater weights have more influence. Therefore, the worlds closer to the higher-weighted local pattern sets are actually closer overall to the set of local pattern sets.

A world w is closer to, or at the same distance from, $\{K_1, K_2, ..., K_n\}$ than w', denoted as

$$w \preceq_{\{K_1, K_2, ..., K_n, \mu\}} w'$$

if, and only if,

$$\sum_{i=1}^{n} (dist(w, K_i) * \mu(K_i)) \leq \sum_{i=1}^{n} (dist(w', K_i) * \mu(K_i)).$$

Clearly, $\preceq_{\{K_1, K_2, ..., K_n, \mu\}}$ is a total pre-order, that is, a total, reflexive and transitive relation on $\mathcal{W}$. A possible world w is *minimal* with respect to

$$\preceq_{\{K_1, K_2, ..., K_n, \mu\}}$$

if, for all $w' \in \mathcal{W}$,

$$w \preceq_{\{K_1, K_2, ..., K_n, \mu\}} w'.$$

Let

$$Min(\mathcal{W}, \preceq_{\{K_1, K_2, ..., K_n, \mu\}})$$

denote the set of possible worlds that are minimal with respect to

$$\preceq_{\{K_1, K_2, \cdots, K_n, \mu\}} .$$

We now define *Synthesize* as follows.

Definition 6.1

$$\Omega(Synthesize(\{K_1, K_2, ..., K_n\}, \mu)) = Min(\mathcal{W}, \preceq_{\{K_1, K_2, ..., K_n, \mu\}}).$$

This means that a possible world is a model of *Synthesize* if, and only if, its overall distance to the set of local pattern sets is minimum. Because the *distance* operator is on the models of each local pattern set, *Synthesize* is independent of the syntactic forms of the local pattern sets.

We now present some properties of *Synthesize*.

Proposition 6.1 *If for all $i \in [1, n]$, $K_i \equiv K_i'$ and $\mu(K_i) = \mu(K_i')$ then*

$$Synthesize(\{K_1, \ K_2, ..., K_n\}, \mu)$$
$$\equiv Synthesize(\{K_1', K_2', ..., K_n'\}, \mu).$$

Proposition 6.1 shows that logically equivalent local pattern sets have the same *local patterns*. Below, Proposition 6.2 shows that the local pattern sets which are inconsistent, or are assigned the weight of zero, can be discarded without affecting the synthesizing.

Proposition 6.2 *If $K_i(i \in [1, n])$ is inconsistent or $\mu(K_i) = 0$ then*

$$Synthesize(\{K_1, K_2, ..., K_n\}, \mu)$$

$$\equiv Synthesize(\{K_1, ..., K_{i-1}, K_{i+1}, ..., K_n\}, \mu).$$

Proof. Proposition 2 follows from the definition of

$$\preceq_{\{K_1, K_2, ..., K_n, \mu\}}$$

and the fact that if K_i is inconsistent, then $dist(w, K_i) = 0$. $\diamondsuit$

Using Proposition 6.2, we can deny a local pattern set from influencing the synthesis by assigning it a zero weight.

Proposition 6.3 *Let $\{K_1, K_2, ..., K_n\}$ be a set of local pattern sets, and μ and μ' be two weight functions such that $\mu(K_i) = c * \mu'(K_i)$ (where $c > 0$) for $i = 1, ..., n$. Then*

$$Synthesize(\{K_1, K_2, ..., K_n\}, \mu) \equiv Synthesize(\{K_1, K_2, ..., K_n\}, \mu').$$

Proof. Since $\mu(K_i) = c * \mu'(K_i)$, for all $w \in \mathcal{W}$,

$$\sum_{i=1}^{n} dist(w, K_i) * \mu(K_i) = \sum_{i=1}^{n} dist(w, K_i) * c * \mu'(K_i)$$

$$= c * \sum_{i=1}^{n} dist(w, K_i) * \mu'(K_i).$$

Hence, for all $w, w' \in \mathcal{W}$, we have

$$\sum_{i=1}^{n} dist(w, K_i) * \mu(K_i) \leq \sum_{i=1}^{n} dist(w', K_i) * \mu(K_i)$$

if, and only if,

$$\sum_{i=1}^{n} dist(w, K_i) * \mu'(K_i) \leq \sum_{i=1}^{n} dist(w', K_i) * \mu'(K_i).$$

From this, the proposition follows.   ◇

For example, suppose μ and μ' are equivalent, μ assigns K_1, K_2, and K_3 with weights 5, 4, and 2, and μ' assigns them 10, 8, and 4. Then

$$Synthesize(\{K_1, K_2, K_3\}, \mu)$$

and

$$Synthesize(\{K_1, K_2, K_3\}, \mu')$$

are equivalent in our logic.

Proposition 6.4 *Let* $\{K_1, K_2, ..., K_n\}$ *be a set of consistent local pattern sets, and* μ *be a weight function. Then*

$$Synthesize(\{K_1, K_2, ..., K_n\}, \mu)$$

is consistent.

Proof. Let w be any possible world, and $P_i (i \in [1, n])$ be the set of all atoms appearing in the local patterns of K_i. Since any local pattern set is finite, P_i is finite. We now prove that, for all $i \in [1, n]$, $dist(w, K_i)$ is a finite number. If K_i is consistent, then there exists at least one world, w_i in $\Omega(K_i)$. Let w' be the possible world that agrees with w_i on the valuations of the atoms in P_i, and agrees with w on the valuations of all other atoms. Then it is clear that $w' \in \Omega(K_i)$. And $dist(w, w')$ is a finite (non-negative) number, since P_i is finite. Hence, $dist(w, K_i)$ (which is less than, or equal to, $dist(w, w')$) is a finite (nonnegative) number. Now that n is a finite (nonnegative) number, $\sum_{i=1}^{n} dist(w, K_i) * \mu(K_i)$ is also a finite (nonnegative) number. Thus, there exists $w \in \mathcal{W}$, such that $\sum_{i=1}^{n} dist(w, K_i) * \mu(K_i)$ is minimum. This means

$$\Omega(Synthesize(\{K_1, K_2, ..., K_n\}, \mu))$$

is not empty — from which the proposition follows.   ◇

Proposition 6.5 *If* $K_1, K_2, ..., K_n$ *are all consistent, and for all* $i \in [1, n]$, $\mu(K_i) \neq 0$, *then*

$$Synthesize(\{K_1, K_2, ..., K_n\}, \mu) \equiv K_1 \wedge K_2 \wedge \cdots \wedge K_n.$$

Proof. Let $W = \Omega(K_1 \wedge K_2 \wedge ... \wedge K_n)$. We prove

$$\Omega(Synthesize(\{K_1, K_2, ..., K_n\}, \mu)) = W$$

from which the proposition follows. Then W is not empty and $\Omega(K_i)$ is not empty, for all $i \in [1, n]$.

Let $w \in W$. For $i \in [1, n]$, $w \in \Omega(K_i)$, and hence $dist(w, K_i) = 0$. It follows that

$$\sum_{i=1}^{n} \mu(K_i) * dist(w, K_i) = 0.$$

Thus,

$$w \preceq_{\{K_1, K_2, \dots, K_n, \mu\}} w'$$

for all $w' \in W$. We have

$$w \in \Omega(Synthesize(\{K_1, K_2, \dots, K_n\}, \mu)).$$

To prove the other direction, let

$$w \in \Omega(Synthesize(\{K_1, K_2, \dots, K_n\}, \mu))$$

and assume $w \notin W$. Then $w \notin \Omega(K_i)$, for some $i \in [1, n]$. Since $\Omega(K_i)$ is not empty, for all $w' \in \Omega(K_i)$, $dist(w, w') > 0$. It follows that

$$dist(w, K_i) > 0.$$

Since $\mu(K_i) \neq 0$,

$$\sum_{i=1}^{n} \mu(K_i) * dist(w, K_i) > 0.$$

From the above proof we know that for all $w' \in W$,

$$\sum_{i=1}^{n} \mu(K_i) * dist(w', K_i) = 0.$$

Hence

$$w \npreceq_{\{K_1, K_2, \dots, K_n, \mu\}} w'$$

which contradicts the fact that

$$w \in \Omega(Synthesize(\{K_1, K_2, \dots, K_n\}, \mu)).$$

$\diamondsuit$

Proposition 6.5 and Proposition 6.2 together have shown the result of *Synthesize* on consistent local pattern sets whose weights are not zero.

6.4 Weighted Majority

To resolve inconsistency, we apply the weighted majority principle to our *Synthesize*. For the inconsistent local patterns X and $\neg X$, our *Synthesize* selects one with higher weight. This principle makes our *Synthesize* produce a when synthesizing the local pattern sets $K_1 = \{a\}$, $K_2 = \{a\}$, and $K_3 = \{\neg a\}$ with the same weight.

Theorem 6.1 *Let p be a local pattern, and the total weights of $K_1, K_2, ...$ and K_n be 1, that is, $\sum_{i=1}^{n} \mu(K_i) = 1$. Then, if the combined weights of the local pattern sets that consistently support p are over $1/2$,*

$$Synthesize(\{K_1, K_2, ..., K_n\}, \mu) \models p.$$

Proof. Assume to the contrary that

$$Synthesize(\{K_1, K_2, ..., K_n\}, \mu) \not\models p.$$

Then there exists

$$w \in Min(W, \preceq_{\{K_1, K_2, ..., K_n, \mu\}})$$

such that $w \not\models p$. Let w_p^- be the possible world that agrees with w on everything except the truth value of p, in which case $w_p^- \models p$. Our task is to derive a contradiction by proving that

$$\sum_{i=1}^{n} \mu(K_i) * dist(w_p^-, K_i) < \sum_{i=1}^{n} \mu(K_i) * dist(w, K_i).$$

Without loss of generality, let $K_1, K_2, ..., K_m$ $(m \leq n)$ be the local pattern sets in $\{K_1, K_2, ..., K_n\}$ that consistently support p. Then $\sum_{i=1}^{m} \mu(K_i) > 1/2$. For $i \in [1, m]$, we prove

$$dist(w_p^-, K_i) \leq dist(w, K_i) - 1.$$

Note that $\Omega(K_i)$ is not empty, because K_i is consistent. Let $w_i \in \Omega(K_i)$ such that

$$dist(w, K_i) = dist(w, w_i).$$

Since $w_i \in \Omega(K_i)$ and $K_i \models p$, $w_i \models p$, then

$$dist(w_p^-, w_i) = dist(w, w_i) - 1$$

because $w_p^- \models p$, where $w \not\models p$ and w_p^- agrees with w on everything except the truth value of p.

$$dist(w_p^-, K_i) \leq dist(w, w_i) - 1 = dist(w, K_i) - 1.$$

For $i \in [m + 1, n]$, we prove

$$dist(w_p^-, K_i) \leq dist(w, K_i) + 1.$$

There are the following cases.

1. K_i is inconsistent. Then

$$dist(w_p^-, K_i) = dist(w, K_i) = 0$$

and we have

$$dist(w_p^-, K_i) \leq dist(w, K_i) + 1.$$

2. K_i is consistent. Let $w_i \in \Omega(K_i)$ be such that $dist(w, w_i) = dist(w, K_i)$. Then

$$dist(w_p^-, w_i) \leq dist(w, w_i) + 1$$

since w_p^- agrees with w on everything except the truth value of p. As $dist(w_p^-, K_i) \leq dist(w_p^-, w_i)$, $i \in [m+1, n]$, we have

$$dist(w_p^-, K_i) \leq dist(w, w_i) + 1 = dist(w, K_i) + 1.$$

Then

$$\sum_{i=1}^{n} dist(w_p^-, K_i) * \mu(K_i) = \sum_{i=1}^{m} dist(w_p^-, K_i) * \mu(K_i)$$

$$+ \sum_{i=m+1}^{n} dist(w_p^-, K_i) * \mu(K_i)$$

$$\leq \sum_{i=1}^{n} dist(w_p^-, K_i) * \mu(K_i)$$

$$- \sum_{i=1}^{m} \mu(K_i) + \sum_{i=m+1}^{m} \mu(K_i)$$

$$< \sum_{i=1}^{n} dist(w_p^-, K_i) * \mu(K_i).$$

This contradicts the fact that

$$w \in Min(W, \preceq_{\{K_1, K_2, ..., K_n, \mu\}}).$$

$\diamond$

The condition in Theorem 6.1 is the *strict* weighted majority. The combined weights of the support for p should be over 50% of the total weight. We now show a *simple* weighted majority condition for *Synthesize*. It suffices that the combined weights of the support for p are greater than the combined weights of the support for $\neg p$.

Proposition 6.6 *Suppose every member in* $\{K_1, K_2, ..., K_n\}$ *supports either* p *or* $\neg p$, *and*

$$\sum_{K_i \models p} \mu(K_i) > \sum_{K_i \models \neg p} \mu(K_i).$$

Then

$$Synthesize(\{K_1, K_2, ..., K_n\}, \mu) \models p.$$

Proof. Similar to that for Theorem 6.1. $\diamond$

While the above theorem and proposition involve literals, we have a theorem for *Synthesize* that concerns arbitrary local patterns. Consider three local pattern sets $K_1 = \{a \vee b, c\}$, $K_2 = \{c\}$, and $K_3 = \{\neg c\}$. Intuitively, $a \vee b$ is a local pattern "specialized" to K_1, and it is not involved in the inconsistency among the local pattern sets, since K_2 and K_3 do not even mention any atom appearing in $a \vee b$. It is desirable that local patterns, such as $a \vee b$, be included in the synthesizing result. The following theorem shows that this is indeed the case.

Theorem 6.2 *Suppose K_j ($j \in [1, n]$) is consistent, and $\mu(K_j) \neq 0$. If $K_j \models \alpha$, and no atom appearing in α is mentioned by any K_i ($i \in [1, n]$ and $i \neq j$), then*

$$Synthesize(\{K_1, K_2, ..., K_n\}, \mu) \models \alpha.$$

Proof. Assume to the contrary that

$$Synthesize(\{K_1, K_2, ..., K_n\}, \mu) \not\models \alpha.$$

Then there exists

$$w \in Min(W, \preceq_{\{K_1, K_2, ..., K_n, \mu\}})$$

such that $w \not\models \alpha$. Let $\mathcal{P}$ be the set of all atoms that appear in α.

Since K_j is consistent, $\Omega(K_j)$ is not empty. Let $w_j \in \Omega(K_j)$ such that $dist(w, K_j) = dist(w, w_j)$. Then, because $w \not\models \alpha$ while $w_j \models \alpha$, w differs from w_j on the valuations of some atoms in $\mathcal{P}$. Let w' be a possible world that agrees with w_j on the valuations of all atoms in P, and agrees with w on all other atoms. Then it is clear that $dist(w', w_j) < dist(w, w_j)$. It follows then that $dist(w', K_j) < dist(w, K_j)$. Now, for all $i \in [1, n]$ and $i \neq j$, K_i does not mention any atom in P, and we have $dist(w', K_j) < dist(w, K_j)$. Since $\mu(K_j) \neq 0$, we have

$$\sum_{i=1}^{n} (dist(w', K_i) * \mu(K_i)) < \sum_{i=1}^{n} (dist(w, K_i) * \mu(K_i)).$$

This contradicts the fact that

$$w \in Min(\mathcal{W}, \preceq_{\{K_1, K_2, ..., K_n, \mu\}}).$$

$\diamond$

In general, within a group, each member is specialized in some areas. Theorem 6.2 shows that the result of *Synthesize* combines the specialized local patterns of the members. Note that in the theorem K_j must be consistent and does not have a zero weight, otherwise it has no effect on the result of synthesizing.

6.5 Mastering Local Pattern Sets

In this section, we show how to model an agent that has absolute priority or seniority within a group, for example, the *master* in a master-slave model. If a group consists of a master and several slaves, the master's opinions always prevail. In database systems, integrity constraints can be viewed as examples of masters that must always be satisfied. In our framework, we can model a master knowledge base by assigning it a weight that is greater than the combined weights of the other local pattern sets in the group. It can be seen that only one master is allowed within a group. The following theorem shows that the opinions of the master local pattern set are always reflected in the synthesizing result.

Theorem 6.3 *For* $k \in [1, n]$, *suppose* K_k *is consistent and* $\mu(K_k) > \sum_{i \neq k} \mu(K_i)$; *then*

$$Synthesize(\{K_1, K_2, ..., K_n\}, \mu) \models K_k.$$

Proof. Assume there exists

$$w \in Min(\mathcal{W}, \preceq_{\{K_1, K_2, ..., K_n, \mu\}})$$

such that $w \not\models K_k$. Since K_k is consistent, $\Omega(K_k)$ is not empty. Let $w_k \in \Omega(K_k)$, such that $dist(w, w_k) = dist(w, K_k)$. Then, since $w \not\models K_k$, $dist(w, w_k) > 0$. Thus, there exists at least one literal p such that $w_k \models p$, while $w \not\models p$. As in the proof of Theorem 6.1, we can prove

$$w_p^- \preceq_{\{K_1, K_2, ..., K_n, \mu\}} w;$$

that is,

$$\sum_{i=1}^n dist(w_p^-, K_i) * \mu(K_i) < \sum_{i=1}^n dist(w, K_i) * \mu(K_i).$$

This contradicts our assumption that

$$w \in Min(\mathcal{W}, \preceq_{\{K_1, K_2, ..., K_n, \mu\}}).$$

$\Diamond$

Note that this theorem holds only when the master K_k is consistent. Since the result of synthesizing is always consistent, it does not imply any inconsistent K_k.

Let IC denote the master local pattern set, referred to as the *integrity constraint* hereafter. Suppose IC is consistent. By the above theorem, the result of synthesizing $\{K_1, K_2, ..., K_n, IC\}$ implies IC, which means that a model of the synthesizing result is also a model of IC. It then seems clear that the models of the result of synthesizing $\{K_1, K_2, ..., K_n, IC\}$ are the models of IC closest to $\{K_1, K_2, ..., K_n\}$. This observation is confirmed by the following theorem.

Theorem 6.4 *Suppose* IC *is consistent, and* $\mu(IC) > \sum_{i=1}^n \mu(K_i)$. *Then*

$$\Omega(Synthesize(\{K_1, K_2, ..., K_n, IC\}, \mu)) = Min(\Omega(IC), \preceq_{\{K_1, K_2, ..., K_n, \mu\}})$$

Proof. Neither the LHS nor RHS of the "=" in the above formula is empty. Let $w \in$ LHS and $w' \in$ RHS. Then $w' \in \Omega(IC)$ and, by Theorem 6.1, we also have $w \in \Omega(IC)$. It follows that $dist(w, IC) = dist(w', IC) = 0$. Let

$$\mathcal{K} = \{K_1, K_2, ..., K_n, IC\}.$$

Assuming $w \notin$ RHS, we have

$$\sum_{i=1}^{n} dist(w', K_i) * \mu(K_i) < \sum_{i=1}^{n} dist(w, K_i) * \mu(K_i).$$

Since $dist(w, IC) = dist(w', IC) = 0$, we have

$$\sum_{K \in \mathcal{K}} dist(w', K) * \mu(K) < \sum_{K \in \mathcal{K}} dist(w, K) * \mu(K).$$

This contradicts the fact that $w \in$ LHS.

Assuming $w' \notin$ LHS, then from Definition 6.1, we have

$$\sum_{K \in \mathcal{K}} dist(w, K) * \mu(K) < \sum_{K \in \mathcal{K}} dist(w', K) * \mu(K).$$

Since $dist(w, IC) = dist(w', IC) = 0$, we have

$$\sum_{i=1}^{n} dist(w, K_i) * \mu(K_i) < \sum_{i=1}^{n} dist(w', K_i) * \mu(K_i).$$

But since $w \in \Omega(IC)$, this contradicts the fact that $w' \in$ RHS. $\Diamond$

Therefore, in the presence of a consistent IC, Definition 6.1 can be simplified. Instead of selecting from $\mathcal{W}$ the worlds closest to $\{K_1, K_2, ..., K_n, IC\}$, we can now select the models of IC that are closest to $\{K_1, K_2, ..., K_n\}$.

It is interesting to consider a special case where there is only one local pattern set K to be synthesized with IC. The above theorems show that $Synthesize(\{K, IC\}, \mu)$ always implies IC. Hence $Synthesize(\{K, IC\}, \mu)$ can also be viewed as a kind of belief revision — revising K by IC, where K is the old local pattern set, and IC represents the new local patterns that must be satisfied. From this, we see that our $Synthesize$ operator collapses to a revision operator when there are only two local pattern sets to be synthesized, one of which is an integrity constraint.

6.6 Examples of Synthesizing Local Pattern Sets

Example 6.1 Let $K_1 = \{a, c\}$, $K_2 = \{a \rightarrow b, \neg c\}$, and $K_3 = \{b \rightarrow e, c\}$, with weights $\mu(K_1) = \mu(K_2) = \mu(K_3) = 0.2$.

Then

$$Synthesize(\{K_1, K_2, K_3\}, \mu) \equiv \{a, a \rightarrow b, b \rightarrow e, c\}$$

We observe that inconsistency among the local pattern sets centers on c. Since all local pattern sets are of equal weight, and two local pattern sets support c while only one opposes c, the result supports c — reflecting the majority opinion. The result also implies that the other local patterns are irrelevant to c, which allows the derivation of the (implicit) local patterns b and e.

Example 6.2 *Suppose K_1, K_2, K_3, their weights are as in Example 6.1, and $K_4 = \{\neg c\}$, with weight $\mu(K_4) = 0.2$.*
    Then

$$Synthesize(\{K_1, K_2, K_3, K_4\}, \mu) \equiv \{a, a \rightarrow b, b \rightarrow e\}.$$

Now in the group of four local pattern sets, half support c and half support $\neg c$. Since all of the local pattern sets have equal weight, c is left undecided. But, as in Example 6.1, the local patterns irrelevant to c are preserved.

Example 6.3 *Suppose K_1, K_2, and K_3 are as in Example 6.1, but their weights are different: $\mu(K_1) = \mu(K_3) = 0.2$, while $\mu(K_2) = 0.4$.*
    Then
$$Synthesize(\{K_1, K_2, K_3\}, \mu) \equiv \{a, a \rightarrow b, b \rightarrow e\}.$$

The inconsistency issue c is left undecided, since the support and opposition of c are balanced. The local pattern set that opposes c has a weight twice as much as the weight of the other two local pattern sets that support c. But, as in the previous examples, the local patterns irrelevant to c are preserved.
    Suppose we have $\mu(K_1) = \mu(K_3) = 0.1$, while $\mu(K_2) = 0.3$. Then

$$Synthesize(\{K_1, K_2, K_3\}, \mu) \equiv \{a, a \rightarrow b, b \rightarrow e, \neg c\}$$

Now the local pattern set that opposes c has a weight greater than half of the total weight of the three local pattern sets. Accordingly, the result of *Synthesize* supports $\neg c$. We get the same result whenever $\mu(K_2) > 0.2$. This result conforms with Theorem 6.1.

Example 6.4 *Suppose $K_1 = \{a\}$, $K_2 = \{a \rightarrow b\}$, $K_3 = \{a, \neg b\}$, and $\mu(K_1) = \mu(K_2) = \mu(K_3) = 0.2$.*
    Then

$$Synthesize(\{K_1, K_2, K_3\}, \mu) \equiv \{a, a \rightarrow b\} \vee \{a, \neg b\}.$$

The synthesized local pattern sets support a, since the majority supports a. For b, it is a striking of balance between $a \rightarrow b$ and $\neg b$. In other words, one local pattern set (K_3) opposes b, but, because the majority supports a, K_2 generates support for b, using its rule $a \rightarrow b$. The opposing and supporting forces are in balance, and hence the issue of b is undecided. Therefore, the result of synthesizing supports the disjunction of $a \rightarrow b$ and $\neg b$.

Example 6.5 *Suppose K_1, K_2, and K_3 are as in Example 6.4, and $\mu(K_1) = \mu(K_2) = 0.1$ while $\mu(K_3) = 0.2$.*
   Then

$$Synthesize(\{K_1, K_2, K_3\}, \mu) \equiv \{a, \neg b\}.$$

Now the opposing force for b is stronger than the supporting force, since K_3 carries a higher weight. Consequently, the synthesized result opposes b.
   Suppose in Example 6.5 the weights are $\mu(K_1) = \mu(K_3) = 0.1$, while $\mu(K_2) = 0.2$. Then

$$Synthesize(\{K_1, K_2, K_3\}, \mu) \equiv \{a, a \to b\}.$$

The result supports b accordingly, because the supporting force of b is stronger than the opposing force.

6.7 A Syntactic Characterization

In this section we present a syntactic characterization of *Synthesize* that defines the result of synthesizing by a syntactic transformation of the local pattern sets to be synthesized.
   Let $DNF(K)$ denote the disjunctive normal form of K. We omit primitive connectives $\wedge$ and $\vee$ in $DNF(K)$, hence $DNF(K)$ is a set of disjuncts, and each disjunct is a set of literals. We require each disjunct in $DNF(K)$ to be satisfiable. If not, the disjunct can be discarded from $DNF(K)$. For technical reasons, when K is inconsistent we define $DNF(K) = \{\emptyset\}$.
   In syntactic characterization, we often need to consider sets of weighted literals. For example, we have a set of literals $D = \{a, \neg a, b\}$, where the literals are associated with weights 1, 2, and 1 respectively. For convenience, we write the weight in the superscripts of the literals. Now, suppose we view D equivalently as $\{a^1, \neg a^1, \neg a^1, b^1\}$, then intuitively, D contains an "inconsistency" represented by the pair $\langle a^1, \neg a^1 \rangle$. We split D into two subsets: $\{a^1, \neg a^1\}$ and $\{\neg a^1, b^1\}$. The first subset contains the inconsistency, and the second subset is the set of D after removing the inconsistency. We call the first subset the *inconsistent part* of D, and the second the *consistent part* of D. The notion of inconsistent and consistent parts of a set of weighted literals is the cornerstone of our syntactic transformation for *Synthesize*. We give the formal definitions below.
   Let D be a set of weighted literals. We define the inconsistent part of D, denoted by $f(D)$, to be the set of all literals of pairs $\langle p^x, \neg p^x \rangle$ (where p is an atom), such that one of p^x and $\neg p^x$ is in D. For the other, say p^x (or $\neg p^x$), there is a $p^{x'}$ (or $\neg p^{x'}$, respectively) in D such that $x' \geq x$. We also define the consistent part of d, denoted by $g(D)$, to be the set of literals in D after "subtracting" the literals in $f(D)$. That is, $g(D) = \{p^x \mid n > 0, \; p^{x'} \in D$ and, if $p^{x''} \in D$, then $x = x' - x''$; otherwise $x = x'\}$.

If it is useful to know that, if we take the union of $f(D)$ and $g(D)$ and conjoin the same literals in the union while adding up their weights, we recover the original D. Note also that $f(D)$ is inconsistent unless it is empty, and $g(D)$ is always consistent, which is why we call the former the *inconsistent part*, and the latter the *consistent part*. We define the *weight* of $f(D)$, denoted by $\mu^I(D)$, to be the sum of the weights of all literals in $f(D)$.

The transformation of *Synthesize* goes as follows. First, we assume the local pattern sets have been put into a disjunctive normal form (DNF). From each (DNF) local pattern set K_i ($i \in [1,n]$), we take one disjunct D_i, and superscribe each literal in D_i with the weight of K_i. We then form a *combination*, denoted by $D_1 \uplus D_2 \uplus ... \uplus D_n$, from the union of $D_1, D_2, ..., D_n$, by conjoining the same literals in the union and adding up the weights of the same literals. The idea of the transformation of *Synthesize* is to select those combinations such that the weights of their inconsistent parts are *minimum*; and the result of *Synthesize* is the disjunction of the consistent parts of those combinations.

Theorem 6.5

$Synthesize(\{K_1, K_2, ..., K_n\}, \mu)$
$$\equiv \bigvee\{\bigwedge g(C) \mid C \text{ is in } S \text{ such that } \mu^I(C) \text{ is minimal}\},$$
where $S = \{D_1 \uplus \cdots \uplus D_n \mid D_i \in DNF(K_i)\}$.

Proof. For a possible world w, and a set of literals D, let $diff(w, D)$ denote the number of literals in D that are not supported by w. That is, $diff(w, D)$ is the cardinality of $\{p \in D \mid w \not\models p\}$. Then we have the following lemma.

Lemma 6.1 *Let W be a possible world, and K be a local pattern set. Then*

$$dist(w, K) = \min_{D \in DNF(K)} diff(w, D).$$

Proof. If K is inconsistent (unsatisfiable), then $DNF(K) = \{\emptyset\}$ and $dist(w, K) = 0$. It is easy to see that the lemma holds. Hence we assume K is satisfiable.

Assume $dist(w, K) > min_{D \in DNF(K)} diff(w, D)$. Let $D' \in DNF(K)$ such that

$$diff(w, D') > min_{D \in DNF(K)} diff(w, D).$$

Then

$$dist(w, K) > diff(w, D').$$

From the definition of DNF, we know that all the disjuncts in $DNF(K)$ are satisfiable, and hence D' is satisfiable. Thus, there does not exist $p \in D'$ such that $\neg p \in D'$. Let w' be a possible world such that $w'(p) = true$ if $p \in D'$. Thus, $w'(p) = false$ if $\neg p \in D'$ and $w'(p) = w(p)$ otherwise. Then it is obvious that $w' \models D'$, and therefore $w' \in \Omega(K)$. It is also easy to see $dist(w, w') = diff(w, D')$. Then, from $dist(w, K) > diff(w, D')$, it follows that $dist(w, K) > dist(w, w')$. However, since $w' \in \Omega(K)$, this contradicts the fact that $dist(w, K) = min_{y \in \Omega(K)} dist(w, y)$.

Conversely, assume $dist(w, K) < min_{D \in DNF(K)} diff(w, D)$. Let $w' \in \Omega(K)$ such that $dist(w, w') = dist(w, K)$. Then

$$dist(w, w') < min_{D \in DNF(K)} diff(w, D).$$

Since $w' \in \Omega(K)$, $w' \models D'$ for some $D' \in DNF(K)$. Then $w' \models p$ for all $p \in D'$. Hence we have $diff(w, D') \leq dist(w, w')$. From

$$dist(w, w') < min_{D \in DNF(K)} diff(w, D)$$

it follows that

$$diff(w, D') < min_{D \in DNF(K)} diff(w, D).$$

Since $D' \in DNF(K)$, this is a contradiction.

Therefore $dist(w, K) = min_{D \in DNF(K)} diff(w, D)$. $\Diamond$

Lemma 6.2 *Let w be any possible world, and D_i be any disjunct in K_i $(i = 1, ..., n)$. Then*

$$\sum \mu(K_i) * diff(w, D_i) \geq \mu^I(D_1 \uplus \cdots \uplus D_n)/2,$$

where the equality holds iff

$$w \models \bigwedge g(D_1 \uplus \cdots \uplus D_n).$$

Proof. From the definitions of $diff$ and g, and the fact that for any pair $\langle p, \neg p \rangle$ in $f(D_1 \uplus \cdots \uplus D_n)$, w implies exactly one of p and $\neg p$. $\Diamond$

We now proceed to prove the main theorem.

Both the RHS and LHS are consistent. Let $w \models$ RHS and $w' \models$ LHS. Then

$$w \models \bigwedge g(D_1 \uplus \cdots \uplus D_n)$$

for some $D_1 \in DNF(K_1)$, ..., $D_n \in DNF(K_n)$ such that

$$\mu^I(D_1 \uplus \cdots \uplus D_n) \leq \mu^I(C)$$

for all $C \in S$. Let $Q_i \in DNF(K_i)$ $(i = 1, ..., n)$ such that

$$diff(w', Q_i) = min_{D \in DNF(K)} diff(w', D).$$

To simplify the notation, we let $\mathcal{D}$ denote $D_1 \uplus \cdots \uplus D_n$, and $\mathcal{Q}$ denote $Q_1 \uplus \cdots \uplus Q_n$. We first obtain:

$$\mu^I(\mathcal{D}) \leq \mu^I(\mathcal{Q}). \tag{6.2}$$

For later development, we prove two inequalities. One concerns w:

$$\sum(dist(w, K_i) * \mu(K_i)) \leq \mu^I(\mathcal{D})/2 \tag{6.3}$$

and the other concerns w':

$$\sum(dist(w', K_i) * \mu(K_i)) \geq \mu^I(\mathcal{Q})/2. \tag{6.4}$$

Since $w \models \bigwedge g(\mathcal{D})$, by Lemma 6.1 we have

$$\sum(diff(w, D_i) * \mu(K_i)) = \mu^I(\mathcal{D})/2.$$

By Lemma 6.2, we have

$$\sum(dist(w, K_i) * \mu(K_i)) = \sum \mu(K_i) * min_{D \in DNF(K_i)} diff(w, D).$$

To prove Eq. (6.3), it suffices to prove

$$\sum \mu(K_i) * min_{D \in DNF(K_i)} diff(w, D) \leq \sum \mu(K_i) * diff(w, D_i). \tag{6.5}$$

Assume to the contrary that

$$\sum \mu(K_i) * min_{D \in DNF(K_i)} diff(w, D) > \sum \mu(K_i) * diff(w, D_i).$$

Then there must be at least one $i \in [1, n]$, such that

$$min_{D \in DNF(K_i)} diff(w, D) > diff(w, D_i).$$

However, since $D_i \in DNF(K_i)$, this is a contradiction. Therefore, we have the inequality (6.5), from which the inequality (6.3) is established.

Now we prove (6.4). By Lemma 6.2 and the definition of Q_i $(1, ..., n)$ we have

$$\sum \mu(K_i) * dist(w', K_i) = \sum \mu(K_i) * diff(w', Q_i). \tag{6.6}$$

By Lemma 6.1 we know $\sum \mu(K_i) * diff(w', Q_i) \geq \mu^I(\mathcal{Q})/2$, from which, together with Eq. (6.6), we obtain (6.4).

Then, the proof of the main theorem is carried out in the following steps:

(a) Assume $w \not\models$ LHS. Then, since $w' \models$ LHS, we have

$$\sum \mu(K_i) * dist(w', K_i) < \sum \mu(K_i) * dist(w, K_i).$$

Using (6.3) and (6.4), we get

$$\mu^I(\mathcal{Q}) < \mu^I(\mathcal{D}).$$

This contradicts (6.2). Hence, $w \models$ LHS.

(b) Assume $w' \not\models$ RHS. Our goal is to derive a contradiction by proving

$$\sum \mu(K_i) * dist(w, K_i) < \sum \mu(K_i) * dist(w', K_i).$$

As $\mu^I(\mathcal{Q}) \leq \mu^I(\mathcal{D})$, there are two cases:

(i) $\mu^I(\mathcal{D}) < \mu^I(\mathcal{Q})$. Using (6.3) and (6.4), we obtain

$$\sum \mu(K_i) * dist(w, K_i) < \sum \mu(K_i) * dist(w', K_i).$$

(ii) $\mu^I(\mathcal{D}) = \mu^I(\mathcal{Q})$. Then

$$\mu^I(\mathcal{Q}) \leq \mu^I(\mathcal{C})$$

for all $C \in S$. It must be the case that $w' \not\models g(\mathcal{Q})$; otherwise $w' \models$ RHS, which contradicts our assumption. Then by Lemma 6.3, we have

$$\sum \mu(K_i) * diff(w', Q_i) > \mu^I(\mathcal{Q})/2.$$

From Eq. (6.6) we obtain $\sum \mu(K_i) * dist(w', K_i) > \mu^I(\mathcal{Q})/2$. Using (6.3), and the fact that

$$\mu^I(\mathcal{D}) = \mu^I(\mathcal{Q})$$

we establish

$$\sum \mu(K_i) * dist(w', K_i) > \sum \mu(K_i) * dist(w, K_i).$$

In both cases we have $\sum \mu(K_i) * dist(w', K_i) > \sum \mu(K_i) * dist(w, K_i)$. This contradicts the fact that $w' \models$ LHS.

The theorem follows from (a) and (b).   ◇

An example of the transformation

Given are three local pattern sets $K_1 = \{a, c\}$, $K_1 = \{a \rightarrow b, \neg c\}$, and $K_3 = \{c\}$, with weights $\mu(K_1) = 1$, $\mu(K_2) = 3$, and $\mu(K_3) = 1$. Their disjunctive normal forms are $DFN(K_1) = \{\{a, c\}\}$, $DFN(K_2) = \{\{\neg a, \neg c\}, \{b, \neg c\}\}$, and $DFN(K_3) = \{\{c\}\}$.

Then $S = \{C_1, C_2\}$, where

$$C_1 = \{a^1, c^1, \neg a^3, \neg c^3, c^1\} = \{a^1, \neg a^3, c^2, \neg c^3\}$$

and

$$C_2 = \{a^1, c^1, b^3, \neg c^3, c^1\} = \{a^1, b^3, c^2, \neg c^3\}.$$

Thus, we have

$$f(C_1) = \{a^1, \neg a^1, c^2, \neg c^2\}$$

and
$$g(C_1) = \{\neg a^2, \neg c^1\}$$
while $f(C_2) = \{c^2, \neg c^2\}$ and $g(C_2) = \{a^1, b^3, \neg c^1\}$. Since $\mu^I(C_1) = 6 > \mu^I(C_2) = 4$,

$$
\begin{aligned}
Synthesize(\{K_1, K_2, K_3\}) &\equiv g(C_2) \\
&= \{a^1, b^3, \neg c^1\} \\
&= \{a, b, \neg c\} \\
&= \{a, a \rightarrow b, \neg c\}.
\end{aligned}
$$

6.8 Summary

In this chapter, we have presented a local pattern synthesizing operator that has desirable properties and is capable of resolving inconsistencies among the local pattern sets. The operator also plausibly incorporates the weights of the local pattern sets within the process of synthesizing.

7. Identifying High-vote Patterns

While traditional multi-database mining algorithms focus on identifying mono-database-mining-like patterns, in this chapter we develop techniques for identifying novel patterns (*high-vote patterns*) in multi-databases by analyzing local patterns. The number of patterns forwarded from, say, company branches, may be so large that browsing the pattern set, and finding interesting patterns from it, could be rather difficult for a head office. In particular, it is more difficult to identify which of the forwarded patterns are really useful for a company's applications. In this chapter we design efficient strategies to search for high-vote patterns from *local patterns* within the branches of a company. As we stated in Chapter 1, *this approach is particularly useful in dual-level applications*. Another technique we develop provides a good human interface, by constructing a fuzzy logic controller.

From the structure of patterns, as described in Chapter 3, a high-vote pattern (e.g., an itemset) can contain a great deal of information concerning the uncertainty of the pattern (the support of the itemset) in local databases. In this case, there can be altogether too much information for users to comprehend. Thus, it is very difficult for users to apply a pattern when making decisions. With this in mind, this chapter also presents a method for analyzing high-vote patterns so that they can be easily understood and applied. High-vote pattern analysis is what users need to consider.

7.1 Introduction

Within a company, each branch, large or small, has equal power to vote for patterns for global decision-making. Some patterns receive votes from most of the branches. These patterns are referred to as *high-vote patterns*. High-vote patterns represent the commonness of the branches. Therefore, these patterns may be far more important in terms of global decision-making.

A high-vote pattern is of the form $P(A, v)$, where A is a local pattern, and v is the vote ratio of A in a multi-database environment which is greater than, or equal to, a minimum vote-ratio ($minVR$) specified by users.

As we have seen, in a multi-database environment a pattern has attributes, such as the name of the pattern, the rate voted for by branches, supports, and confidences for a rule, in branches that vote for the pattern. In other words, a pattern is a super-point of the form

$$P(name, vote, vsupp, vconf).$$

To identify high-vote and suggested patterns from local patterns, the projection of $P(name, vote, vsupp, vconf)$ on $name$ and $vote$ is considered in this chapter. That is, the projection

$$P(name, vote) \tag{7.1}$$

is used to search for high-vote and suggested patterns of interest.

The chapter is organized as follows. We start with studying an illustration of high-vote patterns in Section 7.2. Section 7.3 advocates a model for identifying high-vote patterns. In Section 7.4, we design an algorithm that searches for high-vote patterns. In Section 7.5, a fuzzy logic controller is constructed for providing a good man-machine interface in multi-database mining. Section 7.6 presents an approach for analyzing high-vote patterns. Section 7.7 simply discusses the identification of suggested patterns. Finally, the work in this chapter is summarized in Section 7.8.

7.2 Illustration of High-vote Patterns

Now that multiple databases have been pre-processed, using techniques in Chapters 4 through 6, we develop techniques for mining the quality and consistency of data in each class. For simplicity in this chapter and following chapters, the multi-databases given are regarded as belonging to only one class, and all the data have quality and consistency, except when specified.

As we have pointed out, a multi-branched company must face dual-level decisions: company decisions (global applications) and branch decisions (local applications). To avoid re-mining multiple databases, the local patterns (including local frequent itemsets and local association rules mined in branches) are reused.

For a huge number of local patterns, a company's headquarters often select predictive patterns based on the lift in the top 5%, 10%, or 15%. And these patterns would generally be voted for by most of the company's branches. Hence, reusing local patterns is important, and sometimes necessary. The techniques in this section focus on identifying high-vote patterns from local patterns, which are regarded as novel patterns in multi-databases.

Graphical methods usually attempt to present a set of local patterns in pictorial form, so as to give users an adequate visual description. Therefore, we use the figures below to illustrate, in a concrete form, which patterns among the local patterns are of interest.

It is not easy to grasp the essential characteristics of a large set of local patterns by looking at a listing of the patterns. So, as a rule, we must summarize the patterns through the use of graphical, or numerical, techniques.

Even though, in general, all the patterns from branches are not available to the company, we may still be able to assume a reasonable graphic shape for the relative frequency distribution of the patterns. Of course, we can always construct a frequency, or relative frequency, histogram for a multi-branch company (since its local patterns are known) and use it to make an empirical assessment of the shape of the patterns.

Once a relative frequency distribution is established for an interstate company, we can, by using probability arguments, calculate summarizing numerical measurements such as the mean, variance, and standard deviation. Similar quantities can be calculated directly from the patterns.

Consider four databases $DB1$, $DB2$, $DB3$, and $DB4$ of a company. In Figure 7.1, the distribution of patterns in branches (databases) of the company is depicted, where each local pattern in the databases $DB1$, $DB2$, $DB3$, $DB4$ is a point marked by "r".

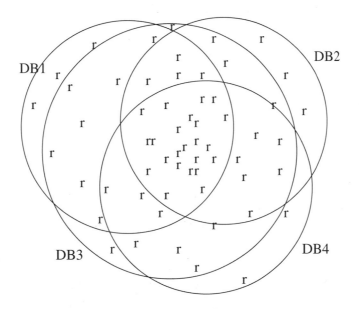

Fig. 7.1. The intersection of four databases

Figure 7.1 displays the distribution of local patterns (patterns) in the four databases. Intuitively, the patterns distributed at the intersection of the four databases would be of the most interest to company headquarters, as they have been voted for by all branches. Figure 7.2 highlights the intersections of interest.

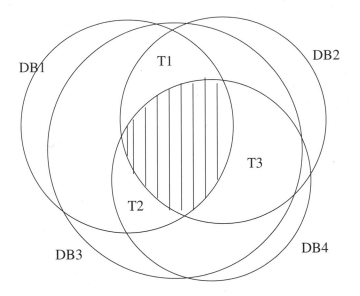

Fig. 7.2. The shaded part of the intersection

In Figure 7.2, the shaded portion is the intersection of $DB1$, $DB2$, $DB3$, and $DB4$. There are also three other parts, $T1$, T_2 and T_3, which may be of interest, where T_1 is the intersection of $DB1$, $DB2$, and $DB3$; $T2$ is the intersection of $DB1$, $DB3$, and $DB4$; and $T3$ is the intersection of $DB2$, $DB3$, and $DB4$.

In real applications, it is common sense that company headquarters would be interested in patterns that are voted for by the majority of its branches. In Figure 7.2, the local patterns that occur in the labeled areas $T1$, $T2$, and $T3$ are of interest. This includes the shaded area. These areas are referred to as *high-vote-pattern areas*, in which the patterns have been voted for by most of the branches of the company.

High-vote patterns, such as "80% of 15 supermarket branches reported that customers like to buy the products of Sunshine", are useful in market forecasting, customer behavior prediction, and global decision-making of an interstate company. Because traditional multi-database mining techniques cannot identify high-vote patterns, they are regarded as relatively novel patterns that describe the distribution of patterns within branches.

7.3 Identifying High-vote Patterns

High-vote patterns can grasp the distribution of patterns in local patterns, and reflect the "commonness" of branches in their voting. High-vote patterns are useful for global applications of interstate companies. This subsection presents techniques for identifying this kind of pattern from local patterns.

In some contexts, each branch, large or small, has equal power to vote for its local patterns when global decisions are being made by the company. Thus, we may expect to obtain some commonness from local patterns. This commonness could be of interest to company headquarters.

We now formally define the patterns below.

Let $D_1, D_2, ..., D_m$ be m databases in the m branches $B_1, B_2, ..., B_m$ of a company, respectively, and LI_i be the set of patterns (local patterns) from D_i $(i = 1, 2, ..., m)$, and

$$LI = \{r_j | r_j \in LI_1 \cup LI_2 \cup \cdots \cup LI_m, 1 \le j \le n\},$$

where $n = |LI_1 \cup LI_2 \cup \cdots \cup LI_m|$.

The table of frequency of patterns voted for by the branches of an interstate company for local patterns is listed in Table 7.1.

Table 7.1 *Frequencies of patterns voted for by branches*

	r_1	r_2	...	r_n
B_1	$a_{1,1}$	$a_{1,2}$	...	$a_{1,n}$
B_2	$a_{2,1}$	$a_{2,2}$	...	$a_{2,n}$
...	...	...	...	...
B_m	$a_{m,1}$	$a_{m,2}$	...	$a_{m,n}$
Voted Number	*voting$_1$*	*voting$_2$*	...	*voting$_n$*

In Table 7.1, B_i is the ith branch $(1 \le i \le m)$, $a_{i,j} = 1$ means that branch B_i votes for pattern r_j (where r_j is a valid pattern in branch B_i), $a_{i,j} = 0$ means that branch B_i does not vote for pattern r_j (where r_j is not a valid pattern in branch B_i) $(1 \le i \le m$ and $1 \le j \le n)$; and $voting_i$ is the number of branches that vote for the ith patterns $(1 \le i \le m)$.

From Table 7.1, the average voting rate can be obtained as

$$AverageVR = \frac{voting(r_1) + voting(r_2) + \cdots + voting(r_n)}{n}, \qquad (7.2)$$

where $voting(r_i) = voting_i/m$, which is the voting ratio of r_i.

The voting rate of a pattern is *high* if it is greater than $AverageVR$. By using $AverageVR$, these patterns can be classified into four classes which are depicted in Figure 7.3.

In Figure 7.3, $votingrate = AverageVR$ is a reference line for measuring the interest of the pattern r_i. Certainly, the farther the voting rate is from the line, the more the interest. If the voting rate of a pattern is in $[x_1, 1]$, the pattern is referred to as a "high-vote pattern", and $[x_1, 1]$ referred to as a *high-vote pattern area*. If the voting rate of a pattern is in $[x_2, x_1)$, the pattern is referred to as a "suggested pattern", and $[x_2, x_1)$ referred to as a *suggested pattern area*. If the voting rate of a pattern is in (x_3, x_2), the pattern is referred to as a "random pattern", and (x_3, x_2) referred to as a *random pattern area*. Random patterns are of no interest to company headquarters. Nor are they considered in this book. If the voting rate of a pattern is in $[0, x_3]$, the pattern is referred to as an "exceptional pattern" and $[0, x_3]$ referred to as an *exceptional pattern area*. For any pattern r, in the exceptional pattern area, r is of interest if it satisfies the conditions that we give in Chapter 8.

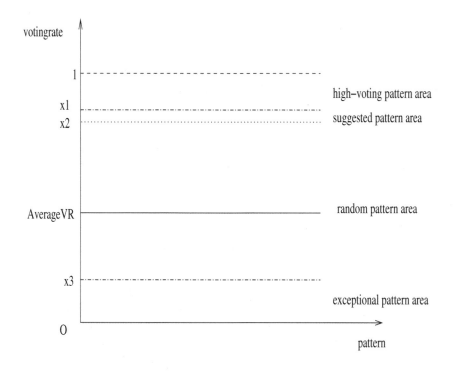

Fig. 7.3. Patterns in local pattern sets

To measure the interestingness of a high-vote pattern r_i, the relationship between the voting rate $voting(r_i)$ and the average voting rate $AverageVR$ is considered. Certainly, if $voting(r_i) > AverageVR$, the pattern r_i refers to a high-vote pattern. Therefore, $voting(r_i) - AverageVR$ satisfies:

$$0 < voting(r_i) - AverageVR \leq 1 - AverageVR.$$

In particular, we have

$$0 < \frac{voting(r_i) - AverageVR}{1 - AverageVR} \le 1.$$

Certainly, the bigger the ratio $(voting(r_i) - AverageVR)/(1 - AverageVR)$, the more interesting the pattern.

Consequently, the interest measure $LPI(r_i)$ of a pattern r_i is defined according to the deviation of the voting rate $voting(r_i)$ from the average voting rate $AverageVR$ and

$$LPI(r_i) = \frac{voting(r_i) - AverageVR}{1 - AverageVR} \tag{7.3}$$

for $1 - AverageVR \ne 0$, where $LPI(r_i)$ is referred to as the interestingness of r_i, given $AverageVR$.

From this interest measure, $LPI(r_i)$ is positively related to the real voting ratio of the pattern r_i. It is highest if the real voting ratio is 1. A pattern r_i in local patterns is an interesting high-vote pattern if its interest measure LPI_i is equal to, or greater than, a threshold — the minimum interest degree $(miniVR)$ given by users or experts. Obviously, for $LPI(r_i)$:

- if $voting(r_i) = AverageVR$, r_i is of no interest, and the interest measure of the pattern is as

$$LPI(r_i) = 0;$$

- if $voting(r_i) - AverageVR > 0$, r_i is a high-vote pattern. When $voting(r_i) = 1$ is the strongest voting rate, r_i is a high-vote pattern of interest, and the interest measure of the pattern is as

$$LPI(r_i) = 1;$$

- again, if $voting(r_i) - AverageVR < 0$, r_i is a low-vote pattern. When $voting(r_i) = 0$ is the weakest voting rate, r_i is a low-vote pattern of interest. The interest measure of this pattern is defined in Chapter 8.

The problem of finding high-vote patterns can now be stated as follows.

Given a set of local pattern sets $LIset$, find all patterns for which interest degrees are equal to, or greater than, $miniVR$.

7.4 Algorithm Design

High-vote patterns reflect the commonness of branches within an interstate company. Finding high-vote patterns in multiple databases is a procedure that identifies all patterns for which interest degrees are equal to, or greater than, $miniVR$. This section presents the algorithm $highvotingPatterns$.

7.4.1 Searching for High-vote Patterns

We now design an algorithm, *highvotingPatterns*, which searches for high-vote patterns.

> **Algorithm 7.1** *highvotingPatterns*
> **begin**
>
> **Input**: LI_i $(1 \leq i \leq M)$: sets of local patterns, *miniVR*: threshold value that is the minimum interest voting ratio;
> **Output**: *FPattern*: set of high-vote patterns;
> (1) **call** the procedure *GoodClass* to generate a classification $class^\alpha$ for M local patterns LI_i;
> (2) **if** $\alpha = 1$ **then**
>   **begin**
>   **input** please suggest a value for α;
>   **call** the procedure *GreedyClass* to generate a classifica-
> tion $class^\alpha$;
>   **end**;
> (3) **let** $FPattern \leftarrow \{\}$;
> (4) **for** each $class_i$ in $class^\alpha$ **do**
>   **begin**
>   (4.1) **let** $FPattern_i \leftarrow \{\}$;
>   **let** pattern set $P \leftarrow \emptyset$;
>   (4.2) **for** a local pattern set LI in $class_i$ **do**
>   **for** each pattern r in LI **do**
>   **begin**
>   **if** $r \in P$ **then**
>   **let** $r_f \leftarrow r_f + 1$;
>   **else**
>   **begin**
>   **let** $P \leftarrow P \cup \{r\}$;
>   **let** $r_f \leftarrow 1$;
>   **end**
>   **end**
>   (4.3) **for** each pattern r in P **do**
>   **if** $LPI(r_f) \geq miniVR$ **then**
>   **let** $FPattern_i \leftarrow FPattern_i \cup \{r\}$;
>   (4.4) **let** $FPattern \leftarrow FPattern \cup \{FPattern_i\}$;
>   **end**
> (5) **output** the high-vote patterns in $FPattern$;
> **end**;

The algorithm *highvotingPatterns* above searches for all high-vote patterns from M given local pattern sets.

Step (1) finds a good classification $class^\alpha$ for the M local pattern sets (i.e., from M databases) using the algorithm $GoodClass$. If there is non-trivial good classification, it requires the inputting of a suggested value for α in Step (2), and it generates a classification $class^\alpha$ for the M local pattern sets using the algorithm $GreedyClass$ (see Chapter 5). Therefore, the databases can also be classified according to applications given by users.

For the above $class^\alpha$, we need to search for high-vote patterns one by one, with respect to the classes. The set of high-vote patterns found in a class is taken as an element of $FPattern$. Step (3) allows the set $FPattern$ to be an empty set.

Step (4) analyzes the patterns for each class $class_i$ in $class^\alpha$. Step (4.1) initializes the set variable $FPattern_i$ that is used to save all high-vote patterns in $class_i$, and the set variable P that is used to save all patterns in $class_i$. Step (4.2) sums up the frequency for each pattern r in $class_i$. Step (4.3) generates all high-vote patterns from set P and saves them in $FPattern_i$, where each pattern r in $FPattern_i$ has a voting ratio $LPI(r_f) \geq miniVR$. Step (4.4) appends $FPattern_i$ into $FPattern$.

Step (5) outputs all high-vote patterns in the given local pattern sets class by class.

7.4.2 Identifying High-vote Patterns: An Example

We now demonstrate the use of the algorithm $highvotingPatterns$.

Example 7.1 *Consider the seven local pattern sets LI_1, LI_2, ..., LI_7 that are obtained from branches B_1, B_2, ..., B_7, respectively.*

$$LI_1 = \{(A, 0.4); (B, 0.5); (C, 0.7); (D, 0.6); (E, 0.9)\},$$
$$LI_2 = \{(A, 0.5); (B, 0.45); (C, 0.5)\},$$
$$LI_3 = \{(A, 0.55); (B, 0.42)\},$$
$$LI_4 = \{(A, 0.51); (C, 0.4); (D, 0.44)\},$$
$$LI_5 = \{(E, 0.38); (F, 0.5); (G, 0.85); (I, 0.44)\},$$
$$LI_6 = \{(E, 0.47); (I, 0.34); (J, 0.6)\},$$
$$LI_7 = \{(E, 0.55); (F, 0.35)\}.$$

Here each local pattern set has several patterns, separated by a semicolon, and each pattern consists of its name and its support in a branch, separated by a comma. Let the minimal voting ratio $miniVR$ equal 0.25.

First, the algorithm $highvotingPatterns$ searches for all high-vote patterns from the seven local pattern sets. After calling $GoodClass$, there is a good classification $class^{0.0375}$ for the seven local pattern sets, and $class^{0.0375}$ has two elements as follows.

$class_1 = \{LI_1, LI_2, LI_3, LI_4\};$

$class_2 = \{LI_5, LI_6, LI_7\}.$

For $class_1$ and $class_2$, the votes of patterns are summed up, as shown in Tables 7.2 and 7.3.

Table 7.2 *Frequency of patterns in $class_1$ voted for by branches*

	A	B	C	D	E
B_1	1	1	1	1	1
B_2	1	1	1	0	0
B_3	1	1	0	0	0
B_4	1	0	1	1	0
Voted Number	4	3	3	2	1

Table 7.3 *Frequency of patterns in $class_2$ voted for by branches*

	E	F	G	I	J
B_5	1	1	1	1	0
B_6	1	0	0	1	1
B_7	1	1	0	0	0
Voted Number	3	2	1	2	1

From the voting ratios of patterns, we can obtain the interest measurements of all patterns. For $class_1$, $AverageVR = 0.65$. Because the voting rates of D and E are less than $AverageVR$, they are not high-vote patterns. For A, B, and C,

$$LPI(A) = \frac{voting(A) - AverageVR}{1 - AverageVR} = \frac{1 - 0.65}{1 - 0.65} = 1;$$

$$LPI(B) = \frac{voting(B) - AverageVR}{1 - AverageVR} = \frac{0.75 - 0.65}{1 - 0.65} \approx 0.286;$$

$$LPI(C) = \frac{voting(C) - AverageVR}{1 - AverageVR} = \frac{0.75 - 0.65}{1 - 0.65} \approx 0.286.$$

For $class_2$, $AverageVR = 0.6$. Because the voting rates of G and J are less than $AverageVR$, they are not high-vote patterns. For E, F, and I,

$$LPI(E) = \frac{voting(E) - AverageVR}{1 - AverageVR} = \frac{1 - 0.6}{1 - 0.6} = 1;$$

$$LPI(F) = \frac{voting(F) - AverageVR}{1 - AverageVR} = \frac{0.667 - 0.6}{1 - 0.6} \approx 0.167;$$

$$LPI(I) = \frac{voting(I) - AverageVR}{1 - AverageVR} = \frac{0.667 - 0.6}{1 - 0.6} \approx 0.167.$$

When $miniVR = 0.25$, high-vote patterns in $FPattern_1$ and $FPattern_2$ are as follows.

$$FPattern_1 = \{(A, 1); (B, 0.75); (C, 0.75)\};$$
$$FPattern_2 = \{(E, 1)\}.$$

Here, each set has several patterns, separated by a semicolon, and each pattern consists of its name and its voting ratio by the branches in a class, separated by a comma.

We can represent high-vote patterns in natural language. For example, let B stand for $i_1 \rightarrow i_2$. Then the high-vote pattern $(B, 0.75)$ can be represented as "75% of the branches agreed that if i_1 then i_2."

7.4.3 Algorithm Analysis

This subsection analyzes the complexity of the algorithm $highvotingPatterns$.

The algorithm $highvotingPatterns$ identifies all high-vote patterns from local patterns. We have a theorem for the algorithm as follows.

Theorem 7.1 *Algorithm highvotingPatterns works correctly.*

Proof: Clearly, in Steps (4) and (5), a set $FPattern$ of high-vote patterns is generated, as it is output for given local pattern sets. We need to show that all high-vote patterns are identified, and all low-vote patterns are given up.

For any local pattern r_i in a class, if $LPI(r_i) < miniVR$ in the loop in Step (4.3), there is a low-vote pattern. It is not appended to $FPattern$. This means that all low-voting patterns are given up.

Or else, if $LPI(r_i) \geq miniVR$ in the loop in Step (4.3), there is a high-vote pattern, and the pattern is appended to $FPattern$. This means that all high-vote patterns are identified.　　　　　　　　　　　　　　　　　◇

In the algorithm $highvotingPatterns$, Steps (1) and (2), we call the procedures $GoodClass$ and $GreedyClass$. The complexities of $GoodClass$ and $GreedyClass$ have been discussed in Chapter 5. So, the complexity of $highvotingPatterns$ can be regarded as consisting of Steps (3) through (5).

In Step (4), there are $m = |class^\alpha|$ classes that are searched for. Assume that n_i is the number of local patterns in the class $class_i$. It needs

$$n_1 * |class_1| + n_2 * |class_2| + \cdots + n_m|class_m|$$

units to save all the local patterns, which is less than, or equal to, mnl, where $n = \{n_1, n_2, ..., n_m\}$, l is the maximum among $|class_1|, |class_2|, ..., |class_m|$, and $|class_i|$ stands for the number of local patterns in the class $class_i$. Also, we need N units to save all the high-vote patterns in $FPattern_1$, ..., $FPattern_m$, and $FPattern$. Certainly $N \leq mn$. Consequently, the space complexity of $highvotingPatterns$ is $O(mnl)$.

Apparently, the time complexity of $highvotingPatterns$ is dominated by the loop in Step (4). Therefore, we have the following theorem.

Theorem 7.2 *The time complexity of highvotingPatterns is $O(m^2 nl)$.*

Proof: For Step (4), m classes need to be processed for identifying high-vote patterns. For a class $class_i$, there are $|class_i|$ local pattern sets and n_i local patterns. Each pattern needs to be checked as to whether it is to be extracted as a high-vote pattern. So, Step (4.2) needs $O(n_i * |class_i|)$ comparisons, and Step (4.3) needs $O(n_i)$ comparisons. Consequently, the time complexity of Step (4) is $m * (n_1 * |class_1| + n_2 * |class_2| + \cdots n_m * |class_m|) \leq m^2 nl$. This means that the time complexity of *highvotingPatterns* is $O(m^2 nl)$.

$$\diamondsuit$$

7.5 Identifying High-vote Patterns Using a Fuzzy Logic Controller

As we have shown, the above algorithm *highvotingPatterns* relies on the assumption that a user can specify $minVR$. However, the user-specified minimum vote-ratio is appropriate to a group of local pattern sets to be mined only if the distribution of patterns in the group of local pattern sets is known. This motivates us to design the mining techniques with local-pattern-set-independence minimum-vote-ratio.

As we have said, the main principle of this section is to provide a good man-machine interface for mining high-vote patterns, represented as the *FLPSIMVR* strategy, which lets users take the commonly used interval $[0, 1]$ into consideration when specifying the minimum-vote-ratio. This means users can specify a relative minimum-vote-ratio with respect to $[0, 1]$, and our mining algorithm converts the relative minimum-vote-ratio into a true minimum-vote-ratio suitable to the group of local pattern sets to be mined. In our mining approach, we first design a fuzzy logic controller for converting the relative minimum-vote-ratio (specified by users) into real minimum-vote-ratios appropriate to different groups of local pattern sets. And then a *FARDIMS*-based algorithm is developed for identifying high-vote patterns. This is formally described in the following subsections.

7.5.1 Needed Concepts in Fuzzy Logic

The fuzzy set, introduced by Zadeh in 1965, is a generalization of the classical set theory that represents vagueness, or uncertainty, in linguistic terms. In a classical set, an element of the universe belongs to, or does not belong to, the set, that is, the membership of an element is crisp — either yes or no. A fuzzy set allows the degree of membership for each element to range over the unit interval $[0, 1]$. Crisp sets always have unique membership functions, while every fuzzy set has an infinite number of membership functions that may represent it.

For a given universe of discourse U, a fuzzy set is determined by a membership function that maps members of U on to a membership range, usually between 0 and 1. Formally, letting U be a collection of objects, a fuzzy set F in U is characterized by a membership function μ_F, which takes values in the interval $[0, 1]$ as follows,

$$\mu_F : U \mapsto [0, 1].$$

Fuzzy logic is a superset of conventional Boolean logic. It offers a better way of dealing with uncertainty in the definition of objects or phenomena. In fuzzy logic, a statement is true to various degrees ranging from completely true through half-true to completely false.

Fuzzy logic control is a nonlinear computer control technology based on fuzzy logic and fuzzy reasoning. The basic idea of a fuzzy logic controller is to imitate the control action of a human operator. It consists of several steps as follows.

System analysis: This analyzes the system to be designed, and determines the input and output variables in addition to their range.

Setting membership functions for input and output variables: A membership function is a function that specifies the degree to which a given input belongs to a set, or is related to a concept. The most common shape of a membership function is a triangular form, although S-function, p-function, trapezoid form, and exponential form are also used.

Setting fuzzy rules: Fuzzy rules are the collection of expert control knowledge required to achieve the control objective. Fuzzy logic rules are always in the form of IF-THEN statements. The IF part, known as the "antecedent", specifies the conditions under which the rule holds. The THEN part, or "consequent", prescribes the corresponding control action. In practice, the fuzzy rules usually have several antecedents that are combined using fuzzy logic operators, such as AND, OR, and NOT. This step is essential in the fuzzy control system. The number of rules is based on the input and output variables and the output precision.

Fuzzification: This is the process of generating membership values for a fuzzy variable using membership functions, or the process of converting a crisp input value to a fuzzy value.

Inference and rule composition subprocess: Matching the fuzzy concepts and rule sets, the degree of fulfillment for the antecedent of each rule is computed, using fuzzy logic operators. The degree of fulfillment determines to what degree the ith rule is valid. There are several ways to combine the all fired rules into a single fuzzy set. These include the "min-max" inference method and "product-sum" inference method.

Defuzzified: This is the process of transforming a fuzzy output of a fuzzy inference system into a crisp output.

The design of our fuzzy logic controller for the $FARDIMS$ strategy follows the above steps, and the corresponding steps are described as follows.

7.5.2 System Analysis

Let $LPSet$ be a set of local pattern sets, and the vote-ratio of patterns in $LPSet$ be distributed in an interval $[a, b]$, where

$$a = Min\{supp(X)|X \text{ is a local pattern in } LPSet\};$$
$$b = Max\{supp(X)|X \text{ is a local pattern in } LPSet\}.$$

For $LPSet$, assume that users specify a relative minimum-vote-ratio ($Minvoteratio$) with respect to $[0, 1]$. Our fuzzy logic controller will convert $Minvoteratio$ into a real minimum-vote-ratio $Realvoteratio$, appropriate to $LPSet$. In our fuzzy logic controller, we select both the user-specified minimum-vote-ratio $Minvoteratio$, and the distribution of local patterns, to be the two input parameters, and the true vote-ratio $Realvoteratio$, as the output parameter.

For the set of local-pattern-sets $LPSet$, the distribution of the vote-ratios of local patterns in $LPSet$, referred to as *vote-ratio distribution*, is very important when generating a suitable $Realvoteratio$. If the vote-ratio distribution in $LPSet$ is symmetrical, the average vote-ratio of all local patterns $AveVR$ is good for estimating $Realvoteratio$. However, the vote-ratio distribution in a set of local pattern sets can have an extreme gradient. Therefore, we take into account the lean of the vote-ratio distribution when generating a $Realvoteratio$ appropriate to the set of local-pattern-sets. For example, assume that most of the local patterns in $LPSet$ have low vote-ratios, and others have extremely high vote-ratios. Then $AveVR$ can be larger than $(a + b)/2$ (the median of these vote-ratios). If the $AveVR$ is still applied when generating $Realvoteratio$, we may discover little patterns from $LPSet$, even though the $Minvoteratio$ is very low. Similarly, when most of the local patterns in $LPSet$ have high vote-ratios, and others have extremely low vote-ratios, the $AveVR$ can be less than $(a+b)/2$. If the $AveVR$ is applied to generating $Realvoteratio$, we may discover a great many high-vote patterns from $LPSet$.

Based on the above analysis, we now define a measure $Lean$ for evaluating the vote-ratio distribution when generating an appropriate $Realvoteratio$ for $LPSet$.

After scanning $LPSet$ once, we can obtain the vote-ratio of all local patterns in $LPSet$, and calculate the average vote-ratio of local patterns. To generate a suitable $Realvoteratio$ for identifying high-vote patterns, we approximate the lean of the vote-ratio distribution using $AveVR$ as follows.

$$Lean = \frac{\sum_{i=1}^{n} 1(VR(i) < AveVR) - \sum_{i=1}^{n} 1(VR(i) > AveVR)}{m}, \qquad (7.4)$$

where $VR(i)$ is the vote-ratio of the ith local pattern, m is the number of local patterns in $LPSet$, and n is the number of local pattern sets in $LPSet$. Using this lean, we can generate an appropriate $Realvoteratio$ for $LPSet$.

7.5.3 Setting Membership Functions for Input and Output Variables

In our fuzzy logic controller, the sets of the fuzzy sets of parameters *Minvoteratio, Lean,* and *Realvoteratio,* are *F_Minvoteratio, F_Lean* and *F_Realvoteratio* as follows.

$$F\_Minvoteratio = \{(VL) \; Very \; Low, (L) \; Low, (SL) \; More \; or \; Less$$
$$Low, (M) \; Medium, (SH) \; More \; or \; Less \; High,$$
$$(H) \; High, (VH) \; Very \; High\}. \tag{7.5}$$
$$F\_Lean = \{(L) \; Left \; Gradient, (S) \; Symmetry,$$
$$(R) \; Right \; Gradient\}; \tag{7.6}$$
$$F\_Realvoteratio = \{(VL^*) \; Very \; Low^*, (L^*) \; Low^*, (SL^*) \; More \; or$$
$$Less \; Low^*, (M^*) \; Medium^*, (SH^*) \; More \; or \; Less$$
$$High^*, (H^*) \; High^*, (VH^*) \; Very \; High^*\}. \tag{7.7}$$

The triangular functions of *Minvoteratio, Lean* (the input parameters), and *Realvoteratio* (the output parameter) are illustrated in Figures 7.4 through 7.6.

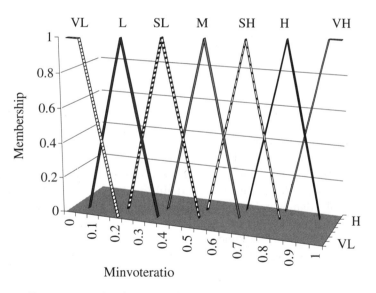

Fig. 7.4. Fuzzy triangular functions for parameter *Minvoteratio*

Figure 7.4 has demonstrated the triangular membership function of *Minvoteratio,* with respect to the fuzzy sets in *F_Minvoteratio.* In Figures 5.1, for a user-specified *Minvoteratio* x, the line *Minvoteratio* $= x$ intersects each fuzzy set in *F_Minvoteratio* at a certain pair of points $(x, \mu_F(x))$, where $\mu_F(x)$ is the degree of x belonging to fuzzy set F. For example, the line $Minvoteratio = 0.24$ intersects L at $(0.24, 0.73)$, and SL at $(0.24, 0.27)$. This says that $\mu_L(0.24) = 0.73$ and $\mu_{SL}(0.24) = 0.27$. In this way, a crisp concept can be converted into a fuzzy concept.

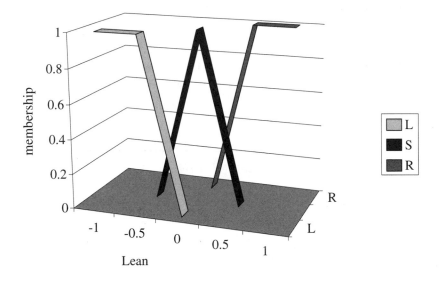

Fig. 7.5. Fuzzy triangular functions for parameter *Lean*

Figure 7.5 demonstrates the triangular membership function of *Lean* with respect to the fuzzy sets in *F_Lean*. Here, for the *Lean* x of a set of local pattern sets, the line $Lean = x$ intersects each fuzzy set in *F_Lean* at a certain point-pair $(x, \mu_F(x))$. For example, the line $Lean = -0.7$ intersects L at $(-0.7, 1.0)$. This says that $\mu_L(-0.7) = 1.0$. And the distribution of local patterns in the set of local pattern sets definitely leans to the left of *AveVR*.

Figure 7.6 demonstrates the triangular membership function of *Realvoteratio*, with respect to the fuzzy sets in *F_Realvoteratio*. This is used for converting a fuzzy concept into a crisp concept. The detailed interpretation of this function is illustrated using examples in the next two subsections.

7.5.4 Setting Fuzzy Rules

In our fuzzy logic controller, for a set of local-pattern-sets, the input parameters *Minvoteratio* and *Lean* are first transformed into fuzzy concepts. Then they are used to generate an output *Realvoteratio* appropriate to the set of local-pattern-sets, using the fuzzy rules. Based on the assumption of input and output parameters, the fuzzy rule FR in our fuzzy logic controller is

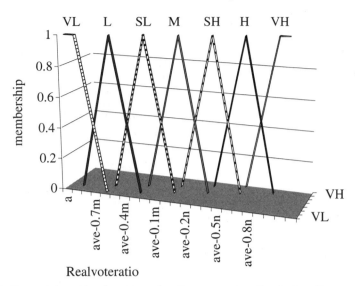

Fig. 7.6. Fuzzy triangular functions for the parameter *Realvoteratio*

IF *Minvoteratio* is $A \wedge$ and *Lean* is B
THEN *Realvoteratio* is C,

where A, B, and C are fuzzy sets.

Table 7.4 gives an example that illustrates the construction of fuzzy rules.

Table 7.4 *Fuzzy rules*

	VL	L	SL	M	SH	H	VH
L	VL^*	SL^*	M^*	SH^*	H^*	VH^*	VH^*
S	VL^*	L^*	SL^*	M^*	SH^*	H^*	VH^*
R	VL^*	VL^*	L^*	SL^*	M^*	SH^*	VH^*

In Table 7.4, the first column is the fuzzy sets in *F_Lean*; the first row is the fuzzy sets in *F_Minvoteratio*; and others are the outputs generated for *Realvoteratio*. Each output is a fuzzy rule. For example, M^* at the intersection of the second row and the fourth column indicates the fuzzy rule: IF *Minvoteratio* is *SL* and *Lean* is *L* THEN *Realvoteratio* is M^*. This means the lean of the local patterns in a set of local pattern sets *Lean* matches the fuzzy set *Left gradient*; the user-specified minimum-vote-ratio for the set of local-pattern-sets *Minvoteratio* matches the fuzzy set, *More or Less Low*; and our fuzzy logic controller outputs the real minimum-vote-ratio *Realvoteratio* which matches the fuzzy set *Medium*.

Using these fuzzy rules, we can convert the user-specified minimum-vote-ratio, for a set of local pattern sets, into a true minimum-vote-ratio appropriate to the set of local-pattern-sets. We do this by considering the lean of the local patterns in the set of local pattern sets.

7.5.5 Fuzzification

Because both input parameters are crisp, we have to map them to fuzzy sets by the membership functions as shown in Figures 7.4 and 7.5. This procedure is a *fuzzification*. Using fuzzification, we can obtain two fuzzy concepts of the two input parameters for our fuzzy logic controller.

Example 7.2 *Consider a set of local-pattern-sets, LPSet. Let the lean of the local patterns in LPSet be Lean = −0.3, and the user-specified minimum-vote-ratio for LPSet be Minvoteratio = 0.24. By the fuzzification, we obtain*

$$\mu_L(0.24) = 0.73;$$
$$\mu_{SL}(0.24) = 0.27;$$
$$\mu_L(-0.3) = 0.6;$$
$$\mu_M(-0.3) = 0.4.$$

This means, if the Minvoteratio is 0.24, then it has a degree 0.73 belonging to the fuzzy set Low *and 0.27 belonging to the fuzzy set* More or Less Low *Similarly, if the Lean is -0.3, then it has a degree 0.6 belonging to the fuzzy set* Left Gradient, *and 0.4 belonging to the fuzzy set* Symmetry.

7.5.6 Inference and Rule Composition

There are several different inference and composition techniques in the literature. The common and simplest methods are the "min-max" and "product-sum" methods. In this paper, we use the min-max method in our fuzzy logic controller.

For the fuzzy rule FR, the min-max method reasons the membership function of an action, according to the input parameters given for FR. We now demonstrate the use of the min-max method with examples.

Example 7.3 *For the input parameters Minvoteratio and Lean in Example 7.2, there are four input cases for the rule FR:*

$$(\mu_L(Minvoteratio = 0.24), \mu_L(Lean = -0.3));$$

$$(\mu_L(Minvoteratio = 0.24), \mu_S(Lean = -0.3));$$

$$(\mu_{SL}(Minvoteratio = 0.24), \mu_L(Lean = -0.3));$$

$$(\mu_{SL}(Minvoteratio = 0.24), \mu_S(Lean = -0.3)).$$

Using the min-max method for the four input cases, we first have

$$\mu_L(Minvoteratio = 0.24) \wedge \mu_L(Lean = -0.3) = Min\{0.73, 0.6\} = 0.6;$$
$$\mu_L(Minvoteratio = 0.24) \wedge \mu_S(Lean = -0.3) = Min\{0.73, 0.4\} = 0.4;$$
$$\mu_{SL}(Minvoteratio = 0.24) \wedge \mu_L(Lean = -0.3) = Min\{0.27, 0.6\} = 0.27;$$
$$\mu_{SL}(Minvoteratio = 0.24) \wedge \mu_L(Lean = -0.3) = Min\{0.27, 0.4\} = 0.27.$$

Or $\mu_{SL^*}(Realvoteratio = x) = 0.6$, $\mu_{L^*}(Realvoteratio = x) = 0.4$, $\mu_{M^*}(Realvoteratio = x) = 0.27$, and $\mu_{SL^*}(Realvoteratio = x) = 0.27$.
We then obtain $\mu_{SL^*}(Realvoteratio = x) = 0.6$ as the desired Realvoteratio, *because,*

$$Max\{0.6, 0.4, 0.27, 0.27\} = 0.6.$$

Example 7.4 *Consider a set of local-pattern-sets, LPSet. Let the lean of the local patterns in LPSet be Lean $= -0.3$, and the user-specified minimum-vote-ratio for LPSet be Minvoteratio $= 0.275$. By fuzzification, we obtain*

$$\mu_L(0.275) = 0.5;$$
$$\mu_{SL}(0.275) = 0.5;$$
$$\mu_L(-0.3) = 0.6;$$
$$\mu_M(-0.3) = 0.4.$$

For the above input parameters Minvoteratio and Lean in Example 7.2, there are four input cases for the rule FR:

$$(\mu_L(Minvoteratio = 0.275), \mu_L(Lean = -0.3));$$
$$(\mu_L(Minvoteratio = 0.275), \mu_S(Lean = -0.3));$$
$$(\mu_{SL}(Minvoteratio = 0.275), \mu_L(Lean = -0.3));$$
$$(\mu_{SL}(Minvoteratio = 0.275), \mu_S(Lean = -0.3)).$$

Using the min-max method for the four input cases, we first have

$$\mu_L(Minvoteratio = 0.275) \wedge \mu_L(Lean = -0.3) = Min\{0.5, 0.6\} = 0.5;$$
$$\mu_L(Minvoteratio = 0.275) \wedge \mu_S(Lean = -0.3) = Min\{0.5, 0.4\} = 0.4;$$
$$\mu_{SL}(Minvoteratio = 0.275) \wedge \mu_L(Lean = -0.3) = Min\{0.5, 0.6\} = 0.5;$$
$$\mu_{SL}(Minvoteratio = 0.275) \wedge \mu_L(Lean = -0.3) = Min\{0.5, 0.4\} = 0.4.$$

Or $\mu_{SL^*}(Realvoteratio = x) = 0.5$, $\mu_{L^*}(Realvoteratio = x) = 0.4$, $\mu_{M^*}(Realvoteratio = x) = 0.5$, and $\mu_{SL^*}(Realvoteratio = x) = 0.4$.
We then obtain

$$\mu_{SL^*}(Realvoteratio = x) = 0.5$$

and

$$\mu_{M^*}(Realvoteratio = x) = 0.5$$

as the desired Realvoteratio *because*

$$Max\{0.5, 0.4, 0.5, 0.5\} = 0.5.$$

For the monotone of Realvoteratio, $\mu_{M^*}(Realvoteratio = x) = 0.5$ is chosen as the final Realvoteratio.

7.5.7 Defuzzification

For high-vote pattern discovery, we need to defuzzify the above fuzzy results. There are dozens of defuzzified methods in the literature. A couple of years ago, Mizumoto surveyed about 10 defuzzification methods, and concluded that each one of them had diverse advantages and disadvantages. One popular approach is the "centroid" method, in which the crisp value of an output variable is generated by finding the center of gravity of the membership function for a fuzzy value. Another one is the "maximum" method, in which one of the variable values at which the fuzzy subset has its maximum truth value is chosen as the crisp value for the output variable. In our fuzzy logic controller, we have chosen the maximum method. We now present the defuzzification in our fuzzy logic controller using this method.

Let $LPSet$ be the set of local-pattern-sets to be mined. Let the $AveVR$ calculated by the system be AS_1, the degree of $Lean$ be $Lean_1$, and the range of the vote-ratio of local patterns be $[a, b]$. Assume that the user-specified minimum-vote-ratio for $LPSet$ is $Minvoteratio = MS_1$.

Using the min-max method, we obtain $\mu_F(Realvoteratio = x) = RS_1$ as the desired $Realvoteratio$, where F is a fuzzy set in $F\_Realvoteratio$, and x is a crisp value in $[a, b]$. That is, IF $Minvoteratio$ is A and $Lean$ is B THEN $Realvoteratio$ is F.

For the above fuzzy rule, there is a subinterval $[c, d] \subseteq [a, b]$ such that, for any x in $[c, d]$, the membership of x belonging to F is $\mu_{H^*}(x) = RS_1$.

For the subinterval $[c, d]$, our defuzzification generates a crisp value $(c + (c + d)/2)/2 = (3c + d)/4$ for $Realvoteratio$.

Below we illustrate the use of the above defuzzification by way of an example.

Example 7.5 *Consider a set of local-pattern-sets $LPSet$ to be mined. Let the $AveVR$ calculated by the system be 0.180, the degree of $Lean$ be 0.243, and the range of the vote-ratio of local patterns be $[0.00012, 0.974]$. Assume that the user-specified minimum-vote-ratio for $LPSet$ is $Minvoteratio = 0.75$. By the fuzzification, we obtain*

$$\mu_{SH}(0.75) = 0.333;$$
$$\mu_H(0.75) = 0.667;$$
$$\mu_S(0.243) = 0.514;$$
$$\mu_R(0.243) = 0.486.$$

Using the min-max method, we have $\mu_{H^*}(Realvoteratio = x) = 0.514$ as the desired Realvotcratio. That is, IF Minvotcratio is H and Lcan is S THEN Realvoteratio is H^*.

For the above fuzzy rule, $[0.540, 0.772] \subseteq [0.00012, 0.974]$ is the desired subinterval such that, for any x in $[0.540, 0.772]$, the membership of x belonging to H^* is $\mu_{H^*}(x) = 0.514$.

For the subinterval $[0.540, 0.772]$, our defuzzification generates a crisp value 0.598 for Realvoteratio.

7.5.8 Algorithm Design

Given a set of local pattern sets, LPSet, the Minvoteratio, and Lean, the following function Getrealsupp is used to yield a real vote-ratio Realvoteratio appropriate to LPSet.

Function 7.1 Getrealsupp begin

Input: LPSet: a set of local-pattern-sets; Minvoteratio: user's minimum vote-ratio;
Output: Realvoteratio: real minimum vote-ratio;

1. scan LPSet; get the vote-ratio of every local pattern;
2. let Averagevoteratio ← {the average voteratio of all localpatterns};
3. let $a \leftarrow 1/|D|$;
4. let $b \leftarrow$ {the maximum voteratio of all localpatterns};
5. let Lean ← {the degree of lean};
6. set subject function of Minvoteratio, Lean, and Realvoteratio as FuncMinvoteratio, FuncLean, and FuncRealvoteratio, respectively;
7. get two fuzzy concepts to describe Minvoteratio and Lean using subject function of Minvoteratio and Lean;
8. generate several fuzzy rules according to the values of input parameters;
9. select the desired fuzzy result rule;
10. depend on the fuzzy result rule; get Realvoteratio;
11. return Realvoteratio.

In the case of having no knowledge concerning the set of local pattern sets to be mined, function Getrealsupp generates an appropriate minimum-vote-ratio according to both the user-specified minimum-vote-ratio and the distribution of local patterns in the set of local pattern sets. Steps 1 to 5 scan the set of local pattern sets once, and obtain the average vote-ratio of all local patterns and $[a, b]$. Step 6 constructs the membership functions of Minvoteratio, Lean, and Realvoteratio. Step 7 generates fuzzy concepts using fuzzification. Steps 8 and 9 generate fuzzy rules according to the values of input parameters, and obtain a unique fuzzy rule. Step 10 defuzzifies the fuzzy concepts and Step 11 returns a scrip value as the *Realvoteratio* for mining the set of local pattern sets *LPSet*.

The function *Getrealsupp* is generally used as a procedure of the algorithm *highvotingPatterns* so as to generate appropriate minimum-vote-ratios for different sets of local-pattern-sets.

7.6 High-vote Pattern Analysis

Although the projection $P(name, vote)$ of $P(name, vote, vsupp, vconf)$ on *name* and *vote* was used in identifying high-vote patterns, all the information attached to high-vote patterns of the form, $P(name, vote, vsupp, vconf)$, should be analyzed for decision-making after searching for all the high-vote patterns. This section presents techniques for high-vote pattern analysis.

A high-vote pattern of the form "association rule" is attached to certain factors, including *name*, *vote*, *vsupp*, and *vconf*. For a very large interstate company, a high-vote association rule may be voted for by a number of branches. So the sets of its vote-ratio and confidence in the different local-pattern-sets can be too large to be browsed by users. Thus, it is rather difficult to apply the rule to decision-making for users. This section analyzes high-vote association rules, and aims at providing descriptions for high-vote association rules such that association rules can be easily understood and applied by users. A clustering procedure is thus designed to obtain different distribution intervals among the vote-ratios and confidences of a high-vote rule.

7.6.1 Normal Distribution

Suppose a high-vote rule $X \rightarrow Y$ has the following supports and confidences in the n local pattern sets that vote for the rule:

$supp_1, conf_1,$

$supp_2, conf_2,$

...

$supp_n, conf_n.$

If these supports follow a normal distribution, we can get an interval to summarize the supports, and a corresponding interval to summarize the confidences. In other words, for $0 \leq a \leq b \leq 1$, let m be the number of supports that belong to interval $[a, b]$. If $m/n \geq \lambda$, then these supports are in a normal distribution, where $0 < \lambda \leq 1$ is the threshold given by domain experts. This means that $[a, b]$ can be taken as the summary of the supports of rule $A \rightarrow B$. For the corresponding confidences, we can estimate an interval as a summary of the confidences of the rule.

In other words, suppose we have a random variable $X \sim N(\mu, \sigma^2)$ and we need the probability

$$P\{a \leq X \leq b\} = \frac{1}{\sigma\sqrt{2\pi}} \int_a^b e^{-(x-\mu)^2/2\sigma^2} dx$$

to satisfy $P\{a \leq X \leq b\} \geq \lambda$ and, $|b - a| \leq \alpha$, where X is a variable for support and is valued from $supp_1, supp_2, ..., supp_n$, and α is the threshold given by domain experts. Again, if these supports are in multiple normal distributions, we can obtain some intervals to summarize the supports and some corresponding intervals to summarize the confidences, where the intervals for confidence might overlap.

Otherwise, we classify the supports into 11 intervals: $[0, 0.1)$, $[0.1, 0.2)$, ..., $[0.9, 1)$, $[1, 1]$, for their summarization, and 11 corresponding intervals to summarize the confidences, where the intervals for confidences might overlap. Certainly, we can also classify the supports into intervals according to the requirements of applications.

From these observations, high-vote rule analysis clusters the supports and confidences of a high-vote rule into different local pattern sets that vote for the rule. This is the same as for many real-world applications. For example, for the increasing sales of milk in an interstate supermarket, there are 20% of branches where sales increase from 20% to 30%; there are 60% of branches where sales increase from 45% to 63%; and there are 20% of branches where sales increase from 87% to 92%. These data allow users to understand and apply the pattern easily. In other words, high-vote pattern analysis is capable of finding operable descriptions for high-vote patterns.

7.6.2 The Procedure of Clustering

For $supp_1, supp_2, ..., supp_n$ of a high-vote rule in n different local-pattern-sets that vote for the rule, let

$$s_{i,j} = 1 - |supp_i - supp_j|$$

be the *closeness* value between $supp_i$ and $supp_j$, and let the closeness value between any two supports be given as listed in Table 7.5.

Table 7.5 *Distance table*

	$supp_1$	$supp_2$	...	$supp_n$
$supp_1$	$s_{1,1}$	$s_{1,2}$	...	$s_{1,n}$
$supp_2$	$s_{2,1}$	$s_{2,2}$	...	$s_{2,n}$
...	...	...	...	...
$supp_n$	$s_{n,1}$	$s_{n,2}$	...	$s_{n,n}$

We can use clustering technology to obtain some intervals for summarizing the supports. To determine the relationship between supports, a closeness degree measure is required. This measure calculates the closeness degree between two supports by using closeness values. We define a simple closeness degree measure as follows,

$$Close(supp_i, supp_j) = \sum (s_{k,i} * s_{k,j}),$$

where k is summed across the set of all supports. In effect, the formula takes the two columns of the two supports being analyzed, multiplying and accumulating the values in each row. The results can be placed in a resultant n by n matrix, called a *support-support matrix*. This simple formula is reflexive, so that the generated matrix is symmetric.

For example, let $\lambda = 0.7$ and $\alpha = 0.08$. And let $minsupp = 0.65$, a high-vote rule $X \rightarrow Y$ with supports $supp_1 = 0.7$, $supp_2 = 0.72$, $supp_3 = 0.68$, $supp_4 = 0.5$, $supp_5 = 0.71$, $supp_6 = 0.69$, $supp_7 = 0.7$, and $supp_8 = 0.91$, in 8 branches. The closeness value between any two supports is given in Table 7.6.

Table 7.6 *Distance relation table*

	$supp_1$	$supp_2$	$supp_3$	$supp_4$	$supp_5$	$supp_6$	$supp_7$	$supp_8$
$supp_1$	1	0.98	0.98	0.8	0.99	0.99	1	0.79
$supp_2$	0.98	1	0.96	0.78	0.99	0.97	0.98	0.81
$supp_3$	0.98	0.96	1	0.82	0.97	0.99	0.98	0.77
$supp_4$	0.8	0.78	0.82	1	0.79	0.81	0.8	0.59
$supp_5$	0.99	0.99	0.97	0.79	1	0.98	0.99	0.8
$supp_6$	0.99	0.97	0.99	0.81	0.98	1	0.99	0.78
$supp_7$	1	0.98	0.98	0.8	0.99	0.99	1	0.79
$supp_8$	0.79	0.81	0.77	0.59	0.8	0.78	0.79	1

The support-support matrix is shown in Table 7.7.

Table 7.7 *Support-support matrix*

	$supp_1$	$supp_2$	$supp_3$	$supp_4$	$supp_5$	$supp_6$	$supp_7$	$supp_8$
$supp_1$		7.0459	7.0855	6.0181	7.125	7.1252	7.1451	5.9546
$supp_2$	7.0459		7.0247	5.9609	7.0664	7.0646	7.0851	5.9164
$supp_3$	7.0855	7.0247		5.9793	7.0648	7.067	7.0936	5.898
$supp_4$	6.0181	5.9609	5.9793		5.9974	6.0068	6.0181	4.971
$supp_5$	7.125	7.0664	7.0648	5.9974		7.1047	7.125	5.9435
$supp_6$	7.141	7.0646	7.067	6.0068	7.1047		7.1252	5.9341
$supp_7$	7.1451	7.0851	7.0936	6.0181	7.125	7.1252		5.9546
$supp_8$	5.9546	5.9164	5.898	4.971	5.9435	5.9341	5.9546	

Note that there are no values on the diagonal, since the table represents the autocorrelation of a support to itself.

Assume 6.9 is the threshold that determines whether two supports are considered close enough to each other to be in the same class. This produces a new binary matrix which we call the *support relationship matrix*. It is shown in Table 7.8.

Table 7.8 *support closeness relationship matrix*

	$supp_1$	$supp_2$	$supp_3$	$supp_4$	$supp_5$	$supp_6$	$supp_7$	$supp_8$
$supp_1$		1	1	0	1	1	1	0
$supp_2$	1		1	0	1	1	1	0
$supp_3$	1	1		0	1	1	1	0
$supp_4$	0	0	0		0	0	0	0
$supp_5$	1	1	1	0		1	1	0
$supp_6$	1	1	1	0	1		1	0
$supp_7$	1	1	1	0	1	1		0
$supp_8$	0	0	0	0	0	0	0	

Cliques require all supports in a cluster to be within the threshold of all other supports. The methodology to create the clusters using cliques is described in Procedure 7.1.

Procedure 7.1 *Cluster*
  Input: $supp_i$: support, λ: threshold value;
  Output: Class: class set of closeness supports;

(1) **let** $i=1$;
(2) **select** $supp_i$ and place it in a new class;
(3) $r = k = i + 1$;
(4) **validate** if $supp_k$ is within the threshold of all supports within the current class;
(5) **if** not, let $k = k + 1$;
(6) **if** $k > n$ (the number of supports) **then**
  $r = r + 1$;
  if $r = n$ **then go to** *(7)* **else**
  $k = r$;
  create a new class with $supp_i$ in it;
  go to *(4)*;
(7) **if** the current class only has $supp_i$ in it and there are other classes with $supp_i$ in them **then**
  delete the current class;
  else $i = i + 1$;
(8) **if** $i = n + 1$ **then go to** *(9)*
  else go to *(2)*;
(9) **eliminate** any classes that duplicate or are elements of other classes.

The procedure *Cluster* is used to generate clusters for the n supports given. First, it generates a new class for $supp_1$. Second, for each new support $supp_k$, it checks if $supp_k$ belongs to an existing class. If it does, $supp_k$ is appended to the class. Otherwise it generates a new class for $supp_k$. Finally, it eliminates the classes that duplicate, or are elements of, other classes.

Applying *Cluster* to the above example in this section, the following classes are created,

Class 1: $supp_1$, $supp_2$, $supp_3$, $supp_5$, $supp_6$, $supp_7$;
Class 2: $supp_4$;
Class 3: $supp_8$.

The rate of Class i can be determined by the following formula.

$$rate_i = \frac{\text{the number of elements in Class } i}{\text{the number of tatol elements}}.$$

For Class 1, $a = 0.68$ and $b = 0.72$. The rate of Class 1 is as follows.

$$rate_1 = \frac{\text{the number of elements in Class 1}}{\text{the number of tatol elements}} = \frac{6}{8} = 0.75.$$

Then we can say there are 75% of branches in which the support of the rule is from 68% to 72%.

For Class 2, $a = 0.5$ and $b = 0.5$. The rate of Class 2 is as follows.

$$rate_2 = \frac{\text{the number of elements in Class 2}}{\text{the number of tatol elements}} = \frac{1}{8} = 0.125.$$

Then we can say there are 12.5% of branches in which the support of the rule is 50%.

For Class 3, $a = 0.91$ and $b = 0.91$. The rate of Class 3 is as follows.

$$rate_3 = \frac{\text{the number of elements in Class 3}}{\text{the number of tatol elements}} = \frac{1}{8} = 0.125.$$

Then we can say there are 12.5% of branches in which the support of the rule is 91%.

We can obtain corresponding intervals for summarizing the confidences of the rule in the same way.

From the above observations, we can conclude that there are 12.5%, 75% and 12.5% of branches in which the support of the rule is 90%, 68% to 72%, and 50%, respectively. In this representation, the rule has become understandable and operable.

Cluster can be taken as a procedure of the algorithm *highvotingPatterns* for the purpose of analyzing the identified high-vote patterns.

The procedure *Cluster* generates the clusters for the n supports of a high-vote association rule. This is a classical cluster algorithm. Its complexity analysis can be found in books dealing with data structures.

7.7 Suggested Patterns

From Figure 7.3, if the voting rate of a pattern is in $[x_2, x_1)$, the pattern is a suggested pattern. The interest measures of suggested patterns are in a small left neighborhood of $miniVR$. Suggested patterns are likely to be high-vote patterns.

A pattern r_i in local patterns has been previously called a *suggested pattern* if its interest measure $LPI(r_i)$ is equal to, or greater than, the threshold $miniVR - \delta$, where δ (> 0) is small enough (as given by users or experts).

For example, let $\delta = 0.09$. Patterns F and I are suggested patterns in Example 7.1 because

$$LPI(F) = 0.167 > miniVR - \delta = 0.25 - 0.09 = 0.16;$$
$$LPI(I) = 0.167 > miniVR - \delta = 0.25 - 0.09 = 0.16.$$

When analyzing local patterns for an interstate company, such a suggested pattern can be so positive that users may wish to ask branches to check whether the pattern can be taken as a high-vote pattern. We stress, however, this is not appropriate for our model of tennis, as a match generates only one winner no matter how close the scores of two players are. In the case of companies, suggested patterns must be distinguished from high-vote patterns because the use of suggested patterns may be high risk. When high-vote patterns are not sufficient to support the global applications of an interstate company, suggested patterns can be used.

Finding suggested patterns in multiple databases is similar to identifying high-vote patterns in a class of multiple databases. The problem of finding suggested patterns can be stated as follows. Given a set of local pattern sets $LIset$ find all patterns for which the interest degrees are equal to or greater than $miniVR - \delta$.

When required, we can also analyze suggested patterns in the same way that we analyze high-vote patterns.

7.8 Summary

Multi-database mining must confront dual-level applications. At the local level, local databases have been mined for local applications. Putting all data together from (a class of) multi-databases into a single database for knowledge discovery leads to (1) a re-analysis of all data and, in particular, (2) the destruction of some information that reflects the distribution of local patterns.

In this chapter, we presented new and effective mining strategies for identifying high-vote and suggested patterns in multiple databases. Also, a method was advocated for analyzing the high-vote patterns that users need to consider. The principal achievements of this chapter are as follows.

(1) A metric for finding high-vote patterns was presented.
(2) A fuzzy logic controller for generating suitable minimum vote-ratios was designed.
(3) A method for analyzing high-vote patterns was presented.

8. Identifying Exceptional Patterns

Techniques for identifying high-vote patterns have been developed in Chapter 7. Another new kind of pattern is the exceptional pattern which reflects the individuality of, say, branches of an interstate company. Exceptional patterns are also of interest to company headquarters in their decision-making.

To identify exceptional patterns, the support dimension of a pattern must be considered. In this way exceptional patterns can be distinguished from high-vote patterns. Accordingly, this chapter develops new techniques for measuring and identifying exceptional patterns by analyzing local patterns.

8.1 Introduction

While high-vote patterns are useful when an interstate company is attempting to reach common decisions, company headquarters are also interested in viewing exceptional patterns, that is, those special decisions which are made at only a few of the branches, perhaps for predicting the sales for a new product. Exceptional patterns reflect the individuality of branches.

Unlike high-vote patterns, however, exceptional patterns can be hidden in local patterns. An exceptional pattern has a low vote.

Existing multi-database mining approaches cannot identify exceptional patterns from multi-databases. In order to search for useful exceptional patterns in multi-databases, we present a new model for measuring the interestingness of exceptional patterns.

On the other hand, to identify exceptional patterns, the support dimension of a pattern must be considered. It would appear that this would distinguish exceptional patterns from high-vote patterns. Accordingly, this chapter develops new techniques for measuring, and identifying, exceptional patterns by analyzing local patterns.

The chapter is organized as follows. In Section 8.2, we begin by advocating a model for measuring the interestingness of exceptional patterns. In Section 8.3, an algorithm is designed to search for exceptional patterns. In this section, we also demonstrate the use of proposed techniques, and analyze the designed algorithms. In Section 8.4, a fuzzy logic controller is constructed for evaluating the minimum interestingness of exceptional patterns. Finally, the chapter is summarized in Section 8.5.

8.2 Interesting Exceptional Patterns

To avoid re-mining multiple databases, a local pattern analysis was advocated in Chapter 3. This section presents a model for identifying, from local patterns, a new kind of pattern, referred to as an *exceptional pattern*.

Indeed, exceptional patterns often present as more glamorous than high-vote patterns in such areas as marketing, scientific discovery, and information safety. For example, "20% of 10 toy branches strongly supported the new toy 'Mulan' which was purchased with rather high frequency." These local patterns can be used to analyze the possible purchasing trends, although "Mulan" has a low-voting rate.

As we have said, exceptional patterns can reflect the individuality of branches. This section presents models for measuring the interestingness of such patterns.

8.2.1 Measuring the Interestingness

To identify exceptional patterns of interest from local patterns, the projection of $P(name, vote, vsupp, vconf)$ on $name$, $vote$, and $vsupp$ is considered. That is, the projection

$$P(name, vote, vsupp)$$

is considered. Recalling Table 7.1, patterns can be classified into four classes by using $AverageVR$. If the voting rate of a pattern is less than $AverageVR$, the pattern might be an exceptional pattern. This means that interesting exceptional patterns are hidden in low-vote patterns. To measure the interestingness of an exceptional pattern r_i, its voting rate and its support in branches must be considered. Therefore, two metrics for interestingness are constructed below.

The first metric is concerned with the relationship between the voting rate $voting(r_i)$ and the average voting rate $AverageVR$. If $voting(r_i) < AverageVR$, the pattern r_i refers to a low-vote pattern. In this case, $voting(r_i) - AverageVR$ satisfies:

$$-AverageVR \leq voting(r_i) - AverageVR < 0$$

In particular, we have

$$0 < \frac{voting(r_i) - AverageVR}{-AverageVR} \leq 1$$

Certainly, the bigger the ratio $(voting(r_i) - AverageVR)/(-AverageVR)$, the more interesting the pattern.

Consequently, one of the interest measures $EPI(r_i)$ of a pattern r_i is defined as the deviation of the voting rate, $voting(r_i)$, from the average voting rate $AverageVR$. And,

$$EPI(r_i) = \frac{voting(r_i) - AverageVR}{-AverageVR} \tag{8.1}$$

for $AverageVR \neq 0$, while $EPI(r_i)$ is referred to as the interestingness of r_i, given $AverageVR$.

From the above interest measure, $EPI(r_i)$ is negatively related to the voting ratio of the pattern r_i. It is at its highest if the voting ratio is 0. A pattern r_i in local patterns is an exceptional pattern if its interest measure, EPI_i, is equal to, or greater than, the threshold minimum interest degree (or minimum vote-ratio-for-exception, written as $minEP$) given by users or experts.

Because an exceptional pattern is a low-vote pattern, it cannot be a valid pattern in the whole dataset that is the union of a class of databases. However, exceptional patterns are those that are strongly supported by only a few branches. That is, exceptional patterns reflect the individuality of such branches. Consequently, the second interesting metric must consider the support dimensions of a pattern.

From local patterns, the support of patterns in branches of an interstate company are listed in Table 8.1.

Table 8.1 *Support of patterns in branches of an interstate company*

	r_1	r_2	$\cdots$	r_n	$minsupp$
B_1	$supp_{1,1}$	$supp_{1,2}$	$\cdots$	$supp_{1,n}$	$minsupp_1$
B_2	$supp_{2,1}$	$supp_{2,2}$	$\cdots$	$supp_{2,n}$	$minsupp_2$
$\cdots$	$\cdots$	$\cdots$		$\cdots$	$\cdots$
B_m	$supp_{m,1}$	$supp_{m,2}$	$\cdots$	$supp_{m,n}$	$minsupp_m$

In Table 8.1, B_i is the ith branch of the interstate company ($1 \leq i \leq m$), and $supp_{i,j} \neq 0$ stands for the support of pattern r_j in branch B_i, when r_j is a valid pattern in B_i. If $supp_{i,j} = 0$, then r_j is not a valid pattern in branch B_i ($1 \leq i \leq m$ and $1 \leq j \leq n$). Meanwhile, $minsupp_i$ is the minimum support used to identify local patterns within the ith branch.

A pattern r_i in local patterns is exceptional if its support in a few branches is fairly high. How strong can a support be for it to be referred to as *high*? In the case of 0.5 and 0.2, 0.5 is obviously higher than 0.2. However, the supports of a pattern are collected from different branches, and local databases in branches may differ in size. For example, let 100 and 100,000 be the number of transactions in databases D_1 and D_2, respectively, and 0.5 and 0.2 be the supports of r_i in D_1 and D_2, respectively. For these supports of r_i, the support 0.5 of r_i in D_1 cannot be simply regarded as high, and the support 0.2 of r_i in D_2 cannot be simply regarded as low.

Consequently, a reasonable measure for high support should be constructed. Although it is difficult to deal with raw data in local databases, the minimum supports in branches are suitable references for determining which of the supports of a pattern are high.

Generally, the higher the support of a pattern in a branch, the more interesting the pattern. Referenced with the minimum support $minsupp_i$ in branch B_i, the interestingness of a pattern r_i in B_i is defined as

$$RI_j(r_i) = \frac{supp_{j,i} - minsupp_j}{minsupp_j}, \qquad (8.2)$$

where $supp_{j,i}$ is the support of r_i in branch B_j.

From the above measure, $RI_j(r_i)$ is positively related to the support of r_j in branch B_i. It is the highest if the support is 1. The pattern r_i in B_i is of interest if RI_i is equal to, or greater than, a threshold, the minimum interest degree ($minEPsup$) given by users or experts. Example 8.1 illustrates the use of this interesting measurement.

Example 8.1 *Consider the support of patterns in four branches given in Table 8.2.*

Table 8.2 *Support of patterns in four branches of an interstate company*

	r_1	r_2	r_3	r_4	$minsupp$
B_1	0.021	0.012	0.018	0	0.01
B_2	0	0.6	0	0.3	0.25
B_3	0	0	0.8	0	0.4
B_4	0.7	1	0	0	0.5

Pattern r_1 is a valid pattern in branches B_1 and B_4 and not a valid pattern in branches B_2 and B_3. The interesting degrees $RI_1(r_1)$ and $RI_4(r_1)$ of r_1 in B_1 and B_4 are as follows.

$$\begin{aligned}
RI_1(r_1) &= \frac{supp_{1,1} - minsupp_1}{minsupp_1} \\
&= \frac{0.021 - 0.01}{0.01} \\
&= 1.1; \\
RI_4(r_1) &= \frac{supp_{4,1} - minsupp_4}{minsupp_4} \\
&= \frac{0.7 - 0.5}{0.5} \\
&= 0.4.
\end{aligned}$$

This means that the interestingness of r_1 in B_1 is higher than that in B_4 though $supp_{1,1} = 0.021 < supp_{4,1} = 0.7$.

The degrees of interest of other patterns are shown in Table 8.3.

Table 8.3 *Interestingness of patterns in branches*

	r_1	r_2	r_3	r_4	$minsupp$
B_1	1.1	0.2	0.8	—	0.01
B_2	—	1.4	—	0.2	0.25
B_3	—	—	1	—	0.4
B_4	0.4	1	—	—	0.5

In Table 8.3, — *means that a pattern is not voted for by any branch.*

From the above discussion, an exceptional pattern r is of interest if

(C1) $EPI(r) \geq miniEP$; and
(C2) $RI_i(r) \geq minEPsup$ for branches that vote for r.

The problem of finding exceptional patterns can now be stated as follows: given a set of local pattern sets $LIset$, find all patterns that satisfy both the conditions (C1) and (C2).

8.2.2 Behavior of Interest Measurements

An exceptional pattern r is of interest if $EPI(r) \geq miniEP$ and $RI_i(r) \geq minEPsup$ for branches that vote for r. Figures 8.1 and 8.2 depict the behavior of the measurements $EPI(r)$ and $RI_i(r)$.

8.3 Algorithm Design

In this chapter we implement the above approach to identify exceptional patterns from local patterns.

8.3.1 Algorithm Design

Below, we design an algorithm *ExceptionalPatterns* for identifying interesting exceptional patterns from local patterns. Then, in the next section, an example is used to illustrate how to search for exceptional patterns from local patterns by way of algorithms.

Algorithm 8.1 *ExceptionalPatterns*
begin
Input: LI_i $(1 \leq i \leq M)$: *sets of local patterns, minEP: threshold value that is the minimal interest degree for the voting ratios of exceptional patterns; minEPsupp: threshold value that is the minimal interest degree for the supports of exceptional patterns in branches;*
Output: *EPattern: set of exceptional patterns of interest;*

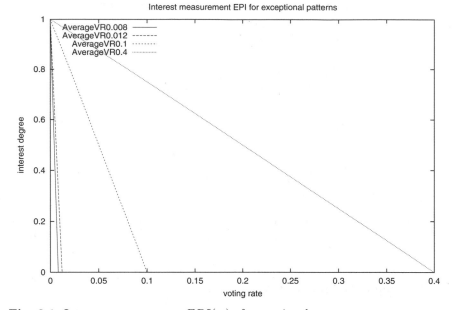

Fig. 8.1. Interest measurement $EPI(r_i)$ of exceptional pattern r_i

(1) **call** the procedure $GoodClass$ to generate a classification $class^\alpha$ for M local patterns LI_i;

(2) **if** $\alpha = 1$ **then**
> **begin**
> > **input** please suggest a value for α;
> > **call** the procedure $GreegyClass$ to generate a classification $class^\alpha$;
>
> **end**;

(3) **let** $EPattern \leftarrow \{\}$;

(4) **for** each $class_i$ in $class^\alpha$ **do**
> **begin**
> > (4.1) **let** $EPattern_i \leftarrow \{\}$; $giveup_i \leftarrow \{\}$;
> > **let** pattern set $E \leftarrow \emptyset$;
> > (4.2) **for** a local pattern set LI in $class_i$ **do**
> > > **for** each pattern r in LI **do**
> > > > **if** $(r \notin giveup_i)$ and $(RI_{LI}(r) < minEPsup)$ **then**
> > > > > **if** $r \in E$ **then**
> > > > > > **let** $E \leftarrow E - \{r\}$; $giveup_i \leftarrow giveup_i \cup \{r\}$;
> > > > >
> > > > > **else**
> > > > > > **if** $r \in E$ **then**
> > > > > > > **let** $r_f \leftarrow r_f + 1$;
> > > > > >
> > > > > > **else**

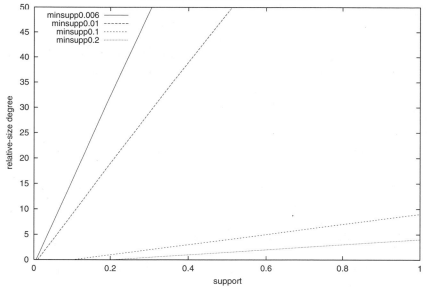

Size measurement RI for supports of patterns

Fig. 8.2. Relative-size $RI(r_i)$ of the support pattern r_i in a branch

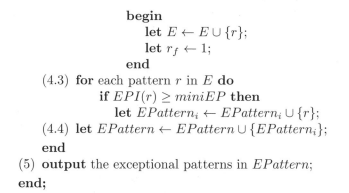

$$\begin{aligned}
&\textbf{begin}\\
&\quad \textbf{let } E \leftarrow E \cup \{r\};\\
&\quad \textbf{let } r_f \leftarrow 1;\\
&\textbf{end}\\
(4.3)\ &\textbf{for } \text{each pattern } r \text{ in } E \textbf{ do}\\
&\quad \textbf{if } EPI(r) \geq miniEP \textbf{ then}\\
&\quad\quad \textbf{let } EPattern_i \leftarrow EPattern_i \cup \{r\};\\
(4.4)\ &\quad \textbf{let } EPattern \leftarrow EPattern \cup \{EPattern_i\};\\
&\textbf{end}\\
(5)\ &\textbf{output } \text{the exceptional patterns in } EPattern;\\
&\textbf{end};
\end{aligned}$$

The algorithm *Exceptionalpatterns* is used to search for all interesting exceptional patterns from M given local pattern sets.

Step (1) finds a good classification $class^\alpha$ for the M local pattern sets (from M databases) using the algorithm *GoodClass*. If there is a nontrivial good classification, it requires the inputting of a suggested value for α as in Step (2), and it generates a classification $class^\alpha$ for the M local pattern sets using the algorithm *GreedyClass* (see Chapter 5). Therefore, the databases can also be classified according to the applications given by users.

For the above $class^\alpha$, we need to search for exceptional patterns for classes one by one. The set of interesting exceptional patterns found in a class is taken as an element of $EPattern$. Step (3) allows the set $EPattern$ to be an empty set.

Step (4) analyzes the patterns for each class $class_i$ in $class^\alpha$. Step (4.1) initializes the set variables $EPattern_i$, $giveup_i$, and E. $EPattern_i$ is used for saving all exceptional patterns in $class_i$, and $giveup_i$ is used for saving the patterns that are given up. E is used to save all patterns in $class_i$. Step (4.2) sums up the frequency for a pattern r that satisfies both $r \notin giveup_i$ and $RI_{LI}(r) \geq minEPsup$ in the local pattern set of $class_i$. Step (4.3) generates all interesting exceptional patterns from the set E, and saves them into $EPattern_i$, where each pattern r in $EPattern_i$ is with $EPI(r) \geq miniEP$ in the local pattern set of $class_i$. Step (4.4) appends $EPattern_i$ into $EPattern$.

Step (5) outputs all exceptional patterns in the given local-pattern-sets class by class.

8.3.2 Identifying Exceptions: An Example

Consider the seven local pattern sets LI_1, LI_2, ..., LI_5 below taken from branches B_1, B_2, ..., B_5, respectively.

$$LI_1 = \{(A, 0.34); (B, 0.45); (C, 0.47); (D, 0.56); (F, 0.8)\};$$
$$LI_2 = \{(A, 0.35); (B, 0.45); (C, 0.46)\};$$
$$LI_3 = \{(A, 0.05); (B, 0.02); (AB, 0.02)\};$$
$$LI_4 = \{(A, 0.38); (B, 0.45); (C, 0.65); (F, 0.68)\};$$
$$LI_5 = \{(A, 0.22); (C, 0.3); (D, 0.61)\}.$$

Here each local pattern set has several patterns, separated by a semicolon, and each pattern consists of its name and its support in a branch, separated by a comma.

Let $minsupp_1 = 0.3$, $minsupp_2 = 0.3$, $minsupp_3 = 0.008$, $minsupp_4 = 0.25$, $minsupp_5 = 0.2$, $miniEP = 0.5$, and $minEPsup = 0.75$.

We now use the algorithm $ExceptionalPatterns$ to search for all exceptional patterns from the five local pattern sets. There is one class,

$$class_1 = \{LI_1, LI_2, LI_3, LI_4, LI_5\}$$

for the given local pattern sets.

For $class_1$, the interestingness of patterns is shown in Table 8.4.

Table 8.4 *Interestingness of patterns in class$_1$*

	A	B	C	D	E	AB	$minsupp$
LI_1	0.133	0.5	0.567	0.867	1.667	–	0.3
LI_2	0.167	0.5	0.533	–	–	–	0.3
LI_3	5.25	1.5	–	–	–	1.5	0.008
LI_4	0.52	0.8	1.6	–	1.72	–	25
LI_5	0.0.1	–	0.5	2.05	–	–	0.2

When $minEPsup = 0.75$, patterns D, F, and AB are selected according to the Step (4.2) in the algorithm *ExceptionalPatterns*. For $class_1$, $AverageVR = 0.6$, and for D, F, and AB,

$$EPI(D) = \frac{voting(D) - AverageVR}{-AverageVR}$$
$$= \frac{0.4 - 0.6}{-0.6}$$
$$\approx 0.333;$$
$$EPI(F) = \frac{voting(F) - AverageVR}{-AverageVR}$$
$$= \frac{0.4 - 0.6}{-0.6}$$
$$\approx 0.333;$$
$$EPI(AB) = \frac{voting(AB) - AverageVR}{-AverageVR}$$
$$= \frac{0.2 - 0.6}{-0.6}$$
$$\approx 0.667.$$

When $miniEP = 0.5$, we can obtain all exceptional patterns in the set *EPattern*. And *EPattern* consists of one element:

$$EPattern_1 = \{(AB, 0.2, (0, 0.25, 0, 0, 0))\}.$$

There is only one interesting exceptional pattern

$$P(AB, 0.2, (0, 0.25, 0, 0, 0))$$

in the given local pattern sets.

8.3.3 Algorithm Analysis

The algorithm *ExceptionalPatterns* identifies all interesting exceptional patterns from local patterns. Therefore, we have a theorem for the procedure as follows.

Theorem 8.1 *The Algorithm ExceptionalPatterns works correctly.*

Proof: Clearly, in Steps (4) and (5), a set $EPattern$ of interesting exceptional patterns is generated, as it is output for given local pattern sets. We need to show that all interesting exceptional patterns are identified, and all uninteresting exceptional patterns are given up.

For any local pattern r_i in a class, all patterns that satisfy the condition (C2) are selected in the loop in Step (4.2) and, if a pattern does not satisfy the condition (C2), the pattern is not appended to E.

Again, if $EPI(r_i) \geq miniEP$ in the loop in Step (4.3), it is an interesting exceptional pattern, and the pattern is appended to $EPattern$. Otherwise, it is not appended to $EPattern$. This means that all interesting exceptional patterns are identified, and all uninteresting exceptional patterns are given up.   ◇

In the algorithm $ExceptionalPatterns$, Steps (1) and (2) refer to the procedures as $GoodClass$ and $GreedyClass$. The complexities of $GoodClass$ and $GreedyClass$ have been discussed in Chapter 5. So, the complexity of $ExceptionalPatterns$ can be regarded as consisting of Steps (3) through (5).

In Step (4), $m = |class^\alpha|$ classes are searched for. Assume that n_i is the number of local patterns in the class $class_i$. We need

$$n_1 * |class_1| + n_2 * |class_2| + \cdots + n_m |class_m|$$

units to save all the local patterns, which are less than, or equal to, mnl, where $n = \{n_1, n_2, ..., n_m\}$, l is the maximum among $|class_1|$, $|class_2|$, ..., $|class_m|$, and $|class_i|$ stands for the number of local patterns in the class $class_i$. Also, we need N units to save all the interesting exceptional patterns in $EPattern_1$, ..., $EPattern_m$, and $EPattern$. Obviously, $N \leq mn$. Consequently, the space complexity of $ExceptionalPatterns$ is $O(mnl)$.

Apparently, the time complexity of $ExceptionalPatterns$ is dominated by the loop in Step (4). Therefore, we have the following theorem.

Theorem 8.2 *The time complexity of $ExceptionalPatterns$ is $O(m^2 nl)$.*

Proof: For Step (4), m classes need to be processed to identify interesting exceptional patterns. For a class $class_i$ there are $|class_i|$ local-pattern-sets and n_i local patterns. Each pattern needs to be checked as to whether the pattern can be extracted as an interesting exceptional pattern. Therefore, Step (4.2) needs $O(n_i * |class_i|)$ comparisons, and Step (4.3) needs $O(n_i)$ comparisons. Consequently, the time complexity of Step (4) is $m * (n_1 * |class_1| + n_2 * |class_2| + \cdots n_m * |class_m|) \leq m^2 nl$. This means that the time complexity of $ExceptionalPatterns$ is $O(m^2 nl)$.

◇

8.4 Identifying Exceptions with a Fuzzy Logic Controller

In this section, we construct a fuzzy logic controller, similar to that in the situation of high-vote pattern discovery, for generating real minimum vote-ratio-for-exception from the relative minimum vote-ratio-for-exception (specified by users).

Because we use Eq. 8.1 to measure the interestingness of exceptional patterns, this fuzzy logic controller (written as $FLCEP$) is similar to that (written as $FLCHVP$) in Chapter 7. Below, we simply describe the fuzzy logic controller.

For a set of local-pattern-sets $LPSet$, assume that users specify a relative minimum-vote-ratio-for-exception ($MinVRforE$) with respect to $[0, 1]$. Our fuzzy logic controller will convert $MinVRforE$ into a real minimum-vote-ratio-for-exception $RealVRforE$ appropriate to $LPSet$. In this fuzzy logic controller, we select both the user-specified minimum-vote-ratio-for-exception $MinVRforE$, and the distribution of local pattern ($Lean$) to be two input parameters, and the true vote-ratio-for-exception $RealVRforE$ as the output parameter.

When the input parameters and output parameter are determined, the fuzzy logic controller $FLCEP$ can be constructed by replacing the input parameters and output parameter of the $FLCHVP$ with the above input parameters and output parameter.

Using the fuzzy logic controller $FLCEP$, we can obtain appropriate minimum-vote-ratio-for-exceptions for different sets of local-pattern-sets.

8.5 Summary

Putting all the data from (a class of) multi-databases into a single dataset can destroy important information. This book develops techniques for identifying the novel patterns, high-vote patterns, and exceptional patterns in multi-databases by analyzing local patterns. As we have explained, exceptional patterns differ from high-vote patterns. Therefore, this chapter has presented techniques for identifying interesting exceptional patterns in multiple databases. Thus, we have:

(1) constructed two metrics for measuring the interestingness of exceptional patterns;
(2) presented an approach for finding exceptional patterns in local patterns of an interstate company;
(3) designed an algorithm to search for interesting exceptional patterns from local patterns; and
(4) evaluated the proposed techniques by experimentation.

9. Synthesizing Local Patterns by Weighting

For the identification of high-vote patterns and exceptional patterns, the projections of a pattern on subspaces were investigated in Chapters 7 and 8. Although each branch of a company, large or small, has equal power to vote for patterns as part of a general company decision, individual branches may be of different importance to their company. Also, local patterns may have different supports within a branch. To take these factors into account, this chapter presents a model for synthesizing global patterns from local patterns by weighting. This model synthesizes association rules with respect to all dimensions: *name*, *vote*, *vsupp*, and *vconf*.

9.1 Introduction

From previous chapters, it would appear to be unrealistic to collect data from different branches for centralized processing because of the potential volume of data. On the other hand, because of data privacy and related issues, it is possible that some databases of an organization can share their association rules, but not their original data. Therefore, mining association rules from different databases and forwarding the rules (rather than the original raw data) to a central company headquarters provides a feasible way of dealing with multiple database problems.

As described previously, patterns in multi-databases are of the form $P(name, vote, vsupp, vconf)$. In Chapters 7 and 8, we have identified high-vote patterns and exceptional patterns from local patterns with respect to only the projection of a pattern. However, although each branch, large or small, has equal power to vote for patterns that ultimately go towards global decision, the head office might place different values on their branches. For example, if the sales of branch A are 4 times of that of branch B in an interstate company, branch A is certainly more important than branch B. The decisions of the company would most likely favor branches with high sales. Also, local patterns may have different supports within branches. For example, suppose the supports of patterns A_1 and A_2 are 0.9 and 0.4 at a branch. Pattern A_1 is certainly more important to the company than pattern A_2. To reflect these factors, this chapter presents a model for synthesizing global patterns from local pattern sets by weighting. Without losing generality, this chapter focuses on the synthesizing of association rules.

However, the number of rules forwarded may be so large that browsing the rule set and finding interesting rules could be rather difficult for central company headquarters. Also, it would be hard to identify which of the forwarded rules (including differing and identical ones) are really useful at the company level. For these reasons, a *rule selection* for improving the synthesizing model is also presented in this chapter. For convenience, we focus on synthesizing association rules.

The rest of the chapter is organized as follows. The motivation for this work is presented in Section 9.2. In Section 9.3, a synthesizing model by weighting is presented. An improvement of the existing synthesizing model by rule selection is explored in Section 9.4. In Section 9.5 the complexity of algorithms is analyzed in a simple way. The chapter is summarized in the last section.

9.2 Problem Statement

Figure 9.1 illustrates the synthesizing process we present for identifying association rules from different branches of a large company. The database DBi ($i = 1, ..., n$) is the local database of the ith branch.

Weighting is a common way to gather, analyze, and synthesize information from different databases in scientific research and applications. For example, consider a diagnosis in a hospital. Let A be a patient, and d_1, d_2, d_3, d_4, and d_5 be 5 medical experts in the hospital with authority weights w_1, w_2, w_3, w_4, and w_5, respectively. After diagnosis, the patient is judged to have one of 4 possible diseases: s_1, s_2, s_3, and s_4. To reach a final conclusion, the experts' diagnoses must be synthesized. Assume b_{ij} is the belief that the patient has the jth disease diagnosed by expert d_i ($i = 1, 2, 3, 4, 5$; $j = 1, 2, 3, 4$). Then the belief that the patient has disease s_j could be synthesized as

$$p_j = \sum_{i=1}^{5} w_i * b_{ij},$$

where $j = 1, 2, 3, 4$. According to the synthesis, we can rank diseases s_1, s_2, s_3, s_4 by p_1, p_2, p_3, p_4, and take the disease with the highest rank as the diagnosed result[1].

---

[1] It is not realistic to rediagnose the patient and aim for consistent results at each diagnosis step taken by the five experts. This is because some steps, such as operations, cannot be repeated, and, also, a rediagnosis can be very expensive.

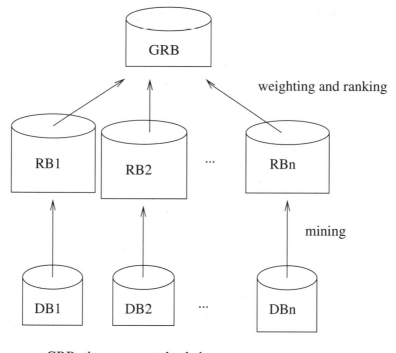

GRB: the aggregated rule base
RBi: all rules in DBi
DBi: the ith data source

Fig. 9.1. The synthesis of association rules by weighting

To synthesize association rules from different databases, the above weighting process is adopted here. In this diagnosis, the synthesis of experts' opinions is relatively straightforward, and the key problem is to allocate a *reasonable weight* to each expert. This chapter examines how to determine proper weights for synthesizing tasks.

In a similar way to that for high-vote patterns, we focus on *high-vote rules* from different databases of a large company. High-vote rules have a better chance of becoming valid rules in the union of all databases than do low-vote rules.

Since putting all association rules together from different databases of a large company might also amass a huge rule set, an efficient algorithm is designed to improve the proposed weighting model. The high-vote rules from different databases are taken as relevant rules, and lower-vote rules as irrelevant rules. In this way, lower-vote rules can be dealt with before rules from different branches are synthesized. Consequently, in Section 9.4, a rule selection procedure is designed for enhancing the assignment of weights.

9.3 Synthesizing Rules by Weighting

We now present a model for synthesizing association rules, when rules are forwarded from the different branch databases of a large company.

Let $D_1, D_2, ..., D_m$ be m different databases from one class of branch (see database classification in Chapter 3), and let S_i be the set of association rules from D_i ($i = 1, 2, ..., m$). For a given rule $X \to Y$, suppose $w_1, w_2, ...,$ w_m are the weights of $D_1, D_2, ..., D_m$, respectively (see Section 9.4.2). Our synthesizing model is defined as follows.

$$supp_w(X \cup Y) = w_1 * supp_1(X \cup Y) + w_2 * supp_2(X \cup Y)$$
$$+ \cdots + w_m * supp_m(X \cup Y),$$
$$conf_w(X \to Y) = w_1 * conf_1(X \to Y) + w_2 * conf_2(X \to Y)$$
$$+ \cdots + w_m * conf_m(X \to Y),$$

where $supp_w(R)$ is the support of R after synthesizing, $conf_w(R)$ is the confidence of R after synthesizing, $supp_i(R)$ is the support of R in D_i, and $conf_i(R)$ is the confidence of R in D_i, $i = 1, 2, ..., m$.

The synthesis of rules in this model is relatively straightforward once all weights are reasonably assigned. To assign weights, we first review Good's idea in Subsection 9.3.1 ([Good 1950]). Then, in the next subsection, the idea is used to determine the weights of association rules and branch databases. A weight synthesizing model is then designed, and an example is given in Subsection 9.3.3.

9.3.1 Weight of Evidence

To allocate weights, Good defines the weight in favor of a hypothesis H provided by evidence E as follows.

$$woe(H : E) = log \frac{O(H|E)}{O(H)}, \tag{9.1}$$

where $O(x)$ stands for the odd values of x. He thinks $woe(H : E)$ is a concept "almost as important as that of probability itself." Good elucidates simple natural desiderata for the formalization of the notion of weight of evidence, including an "additive property":

$$woe(H : E_1 \wedge E_2) = woe(H : E_1) + woe(H : E_2|E_1). \tag{9.2}$$

This property states that the weight in favor of a hypothesis provided by two pieces of evidence is equal to the weight provided by the first piece of evidence, plus the weight provided by the second piece of evidence, conditional upon our having previously observed the first. Starting from these desiderata, Good is able to show that, up to a constant factor, the weight of evidence must take the form given in the definition of weight. From the definition, it follows directly that

$$log\ O(H|E) = log\ O(H) + woe(H:E).$$

That is, if we think on a log-odds scale, our final belief in a hypothesis is equal to our initial belief, plus the weight of whatever evidence with which we are presented. Log-odds represent an attractive scale because weights accumulate additively; and also because the entire range from $-\infty$ to $+\infty$ is used.

It is obvious that either log-odds, or the weight of evidence, can be used to synthesize the association rules forwarded from different databases. For simplicity, weights are generally normalized into the interval $[0,1]$ in the following account. Furthermore, for convenience, Good's idea suggests that the weight of each rule is almost as important as its vote in the databases, and, therefore, the vote of a rule is used to evaluate the rule's weight.

9.3.2 Solving Weights of Databases

In order to synthesize association rules from different databases in the branches of a company, the weight for each database must be determined. It would appear that if all databases were of similar size, the weight of each database could be determined by the rules discovered from it. Let $D_1, D_2, ..., D_m$ be m different databases in the branches of a company; S_i the set of association rules from D_i $(i = 1, 2, ..., m)$; and $S = \{S_1, S_2, ..., S_m\}$. According to Good's definition on weight, *the vote of a rule R in S* can be used to assign R a weight w_R. In practice, for corporate profitability, a head office would be interested in rules that are supported, or voted for, by most of its branches. High-vote rules have a greater chance of becoming valid in the union of all databases than do low-vote rules. Hence, the higher the vote of a rule, the greater the weight of the rule should be.

In the meantime, the intersupport relationship between a database and its rules can be applied to determine the weight of the database. If a database supports a larger number of high-vote rules, the weight of the database should also be higher. The above idea is now illustrated by way of an example.

Let $minsupp = 0.2$ and $minconf = 0.3$, and let the following rules be mined from three databases.

(1) S_1 is the set of association rules from database $D1$:
   $A \wedge B \rightarrow C$ with $supp = 0.4, conf = 0.72$;
   $A \rightarrow D$ with $supp = 0.3, conf = 0.64$;
   $B \rightarrow E$ with $supp = 0.34, conf = 0.7$;
(2) S_2 is the set of association rules from database $D2$:
   $B \rightarrow C$ with $supp = 0.45, conf = 0.87$;
   $A \rightarrow D$ with $supp = 0.36, conf = 0.7$;
   $B \rightarrow E$ with $supp = 0.4, conf = 0.6$;

(3) S_3 is the set of association rules from database $D3$:

$A \wedge B \to C$ with $supp = 0.5, conf = 0.82$;

$A \to D$ with $supp = 0.25, conf = 0.62$.

Assume $S' = \{S_1, S_2, S_3\}$. Then there is a total of four rules in S':

$R_1 \ A \wedge B \to C$

$R_2 \ A \to D$

$R_3 \ B \to E$

$R_4 \ B \to C$

From the above rules mined from different databases, there are two databases that support (vote for) rule R_1, [2] three databases that support (vote for) rule R_2, two databases that support (vote for) rule R_3, and one database that supports (votes for) rule R_4. Following Good's weight of evidence, the vote of a rule in S' is used to assign a weight to the rule. After normalization, the weights are assigned as follows.

$$w_{R1} = \frac{2}{2 + 3 + 2 + 1} = 0.25;$$

$$w_{R2} = \frac{3}{2 + 3 + 2 + 1} = 0.375;$$

$$w_{R3} = \frac{2}{2 + 3 + 2 + 1} = 0.25;$$

$$w_{R4} = \frac{1}{2 + 3 + 2 + 1} = 0.125.$$

As we have seen, rule R_2 has the highest vote and the highest weight, and rule R_4 has the lowest vote and the lowest weight. Now, let $S = \{S_1, S_2, ..., S_m\}$ and $R_1, R_2, ..., R_n$ be all rules in S. Then the weight of R_i is defined as follows.

$$w_{Ri} = \frac{Num(R_i)}{\sum\limits_{j=1}^{n} Num(R_j)}, \tag{9.3}$$

where $i = 1, 2, ..., n$; and $Num(R)$ is the number of databases that contain rule R, or the vote of R in S.

Meanwhile, if a database supports (votes for) a larger number of high-vote rules, the weight of the database should also be higher. If the rules from a database are rarely present in other databases, the database would be assigned a lower weight. To implement this argument, the sum of the multiplications of the weights of rules, and their votes, can be used to assign weights to the branch databases. For the above rule set S', we have

---

[2] This support differs from the support defined in Chapter 2. Here, the support is the number of databases that vote for the rule.

$$w_{D1} = 2 * 0.25 + 3 * 0.375 + 2 * 0.25 = 2.125;$$
$$w_{D2} = 1 * 0.125 + 2 * 0.25 + 3 * 0.375 = 2;$$
$$w_{D3} = 2 * 0.25 + 3 * 0.375 = 1.625.$$

After normalization, the weights of the three databases are assigned as follows.

$$w_{D1} = \frac{2.125}{2.125 + 2 + 1.625} = 0.3695;$$

$$w_{D2} = \frac{2}{2.125 + 2 + 1.625} = 0.348;$$

$$w_{D3} = \frac{1.625}{2.125 + 2 + 1.625} = 0.2825.$$

As we have seen, database D_1 supports (votes for) the most rules with high weights, and it has the highest weight; database D_3 supports (votes for) the fewest rules with high weights, and it has the lowest weight.

Let $D_1, D_2, ..., D_m$ be m different databases in the branches of a company, S_i the set of association rules from D_i $(i = 1, 2, ..., m)$, $S = \{S_1, S_2, ..., S_m\}$, and $R_1, R_2, ..., R_n$ be all rules in S. Then the weight of D_i is defined as follows.

$$w_{Di} = \frac{\sum\limits_{R_k \in S_i} Num(R_k) * w_{R_k}}{\sum\limits_{j=1}^{m} \sum\limits_{R_h \in S_j} Num(R_h) * w_{R_h}}, \tag{9.4}$$

where $i = 1, 2, ..., m$.

After all databases have been assigned weights, the association rules can be synthesized by the weights of the databases. The synthesizing process is as follows.

For rule R_1: $A \wedge B \to C$,

$$
\begin{aligned}
supp(A \cup B \cup C) &= w_{D1} * supp_1(A \cup B \cup C) + w_{D3} * supp_3(A \cup B \cup C) \\
&= 0.3695 * 0.4 + 0.2825 * 0.5 \\
&= 0.28905;
\end{aligned}
$$

$$
\begin{aligned}
conf(A \wedge B \to C) &= w_{D1} * conf_1(A \wedge B \to C) + w_{D3} \\
&\quad * conf_3(A \wedge B \to C) \\
&= 0.3695 * 0.72 + 0.2825 * 0.82 \\
&= 0.49769.
\end{aligned}
$$

For rule R_2: $A \rightarrow D$,

$$supp(A \cup D) = w_{D1} * supp_1(A \cup D) + w_{D2}$$
$$* supp_2(A \cup D)w_{D3} * supp_3(A \cup D)$$
$$= 0.3695 * 0.3 + 0.348 * 0.36 + 0.2825 * 0.25$$
$$= 0.306755;$$

$$conf(A \rightarrow D) = w_{D1} * conf_1(A \rightarrow D)$$
$$+ w_{D2} * conf_2(A \rightarrow D) + w_{D3} * conf_3(A \rightarrow D)$$
$$= 0.3695 * 0.64 + 0.348 * 0.7 + 0.2825 * 0.62$$
$$= 0.68043.$$

For rule R_3: $B \rightarrow E$,

$$supp(B \cup E) = w_{D1} * supp_1(B \cup E) + w_{D2} * supp_2(B \cup E)$$
$$= 0.3695 * 0.34 + 0.348 * 0.4$$
$$= 0.26483;$$

$$conf(B \rightarrow E) = w_{D1} * conf_1(B \rightarrow E) + w_{D2} * conf_2(B \rightarrow E)$$
$$= 0.3695 * 0.7 + 0.348 * 0.6$$
$$= 0.46745.$$

For rule R_4: $B \rightarrow C$,

$$supp(B \cup C) = w_{D2} * supp_2(B \cup C)$$
$$= 0.348 * 0.45$$
$$= 0.1566;$$
$$conf(B \rightarrow C) = w_{D2} * conf_2(B \rightarrow C)$$
$$= 0.348 * 0.87$$
$$= 0.30276.$$

The above rules are ranked R_2, R_1, R_3, and R_4 by their supports. According to this ranking, high-rank rules can be used in applications.

Note that it is not difficult to find many other methods for assigning weights to given databases. For example, we can also use the size of databases to assign weights to the databases. For D_1, D_2, and D_3, let $|D_1|$, $|D_2|$, and $|D_3|$ be 30, 25, and 45, respectively. We can get

$$w_{D1} = \frac{|D_1|}{|D_1| + |D_2| + |D_3|} = \frac{30}{30 + 25 + 45} = 0.3;$$

$$w_{D2} = \frac{|D_2|}{|D_1| + |D_2| + |D_3|} = \frac{25}{30 + 25 + 45} = 0.25;$$

$$w_{D3} = \frac{|D_3|}{|D_1| + |D_2| + |D_3|} = \frac{45}{30 + 25 + 45} = 0.45.$$

Also, we can use sales within branches (of, e.g., supermarkets) to assign weights to the branches. More specifically, we can synthesize multiple factors to assign weights to the branch databases. However, constructing ingenious models for assigning weights is not our main goal in this book. Using Good's idea to assign weights to databases is, however, consistent with the work in Chapter 4, when we focus on high-vote patterns in local patterns.

9.3.3 Algorithm Design

Let $D_1, D_2, ..., D_m$ be m databases, S_i the set of association rules from D_i ($i = 1, 2, ..., m$), $supp_i$ and $conf_i$ the support and confidence of rules in S_i; and $minsupp$ and $minconf$ the threshold values given by the user. A synthesizing algorithm for association rules in different databases is designed as follows.

Algorithm 9.1 *Synthesizing*

Input: $S_1, S_2, ..., S_m$: *rule sets; minsupp, minconf: threshold values;*
Output: $X \to Y$: *synthesized association rules;*

(1) **let** $S \leftarrow \{S_1 \cup S_2 \cup \cdots \cup S_m\}$;
(2) **for** each rule R in S **do**
   let $Num(R) \leftarrow$ the number of databases that contain rule R in S;
   let $w_R \leftarrow \dfrac{Num(R)}{\sum\limits_{R' \in S} Num(R')}$;
(3) **for** $i = 1$ **to** m **do**
   let $w_i \leftarrow \dfrac{\sum\limits_{R_k \in S_i} Num(R_k) * w_{R_k}}{\sum\limits_{j=1}^{m} \sum\limits_{R_h \in S_j} Num(R_h) * w_{R_h}}$;
(4) **for** each rule $X \to Y \in S$ **do**
   let $supp_w \leftarrow w_1 * supp_1 + w_2 * supp_2 + \cdots + w_m * supp_m$;
   let $conf_w \leftarrow w_1 * conf_1 + w_2 * conf_2 + \cdots + w_m * conf_m$;
(5) **rank** all rules in S by their supports;
(6) **output** the high-rank rules in S whose support and confidence are at least *minsupp* and *minconf* respectively;
(7) **end all**.

The *Synthesizing* algorithm above generates high-rank rules from the association rule sets $S_1, S_2, ..., S_m$, where each high-rank rule has a high vote support and confidence. Step (2) assigns a weight to each rule in S according to its vote. Step (3) assigns a weight to each database (and therefore its corresponding rule set) by the number of high-vote rules that the rule set supports. Step (4) synthesizes the support and confidence of each rule in S by the weights of different databases. We rank the rules of S according to the weighted supports in Step (5). The output in Step (6) consists of the high-ranking rules selected in accordance with user requirements.

9.4 Improvement of Synthesizing Model

The number of rules forwarded may be so large that finding interesting rules can be time consuming. In this section, a procedure of rule selection is constructed, which enhances the synthesizing model by coping with low-vote rules.

9.4.1 Effectiveness of Rule Selection

Putting all association rules together from the different databases of a large company might also amass a huge rule set. To overcome this problem, an efficient algorithm is designed to improve the proposed synthesizing approach.

Using the synthesizing model in Subsection 9.3.2, a high weight is assigned to a database that supports (votes for) more high-vote rules, and a lower weight is assigned to a database that supports (votes for) less high-vote rules. However, this model can be enhanced by rule selection. Two examples are used to illustrate the effectiveness of rule selection.

Example 9.1 *Let $D_1, D_2, ..., D_{11}$ be 11 different databases, S_i the set of association rules from D_i ($i = 1, 2, ..., 11$), $S_i = \{R_1 : X \to Y\}$ when $i = 1, 2, ..., 10$, and $S_{11} = \{R_2 : X_1 \to Y_1, ..., R_{11} : X_{10} \to Y_{10}\}$. Then we have*

$$w_{R1} = \frac{Num(R_1)}{\sum\limits_{j=1}^{11} Num(R_j)} = \frac{10}{10 + \sum\limits_{j=1}^{10} 1} = 0.5,$$

$$w_{Ri} = \frac{Num(R_i)}{\sum\limits_{j=1}^{11} Num(R_j)} = \frac{1}{10 + \sum\limits_{j=1}^{10} 1} = 0.05,$$

where $i = 2, 3, ..., 11$.
    So,

$$w_{Di} = \frac{\sum\limits_{R_k \in S_i} Num(R_k) * w_{R_k}}{\sum\limits_{j=1}^{m} \sum\limits_{R_h \in S_j} Num(R_h) * w_{R_h}}$$

$$= \frac{10 * 0.5}{\sum\limits_{j=1}^{10} 10 * 0.5 + \sum\limits_{j=1}^{10} 1 * 0.05}$$

$$= 0.099,$$

where $i = 1, 2, ..., 10.$

$$w_{D11} = \frac{\sum\limits_{R_k \in S_{11}} Num(R_k) * w_{R_k}}{\sum\limits_{j=1}^{m} \sum\limits_{R_h \in S_j} Num(R_h) * w_{R_h}}$$

$$= \frac{\sum\limits_{j=1}^{10} 1 * 0.05}{\sum\limits_{j=1}^{10} 10 * 0.5 + \sum\limits_{j=1}^{10} 1 * 0.05}$$

$$= 0.01$$

From the above example, although S_{11} has 10 rules, w_{D11} is still very low, due to the fact that S_{11} does not contain high-vote rules.

Example 9.2 *In Example 9.1, if* $S_{11} = \{R_2 : X_1 \to Y_1, ..., R_{91} : X_{90} \to Y_{90}\}$, *then we have*

$$w_{R1} = \frac{Num(R_1)}{\sum\limits_{j=1}^{11} Num(R_j)} = \frac{10}{10 + \sum\limits_{j=1}^{90} 1}$$

$$= 0.1$$

$$w_{Ri} = \frac{Num(R_i)}{\sum\limits_{j=1}^{11} Num(R_j)} = \frac{1}{10 + \sum\limits_{j=1}^{90} 1}$$

$$= 0.01.$$

where $i = 2, 3, ..., 91.$

So,

$$w_{Di} = \frac{\displaystyle\sum_{R_k \in S_i} Num(R_k) * w_{R_k}}{\displaystyle\sum_{j=1}^{m} \sum_{R_h \in S_j} Num(R_h) * w_{R_h}}$$

$$= \frac{10 * 0.1}{\displaystyle\sum_{j=1}^{10} 10 * 0.1 + \sum_{j=1}^{90} 1 * 0.01}$$

$$= 0.09174.$$

where $i = 1, 2, ..., 10$.

$$w_{D11} = \frac{\displaystyle\sum_{R_k \in S_{11}} Num(R_k) * w_{R_k}}{\displaystyle\sum_{j=1}^{m} \sum_{R_h \in S_j} Num(R_h) * w_{R_h}}$$

$$= \frac{\displaystyle\sum_{j=1}^{90} 1 * 0.01}{\displaystyle\sum_{j=1}^{10} 10 * 0.1 + \sum_{j=1}^{90} 1 * 0.01}$$

$$= 0.0826.$$

In this case, w_{D11} becomes higher. Although w_{D11} cannot cause rules R_i ($2 \le i \le 91$) to become valid rules in book, the support and confidence of R_1 are slightly weakened by w_{D11}. The larger the number of rules in S_{11}, the more the other rules are weakened.

From the above we can see that there are many low-support association rules in local pattern sets, and that they have almost no impact on the weights of branch databases. This means that, for efficiency, these rules can be eliminated.

9.4.2 Process of Rule Selection

As we have seen in Examples 9.1 and 9.2, R_1 is the highest-vote rule extracted from $S = \{S_1, S_2, ..., S_{11}\}$. The rules with a lower vote (e.g., less than 2) can be taken as noise. For efficiency purposes, these noises could be wiped out before the databases are assigned weights. To eliminate the noise, because our goal is to extract high-vote rules from different databases, we can take the high-vote rules as relevant rules and the lower-vote rules as irrelevant rules. In this way, we can cope with abundance and redundancy of rules before the databases are assigned weights. For this, a new algorithm is constructed that selects rules from local pattern sets.

Procedure 9.1 *RuleSelection(S)*

Input: *γ: minimum voting degree, S: set of N rules, m: number of databases;*
Output: *S: reduced set of rules*

(1) **for** $i = 1$ **to** N
$\qquad$ let $Num(R_i) \leftarrow$ the number of databases that contain rule R_i in S;
$\qquad$ **if** $(Num(R_i)/m < \gamma)$
$\qquad\qquad S \leftarrow S - \{R_i\}$;
$\qquad$ **end for**;
(2) **output** S;
$\qquad$ **end procedure**;

The *RuleSelection* procedure above generates a reduced rule set S from the original N rules. If a rule R_i does not have a vote that meets γ, it is erased from S. Here γ is the user-specified minimum voting degree for different databases, and $0 \leq \gamma \leq 1$. For example, if the user is interested in rules that have a voting degree equal to, or greater than, 80%, then 80% is the users' minimum interest degree, and γ is 0.8.

After all the low-vote rules (those votes that do not meet γ) are deleted, S can be significantly reduced. An example is used below to illustrate the effect on weights by wiping out low-vote rules.

Example 9.3 *Let $D_1, D_2, ..., D_{10}$ be 10 different databases, S_i the set of association rules from D_i ($i = 1, 2, ..., 10$), $S_i = \{R_1 : X \to Y\}$ when $i = 1, 2, ..., 9$, and $S_{10} = \{R_1 : X \to Y, R_2 : X_1 \to Y_1, ..., R_{11} : X_{10} \to Y_{10}\}$. Then we have,*

$$w_{R1} = \frac{Num(R_1)}{\sum_{j=1}^{11} Num(R_j)} = \frac{10}{10 + \sum_{j=1}^{10} 1} = 0.5,$$

$$w_{Ri} = \frac{Num(R_i)}{\sum_{j=1}^{11} Num(R_j)} = \frac{1}{10 + \sum_{j=1}^{10} 1} = 0.05,$$

where $i = 2, 3, ..., 11$.
$\quad$ *So,*

$$w_{Di} = \frac{\sum_{R_k \in S_i} Num(R_k) * w_{R_k}}{\sum_{j=1}^{m} \sum_{R_h \in S_j} Num(R_h) * w_{R_h}}$$

$$= \frac{10 * 0.5}{\sum\limits_{j=1}^{9} 10 * 0.5 + 10 * 0.5 \sum\limits_{j=1}^{10} 1 * 0.05}$$

$$= 0.099,$$

where $i = 1, 2, ..., 9$.

$$w_{D10} = \frac{\sum\limits_{R_k \in S_{11}} Num(R_k) * w_{R_k}}{\sum\limits_{j=1}^{m} \sum\limits_{R_h \in S_j} Num(R_h) * w_{R_h}}$$

$$= \frac{10 * 0.5 + \sum\limits_{j=1}^{10} 1 * 0.05}{\sum\limits_{j=1}^{9} 10 * 0.5 + 10 * 0.5 \sum\limits_{j=1}^{10} 1 * 0.05}$$

$$= 0.109.$$

Because the vote of R_i is 1 ($2 \leq i \leq 11$), the rules R_i ($2 \leq i \leq 11$) can all be wiped out if $\gamma > 0.1$. After wiping out these rules, we have $w_{Di} = 0.1$, where $i = 1, 2, ..., 10$. The errors between the original weights and the changed weights for databases D_i ($1 \leq i \leq 9$) are all $|0.1 - 0.099| = 0.001$, and the error for D_{10} is $|0.1 - 0.109| = 0.009$.

9.4.3 Optimized Algorithm

Rule selection can be used to improve the performance of the synthesizing model by eliminating low-vote rules from the given rule set. The optimized algorithm is designed based on the algorithm *Synthesizing* by embedding a procedure *RuleSelection* as follows.

Algorithm 9.2 *RuleSynthesizing*

Input: *$S_1, S_2, ..., S_m$: rule sets; minsupp, minconf: threshold values;*
Output: *$X \rightarrow Y$: synthesized association rules;*

(1) **let** $S \leftarrow \{S_1 \cup S_2 \cup ... \cup S_m\}$;
(2) **call** RuleSelection(S);
(3) **for** each rule R in S **do**
    let $w_R \leftarrow \dfrac{Num(R)}{\sum\limits_{R' \in S} Num(R')}$;

(4) **for** $i = 1$ **to** m **do**

$$\text{let } w_i \leftarrow \frac{\displaystyle\sum_{R_k \in S_i} Num(R_k) * w_{R_k}}{\displaystyle\sum_{j=1}^{m} \sum_{R_h \in S_j} Num(R_h) * w_{R_h}};$$

(5) **for** each rule $X \rightarrow Y \in S$ **do**

let $supp_w \leftarrow w_1 * supp_1 + w_2 * supp_2 + \cdots + w_m * supp_m$;

let $conf_w \leftarrow w_1 * conf_1 + w_2 * conf_2 + \cdots + w_m * conf_m$;

(6) **rank** all rules in S by their supports;

(7) **output** the high-rank rules in S whose support and confidence are at least *minsupp* and *minconf*, respectively;

(8) **end all**.

The *RuleSynthesizing* algorithm above generates high-rank rules from the association rule sets $S_1, S_2, ..., S_m$. It is slightly different from the algorithm *Synthesizing* in that it calls in the procedure of rule selection in Step (2). Low-vote rules in S are given up in this step.

9.5 Algorithm Analysis

Because there is only a small difference between the algorithms *RuleSynthesizing* and *Synthesizing*, only the procedure *RuleSelection* and the algorithm *RuleSynthesizing* are analyzed in this section.

9.5.1 Procedure *RuleSelection*

The procedure *RuleSelection* generates a reduced rule set from the original rule set by eliminating low-vote rules. Thus, we have a theorem for the procedure as follows.

Theorem 9.1 *Procedure RuleSelection works correctly.*

Proof: In Steps (1) and (2), a set of selected rules is generated and output for a given rule set. We need to show that all high-vote rules are selected, and all low-vote rules are deleted.

For any rule $R_i \in S$ $(1 \leq i \leq N)$, if $Num(R_i)/m < \gamma$, it is a low-vote rule, and is eliminated from the rule set S. Here, S is the rule set from given databases, N the number of rules in S, and m the number of these databases. This means that all low-vote rules in S are deleted.

In the loop in Step (1), for a rule $R_i \in S$ $(1 \leq i \leq N)$, if $Num(R_i)/m \geq \gamma$, it is a high-vote rule, and is not eliminated from the rule set S. This means that all high-vote rules in S are selected.   ◇

In Procedure *RuleSelection*, the rules in m databases need to be input. We need

$$|Rule(D_1)| + |Rule(D_2)| + \cdots + |Rule(D_m)|$$

units to save all rules for the databases, which are less than, or equal to, $m * n$, where n is the maximum among $|Rule(D_1)|$, $|Rule(D_2)|$, ..., $|Rule(D_m)|$ and $|Rule(D_i)|$ stands for the number of rules in the rule set $Rule(D_i)$ of D_i. Also, we need N units to save all rules in S. Consequently, the space complexity of $RuleSelection$ is $O(N + mn)$.

It appears that the time complexity of $RuleSelection$ is dominated by the loop in Step (1). Therefore, we have the following theorem.

Theorem 9.2 *The time complexity of RuleSelection is $O(Nnm)$.*

Proof: For Step (1), the voting numbers of N rules in S need to be computed from the rule sets of the given databases. The voting number of each rule needs to access m rule sets of the databases. Accessing a rule set requires, at most, n comparisons, where n is the maximum among $|Rule(D_1)|$, $|Rule(D_2)|$, ..., $|Rule(D_m)|$. Therefore, the time complexity of Step (1) is $O(Nnm)$. This means that the time complexity of $RuleSelection$ is $O(Nnm)$.

$\diamond$

Note that it is possible to eliminate a rule that is strongly supported by a few of the databases when it receives a low vote. As we have seen in Chapter 5, an exceptional rule can be identified if it satisfies the conditions of exceptional rules. Thus, rule selection is a safe method of searching for rules of interest in multi-databases.

9.5.2 Algorithm *RuleSynthesizing*

Algorithm *RuleSynthesizing* is for generating high-rank rules from the given rule sets $S_1, S_2, ..., S_m$. We have a theorem for the algorithm as follows.

Theorem 9.3 *Algorithm RuleSynthesizing works correctly.*

Proof: In Steps (5), (6), and (7), a set of high-rank rules is generated and output for a set of given databases. We need to show that all selected rules are synthesized.

We know that each selected rule in S is synthesized by weighting in Step (5).

$\diamond$

In algorithm *RuleSynthesizing*, the space complexity of Steps (1) and (2) is $O(N + mn)$, as estimated in procedure $RuleSelection$. In Step (3), we need N' units to save the weights for all rules in S, where $N' \leq N$ is the number of selected rules in S. In Step (4), we need m units to save the weights for the m databases. In Step (5), we need $3N'$ units to save the supports and confidences for all rules in S. Thus, the space complexity of $RuleSynthesizing$ is $O(N + mn + N' + m + 3N') = O(N + mn)$.

The time complexity of *RuleSynthesizing* is determined in Steps (2) to (6). The time complexity of Step (2) is $O(Nnm)$. This is the time complexity of the procedure *RuleSelection*. The time complexity of Step (3) is $O(N')$. The time complexity of Step (4) is $O(m)$. The time complexity of Step (5) is $O(2N')$. The time complexity of Step (6) is $O(N')$. Therefore, the time complexity of *RuleSynthesizing* is $O(Nnm + N' + m + 2N' + N') = O(Nmn)$.

9.6 Summary

Most research efforts into dealing with large databases by data mining have concentrated on scaling up inductive algorithms. See [Provost-Kolluri 1999]. These efforts include the design of fast induction algorithms, data partitioning, and the use of relational representations. The approach presented in this chapter is more appropriate when data come from a variety of databases.

To make use of the association rules discovered from different databases, we have presented a synthesizing model by weighting. When the database for each of the mined association rules was identified, a model was constructed to synthesize these rules. In particular, a rule selection procedure was constructed to improve the efficiency of the weighting model.

Differing from bagging and boosting, the proposed approach can capture characteristics of databases, and can synthesize rules from different databases into a centralized rule set. The proposed approach differs from the incremental batch learning in [Clearwater-CHB 1989] and the multi-layer induction in [Wu-Lo 1998], in that databases can be mined concurrently. Also, the sequentiality of subsets in batch learning and multi-layer induction in the synthesizing model is not important. The synthesizing model is also different from the stacked generalization in [Wolpert 1992, Ting-Witten 1997], because the original data (from different databases) are not required in the synthesizing model. The differences between the synthesizing model for parallel and distributed data mining and for meta-learning were reviewed in Chapter 2.

10. Conclusions and Future Work

Research into multi-database mining has become important, imperative, and challenging with the increasing development of multi-databases. Although data in multi-databases can be merged into a single dataset for knowledge discovery, such merging can lead to many problematic issues such as tremendous amounts of data, the destruction of data distributions, and the infiltration of uninteresting attributes, as well as security and privacy concerns. In particular, some concepts, such as regularity, causal relationships, and rules cannot be discovered if we simply search the merged single dataset, since the knowledge is essentially hidden within the multi-databases (Zhong-Yao-Ohsuga 1999). To deal with multi-database mining problems, this book has designed a new and effective strategy for multi-database mining. This strategy consists of a process for analyzing local patterns, which allows (a) the achievement of high performance in novel and quality pattern discovery; and (b) pattern discovery to become a realistic support for dual-level applications. We now conclude by outlining the key techniques presented in this book and looking towards the future.

10.1 Conclusions

There are several factors that point to the importance of improvements in multi-database mining. (1) there are a growing number of multi-databases serving organizations, both public and private; (2) there are essential differences between mono- and multi-database mining; and (3) various limitations still exist with present multi-database mining techniques. With these factors in mind, we have presented a new strategy for the development of multi-database mining systems.

In a multi-database environment, a pattern has certain attributes, including the name of the pattern, the rate voted for by, for example, branches of a company, and supports and confidences in those branches. That is, as stated in Chapter 3, a pattern is a *super-point* of the form

$$P(name, vote, vsupp, vconf).$$

While collecting all the data from databases to generate a mono-dataset for discovery purposes, traditional multi-database mining merges the vector-dimensions *vsupp* and *vconf* into single-dimensions *supp* and *conf*, respectively. Consequently, such merging leads to the destruction of data distributions. More important, some patterns cannot be discovered, because they are essentially hidden within these databases.

Moving on from traditional multi-database mining, we have presented innovations to key techniques that have not been satisfactorily dealt with previously. These techniques include application-independent database classification and local pattern analysis for identifying useful patterns in multi-databases. Key contributions are as follows.

1. The importance and challenges of multi-database mining were outlined in Chapter 1. Due to essential differences between mono- and multi-databases, a new process of multi-database mining was presented.
2. For the reuse of local patterns, a local pattern analysis, inspired by competition in sports, was advocated in Chapter 3.
3. A logical framework was constructed in Chapter 4, for identifying quality knowledge from different data-sources (multi-databases).
4. An application-independent technique was presented in Chapter 5, for developing database clustering.
5. A logical framework was constructed in Chapter 6, for resolving confliction within multiple databases.
6. By analyzing local patterns, an effective and efficient algorithm was designed in Chapter 7, for identifying a new kind of pattern (a "high-vote pattern"). Another technique developed in this chapter provides a good human interface by constructing a fuzzy logic controller. In particular, this chapter presented a means of analyzing high-vote patterns so that they can be easily understood and applied.
7. To deal with the individuality of branches of an interstate company, Chapter 8 presented an approach for identifying another kind of new pattern, known as an "exceptional pattern." As in Chapter 7, we constructed a fuzzy logic controller for generating real minimum vote-ratio-for-exception from the relative minimum vote-ratio-for-exception (specified by users).
8. In Chapter 9, in order to consider the weight of branches within a multi-branch organization, an approach was built to synthesize local patterns by weighting. In particular for efficiency, a rule selection method was presented.
9. The proposed techniques were evaluated by way of experiments. The experimental results show that these techniques are effective, efficient, and promising.

The techniques that we have presented are very different from those of traditional multi-database mining, because we focus on the analysis of local patterns. Below are four positive features of the techniques presented in this book.

(1)   *The new mining techniques and methodologies developed in this book can significantly increase the efficiency of multi-database mining systems.* Traditional multi-database mining techniques were further developed to search for patterns, using existing mono-database mining. Although data in multi-databases can be merged into a single dataset, such merging can lead to problems such as tremendous amounts of data, the destruction of data distributions, and the infiltration of uninteresting attributes. In particular, some concepts, such as regularity, causal relationships and patterns cannot be discovered if we simply search a single dataset, since the knowledge is essentially hidden within the multi-databases. It is a difficult task to effectively exploit the potential ability of mining systems, and it is one of the key issues essential to achieving an effective design for mining strategies.

Our multi-database mining strategies have focused on identifying quality patterns, including high-vote patterns, exceptional patterns, and global patterns, based on local pattern analysis. Using previous techniques, patterns could be only searched for in the same way as they were in single-database mining. They were not able to discover high-vote patterns, exceptional patterns, and global patterns in multi-databases. These patterns are regarded as novel patterns. Therefore, our data preparation techniques have the potential to deliver quality data and knowledge. This is necessary when quality decisions need to be made.

(2)   *The new mining techniques and methodologies developed in this book can significantly improve the performance of multi-database mining systems.* In real-world applications, company headquarters must tackle huge amounts of data and local patterns. For example, different branches of Wal-Mart receive 20 million transactions a day. This is more than the rate at which data can be feasibly collected and analyzed using today's computing power. Also, because privacy is a very sensitive issue, and safeguarding its protection in a data-source is of extreme importance, sharing knowledge (rather than the original raw data) can be a feasible way to deal with multi-database problems. Because of this, the development of a high-performance system for mining multi-databases is crucial.

This book has developed group pattern discovery systems for identifying potentially useful patterns from multiple databases, based on local pattern analysis. As we have demonstrated, previous techniques are inadequate for mining these patterns. Our local pattern analysis reduces search costs and generates much more useful information. In particular, our work on data preparation cuts down significantly the amount of data required for a multi-database mining application. Further efficiency is achieved by our pattern selection strategies.

(3)   *The new mining techniques and methodologies developed can significantly add to the automation of multi-database mining systems.* Like mono-database mining, traditional multi-database mining techniques rely

on the assumption that users can specify some thresholds. However, the user-specified thresholds are appropriate to a set of databases to be mined only if the distribution of patterns in the set of databases is known. This motivates us to design mining techniques with database-independence thresholds.

Our multi-database mining strategies have provided a good human-computer interface for multi-database mining systems, which allows users to take the commonly used interval $[0, 1]$ into consideration when specifying the thresholds. This means users can specify relative thresholds with respect to $[0, 1]$, and our mining algorithm converts the relative thresholds into true thresholds suitable for multi-database mining applications. This has been implemented by designing fuzzy logic controllers.

(4)   *In this book we have created several multi-database mining techniques and methodologies to deal with key problems that have not been satisfactorily solved before.* For multi-database mining we have dealt with two problems: how to prepare quality data for multiple database mining, and how to efficiently identify potentially useful patterns. Existing multi-database mining strategies collect all the data from these databases to amass a huge database for searching using mono-database mining techniques. This leads to not only expensive search cost, but also the disguising of useful patterns.

For efficient multi-database mining, the key problem is how to identify quality patterns for supporting various kinds of applications. We have studied new strategies in dealing with this very difficult problem. The first strategy was to design group data preparation systems for improving the quality of data and knowledge. The second strategy was to develop group pattern discovery systems based on our local pattern analysis for identifying novel, and potentially useful, patterns. The new strategies in this book are very different from traditional multi-database mining strategies.

10.2 Future Work

An important contribution of this book is the proposal of data preparation techniques. Although the effectiveness of the techniques is reasonably good, the approaches should be studied more comprehensively, and improved. In particular, more techniques for data preparation should be developed.

Our case studies in this book concern analyzing local patterns within an interstate company. By analyzing local patterns, three kinds of patterns — high-vote patterns, exceptional patterns, and global patterns — have been identified. Our work aims to introduce a practical way of attacking multi-database mining problems. In this way, we expect to discover patterns that have, up until now, been concealed within multi-databases.

The data that are distributed in multiple databases present many complications, and associated mining tasks and mining approaches are diverse. Therefore, many challenging research issues have emerged. Important tasks that present themselves to multi-database mining researchers, and multi-database mining system and application developers, are listed below:

- establishment of a powerful representation for patterns in distributed data;
- development of efficient and effective multi-database mining strategies and systems;
- design of database-independent multi-database mining strategies and systems;
- construction of interactive and integrated multi-database mining environments; and
- exploration of secure machines for multi-database mining.

Moreover, with the advance of Internet techniques, the Web is rapidly becoming flooded with information. All companies, large and small, are facing inevitable challenges brought about by information technological developments. The challenges create not only risks, but also opportunities. To *minimize* risks and *maximize* potential benefits, it has become very important for companies making competitive decisions to be able to use their information effectively and efficiently. Multi-database mining, as an important data analysis tool, provides useful ways for decision-makers to deal with distributed data. Consequently, efforts to solve multi-database mining problems will have a great impact on both public and private organizations and academia. It must be kept in mind, too, that, when a large amount of interrelated data is available, and can be effectively analyzed by anyone, it can pose a threat to data security and can be used to invade privacy. It is therefore a challenging task to develop effective techniques that prevent the disclosure of sensitive information during multi-database mining. This is especially true now that the use of multi-database mining systems is rapidly increasing in various domains ranging from business analysis and customer analysis, to medicine and government.

References

[Aggarawal-Yu 1998] C. Aggarawal and P. Yu, A new framework for itemset generation. In: *Proceedings of Symposium on Principles of Database Systems*, 1998: 18–24.

[Agrawal-Shafer 1996] R. Agrawal and J. Shafer, Parallel mining of association rules. *IEEE Transactions on Knowledge and Data Engineering*, 8(6) (1996): 962–969.

[Agrawal-Srikant 1994] R. Agrawal and R. Srikant, Fast algorithms for mining association rules. In: *Proceedings of International Conference on Very Large Data Bases*, 1994: 487–499.

[Agrawal-Imielinski-Swami 1993] R. Agrawal, T. Imielinski, and A. Swami, Database mining: A performance perspective. *IEEE Transactions on Knowledge and Data Engineering*, 5(6) (1993): 914–925.

[Albert 2000] J. Albert, Theoretical foundations of schema restructuring in heterogeneous multidatabase systems. In: *Proceedings of International Conference on Information and Knowledge Management*, 2000: 461–470.

[Aronis et al. 1997] J. Aronis, F. Provost, and B. Buchanan, The WoRLD: Knowledge discovery from multiple distributed databases. In: *Proceedings of tenth International Florida AI Research Symposium*, 1997: 337–341.

[Bayardo 1998] B. Bayardo, Efficiently mining long patterns from databases. In: *Proceedings of ACM International Conference on Management of Data*, 1998: 85–93.

[Berry 1994] J. Berry, Database marketing. *Business Week*. 5 September 1994: 56–62

[Breitbart-ST 1990] Y. Breitbart, A. Silberschatz, and G. Thompson: Reliable transaction management in a multidatabase system. In: *Proceedings of ACM International Conference on Management of Data*, 1990: 215–224.

[Bright-HP 1992] M. Bright, A. Hurson, and S. Pakzad, A taxonomy and current issues in multidatabase systems. *IEEE Computer*, 25(3) (1992): 50–60.

[Brin-Motwani-Silverstein 1997] S. Brin, R. Motwani, and C. Silverstein, Beyond market baskets: Generalizing association rules to correlations. In: *Proceedings of the ACM SIGMOD International Conference on Management of Data*, 1997: 265–276.

[Brin-Motwani-Ullman-Tsur 1997] S. Brin, R. Motwani, J. Ullman, and S. Tsur, Dynamic itemset counting and implication rules for market basket data. In: *Proceedings of the ACM SIGMOD International Conference on Management of Data*, 1997: 255–264.

[Cai et al. 1991] Y. Cai, N. Cercone, and J. Han, Attribute-oriented induction in relational databases. In: G. Piatetsky-Shapiro and W. Frawley, *Knowledge Discovery in Databases*, Menlo Park, CA, AAAI Press, 1991: 213–228.

[Chan 1996] P. Chan, An extensible meta-learning approach for scalable and accurate inductive learning. *PhD Dissertation*, Dept. of Computer Science, Columbia University, New York, 1996.

[Chattratichat et al. 1997] J. Chattratichat, J. Darlington, M. Ghanem, Y. Guo, H. Huning, M. Kohler, J. Sutiwaraphun, H. To, and D. Yang, Large scale data mining: challenges and responses. In: *Proceedings of International Conference on Knowledge Discovery and Data Mining*, 1997: 143–146.

[Chen 1998] X. Chen, Ilias Petrounias: A framework for temporal data mining. In: *Proceedings of Ninth International Conference on Database and Expert Systems Applications*, Vienna, Austria, August 24–28, 1998: 796–805.

[Chen-Han-Yu 1996] M. Chen, J. Han, and P. Yu, Data mining: An overview from a database perspective. *IEEE Transactions on Knowledge and Data Engineering*, 8(6) (1996): 866–881.

[Cheung-Han-Ng-Wong 1996] D. Cheung, J. Han, V. Ng, and C. Wong, Maintenance of discovered association rules in large databases: An incremental updating technique. In: *Proceedings of International Conference on Data Engineering*, 1996: 106–114.

[Cheung-Ng-Fu-Fu 1996] D. Cheung, V. Ng, A. Fu, and Y. Fu, Efficient mining of association rules in distributed databases, *IEEE Transactions on Knowledge and Data Engineering*, 8(6) (1996): 911–922.

[Clearwater-CHB 1989] S. Clearwater, T. Cheng, H. Hirsh, and B. Buchanan, Incremental batch learning. In: *Proceedings of the Sixth International Workshop on Machine Learning*. Ithaca, New York, Morgan-Kaufmann, June 26-27, 1989: 366–370.

[Cooper 1997] G. Cooper, A simple constraint-based algorithm for efficiently mining observational databases for causal relationships. *Data Mining and Knowledge Discovery*, 2(1997).

[Cromp 1993] R. Cromp and W. Campbell: Data mining of multi-dimensional remotely sensed images. In: *Proceedings of the Second International Conference on Information and Knowledge Management*, Washington, DC, November 1–5, 1993. ACM 1993: 471–480.

[Dong-Li 1998] G. Dong and J. Li, Interestingness of discovered association rules in terms of neighborhood-based unexpectedness. In: *Proceedings of the second Pacific–Asia Conference on Knowledge Discovery and Data Mining*, 1998: 72–86.

[Dong-Li 1999] G. Dong and J. Li, Efficient mining of emerging patterns: Discovering trends and differences. In: *Proceedings of International Conference on Knowledge Discovery and Data Mining*, 1999: 43–52.

[Durrett 1996] R. Durrett, *Probability: Theory and examples*, Duxbury Press, Grzybowska 37A, 00-855 Warsaw, 1996.

[Ester et al. 1997] M. Ester, H. Kriegel, and J. Sander, Spatial data mining: A database approach. In: *Proceedings of SDD97*, Berlin, Germany, 1997: 47–66.

[Fayyad-Piatetsky-Smyth 1996] U. M. Fayyad, G. Piatetsky-Shapiro, and P. Smyth, From data mining to knowledge discovery: An overview. In: *Advances in Knowledge Discovery and Data Mining*. AAAI Press/MIT Press, 1996: 1–36.

[Fayyad-Simoudis 1997] U. M. Fayyad and E. Simoudis, Data mining and knowledge discovery. In: *Proceedings of International Conference on Knowledge Discovery and Data Mining*, 1997: 3–16.

[Fayyad-Stolorz 1997] U. Fayyad and P. Stolorz, Data mining and KDD: Promise and challenges. *Future Generation Computer Systems*, 13 (1997): 99–115.

[Feldman et al. 1999] R. Feldman, Y. Aumann, M. Fresko, O. Liphstat, B. Rosenfeld, and Y. Schler, Text mining via information extraction. In: Jan M. Zytkow, Jan Rauch (Eds.): *Principles of Data Mining and Knowledge Discovery*, Third

European Conference, PKDD '99, Prague, Czech Republic, September 15-18, 1999: 165–173.

[Frawley-Piatetsky 1992] W. Frawley, G. Piatetsky-Shapiro, and C. Matheus, Knowledge discovery in databases: An overview. *AI Magazine*, 13(3) (1992): 57–70.

[Good 1950] I. Good, *Probability and the Weighting of Evidence*. Charles Griffin, London, 1950.

[Grecu 1998] D. Grecu and L. Becker, Coactive learning for distributed data mining. In: *Proceedings of International Conference on Knowledge Discovery and Data Mining*, 1998: 209–213

[Grossman-BRMT 2000] R. Grossman, S. Bailey, A. Ramu, B. Malhi and A. Turinsky, The preliminary design of Papyrus: A system for high performance, distributed data mining over clusters. In: *Advances in Distributed and Parallel Knowledge Discovery*, AAAI Press/The MIT Press, 2000: 259–275.

[Guo 1999] Y. Guo and J. Sutiwaraphun, Probing knowledge in distributed data mining. In: *Proceedings of The Third Pacific–Asia Conference on Knowledge Discovery and Data Mining*, 1999: 443–452

[Halpern-Moses 1992] J. Halpern and Y. Moses, A guide to completeness and complexity for modal logics of knowledge and belief. *Artificial Intelligence*, 54 (1992): 319-379.

[Han-Karypis-Kumar 1997] E. Han, G. Karypis, and V. Kumar, Scalable parallel data mining for association rules. In: *Proceedings of ACM International Conference on Management of Data*, 1997: 277–288.

[Han-KK 2000] E. Han, G. Karypis, and V. Kumar, Scalable parallel data mining for association rules. *IEEE Transactions on Knowledge and Data Engineering*, 12 2(2000): 377–352.

[Han 1999] J. Han, Data mining. In: J. Urban and P. Dasgupta (Eds.), *Encyclopedia of Distributed Computing*, Kluwer Academic, 1999.

[Han-Cai-Cercone 1992] J. Han, Y. Cai, and N. Cercone, Knowledge discovery in databases: An attribute-oriented approach. In: *Proceedings of International Conference on Very Large Data Bases*, Canada, 1992: 547–559.

[Han-Cai-Cercone 1993] J. Han, Y. Cai, and N. Cercone, Data-driven discovery of quantitative rules in relational databases. *IEEE Transactions on Knowledge and Data Engineering*, 5(1) (1993): 29–40.

[Han-Huang-Cercone-Fu 1996] J. Han, Y. Huang, N. Cercone, and Y. Fu, Intelligent query answering by knowledge discovery techniques. *IEEE Transactions on Knowledge and Data Engineering*, 8(3) (1996): 373–390.

[Han-Pei-Yin 2000] J. Han, J. Pei, and Y. Yin, Mining frequent patterns without candidate generation. In: *Proceedings of ACM International Conference on Management of Data*, 2000: 1–12.

[Han 1997] K. Han, J. Koperski, and N. Stefanovic, GeoMiner: A system prototype for spatial data mining, *SIGMOD Record* 26(2) (1997): 553–556.

[Heckerman 1995] D. Heckerman, D. Geiger, and D. Chickering, Learning Bayesian networks: The combinations of knowledge and statistical data. *Machine Learning*, 20(1995): 197–243.

[Hosking-Pednault-Sudan 1997] J. Hosking, E. Pednault and M. Sudan, A statistical perspective on data mining. *Future Generation Computer Systems*, 13 (1997): 117–134.

[Hurson-BP 1994] A. Hurson, M. Bright, and S. Pakzad, *Multidatabase systems: An advanced solution for global information sharing*. IEEE Computer Society press, Los Alamitos, CA, 1994.

[Hussain 2000] F. Hussain, H. Liu, E. Suzuki, and H. Lu, Exception rule mining with a relative interestingness measure. In: *Proceedings of PAKDD2000*, 2000: 86–97.

[Hwang 1999] S. Hwang, S. Ho, and J. Tang, Mining exception instances to facilitate workflow exception handling. In: *Proceedings of DASFAA*, 1999: 45–52.

[Kaplan 1966] D. Kaplan, Review of "A semantic analysis of modal logic I: normal modal propositional calculi". *Journal of Symbolic Logic*, 31 (1966): 120-122.

[Kargupta-HS 1997] H. Kargupta, I. Hamzaoglu, and B. Stafford, Scalable, distributed data mining — An agent architecture. In: *Proceedings of International Conference on Knowledge Discovery and Data Mining*, 1997: 211–214.

[Kargupta-HSJ 2001] H. Kargupta, W. Huang, K. Sivakumar, and E. Johnson; Distributed clustering using collective principal component analysis. *Knowledge and Information Systems*, 3(4) (2001): 422–448.

[Kargupta-HSPW 2000] H. Kargupta, W. Huang, K. Sivakumar, B. Park, and S. Wang, Collective principal component analysis from distributed, heterogeneous data. In: *Principles of Data Mining and Knowledge Discovery*, 2000: 452–457.

[Kohavi-John 1997] R. Kohavi, and G. John, Wrappers for feature subset selection. *Artificial Intelligence*, 97(1997): 273–324.

[Konieczny-Perez 1997] S. Konieczny, R. Perez, Merging with integrity constraints. In: *Proceedings of the European Conference on Symbolic and Quantitative Approaches to Reasoning and Uncertainty*, London, UK, July 5-9, 1999: 233-244.

[Kripke 1963] S. Kripke, A semantical analysis of modal logic. I: Normal modal propositional calculi. *Z. Math. Logik Grundl. Math.* 9 (1963): 67-96.

[Krishnaswamy 2000] S. Krishnaswamy, A. Zaslavsky, and S. Loke, An architecture to support distributed data mining services in e-commerce environments. In: *Proceedings of Second International Workshop on Advance Issues of E-Commerce and Web-Based Information Systems (WECWIS 2000)*, 8-9 June 2000, Milpitas, CA, IEEE Computer Society, 2000: 239–246.

[Krishnaswamy 2002] S. Krishnaswamy, A. Zaslavsky, and S. Loke, Techniques for estimating the computation and communication costs of distributed data mining. In: *Proceedings of International Conference on Computational Science*, Amsterdam, The Netherlands, April 21–24, 2002: 603–612.

[Lamarre-Shoham 1994] P. Lamarre and Y. Shoham, Knowledge, certainty, belief and conditionalisation. In: *Principles of Knowledge Representation and Reasoning: Proc. Fourth International Conference (KR'94)*, 1994: 415-424.

[Lesser 1998] V. Lesser, B. Horling, F. Klassner, A. Raja, T. Wagner, and S. Zhang. A next generation information gathering agent. In: *Proceedings of the 4th International Conference on Information Systems, Analysis, and Synthesis; in conjunction with the World Multiconference on Systemics, Cybernetics, and Informatics (SCI'98)*, Orlando, FL, July 1998.

[Lesser 2000] V. Lesser, B. Horling, F. Klassner, A. Raja, T. Wagner, and S. Zhang, BIG: An company for resource-bounded information gathering and decision making. *Artificial Intelligence Journal, Special Issue on Internet Information Agents*, 118(1-2) (2000): 197-244.

[Lin 1995] J. Lin. *Frameworks for dealing with confliction information and applications*. Ph.D. Thesis, Dept. of Computer Science, University of Toronto, 1995.

[Litwin 1985] W. Litwin, An overview of the multidatabase system MRDSM. In: *Proceedings of ACM Annual Conference*, 1985: 524–533.

[Liu 1999] H. Liu, H. Lu, L. Feng, and F. Hussain, Efficient search of reliable exceptions. In: *Proceedings of The Third Pacific–Asia Conference on Knowledge Discovery and Data Mining*, 1999: 194–204.

[Wu-Zhang-Zhang 2004] X. Wu, C. Zhang and S. Zhang, Database classification for multi-database mining, *Information Systems*, accepted, forthcoming (Available online).

[Yan-Zhang-Zhang 2003] Xiaowei Yan, Chengqi Zhang and Shichao Zhang, Towards databases mining: Preprocessing collected data. *Applied Artificial Intelligence*, 17 (5-6) (2003): 545–561.

[Yao-Liu 1997] J. Yao and H. Liu, Searching multiple databases for interesting complexes. In: *Proceedings of Pacific-Asia Conference on Knowledge Discovery and Data Mining*, 1997: 198–210.

[Zhang 1989] S. Zhang, Discovering knowledge from databases. In: *Proceedings of National Conference on Artificial Intelligence and Its Applications*, Beijing, 1989: 161–164.

[Zhang 1993] S. Zhang, Premonitory dependency based on historical data. *Chinese Journal of Computing Technology*, 20(3)(1993): 50–54

[Zhang 1999] S. Zhang, Aggregation and maintenance for databases mining. *Intelligent Data Analysis: An International Journal*, 3(6) (1999): 475–490.

[Zhang 2000] S. Zhang, A nearest neighborhood algebra for probabilistic databases. *Intelligent Data Analysis: An International Journal*, 4(1), 2000: 29-49.

[Zhang 2001] S. Zhang, *Knowledge Discovery in Multi-databases by Analyzing Local Instances*. PhD Thesis, Deakin University, November 2001.

[Zhang-Liu 2002] S. Zhang and L. Liu, Causality discovery in databases. In: *Proceedings of ICAIS'2002*, 2002.

[Zhang-Qin 1997] S. Zhang and Z. Qin, A robust learning model. *Computer Sciences*, 24(4) (1997): 34–37.

[Zhang-Qiu-Luo 1999] S. Zhang, Y. Qiu, and X. Luo, Weighted values acquisition from applications. In: *Proceedings of Eighth International Conference on Intelligent Systems*, 1999: 24–26.

[Zhang-Wu 2001] S. Zhang and X. Wu, Large scale data mining based on data partitioning. *Applied Artificial Intelligence*, 15(2) (2001): 129–139.

[Zhang-Wu-Zhang 2003] S. Zhang, X. Wu, and C. Zhang, Multi-database mining. *The IEEE Computational Intelligence Bulletin*, 1(1) (2003): 5–13.

[Zhang-WZS 2003] S. Zhang, X. Wu, C. Zhang and K. Su, Identifying quality knowledge from different data sources. In: *Proceedings of ICDM '03 Workshop on Foundations and New Directions of Data Mining*, Melbourne, FL, November 19, 2003: 234–242.

[Zhang-Yan 1992] S. Zhang and X. Yan, CTRCC: An analogical forecast model. In: *Proceedings of ICYCS'91*, 1991: 553–556.

[Zhang-Zhang 1998] S. Zhang and C. Zhang, A method of learning probabilities in Bayesian networks. In: *Proceedings of ICCIMA'98*, Australia, 1998: 119–124.

[Zhang-Zhang 2001a] S. Zhang and C. Zhang, Mining small databases by collecting knowledge. In: *Proceedings of DASFAA01*, 2001: 174–175.

[Zhang-Zhang 2001b] C. Zhang and S. Zhang, Collecting quality data for database mining. In: *Proceedings of the Fourtennth Australian Joint Conference on Artificial Intelligence*, 2001: 593–604.

[Zhang-Zhang 2001c] S. Zhang and C. Zhang, Estimating itemsets of interest by sampling. In: *Proceedings of the Tenth IEEE International Conference on Fuzzy Systems*, 2001.

[Zhang-Zhang 2001d] S. Zhang and C. Zhang, Pattern discovery in probabilistic databases. In: *Proceedings of The Fourteenth Australian Joint Conference on Artificial Intelligence*, 2001: 619–630.

[Zhang-Zhang 2002a] C. Zhang and S. Zhang, *Association Rules Mining: Models and Algorithms*. Lecture Notes on Computer Science, Volume 2307, Springer-Verlag, New York, 2002.

[Liu-Lu-Yao 1998] H. Liu, H. Lu, and J. Yao, Identifying relevant databases for multidatabase mining. In: *Proceedings of Pacific–Asia Conference on Knowledge Discovery and Data Mining*, 1998: 210–221.

[Liu-Lu-Yao 2001] H. Liu, H. Lu, and J. Yao, Toward multidatabase mining: Identifying relevant databases. *IEEE Transactions on Knowledge and Data Engineering*, 13(4) (2001): 541-553.

[Liu-Motoda 1998] H. Liu and H. Motoda *Feature Selection for Knowledge Discovery and Data Mining*, Kluwer Academic, Hingham, MA, July 1998.

[Liu-Motoda 2001] H. Liu and H. Motoda, *Instance Selection and Construction for Data Mining*. Kluwer Academic, Hingham, MA, February 2001.

[Massey-Newing 1994] J. Massey and R. Newing, Trouble in mind. *Computing*. May 1994: 44–45.

[Ng 1994] R. Ng and J. Han, Efficient and effective clustering methods for spatial data mining. In: *Proceedings of the Twentieth International Conference on Very Large Data Bases*, September 12-15, 1994, Santiago de Chile, Chile. Morgan–Kaufmann, 1994: 144–155.

[Oguchi 1999a] M. Oguchi and M. Kitsuregawa, Dynamic remote memory acquiring for parallel data mining on PC cluster: Preliminary performance results. In: P. Sloot, M. Bubak, A. Hoekstra, and B. Hertzberger (Eds.): *High-Performance Computing and Networking, seventh International Conference, HPCN Europe 1999*, Amsterdam, The Netherlands, April 12–14, 1999, Proceedings. Lecture Notes in Computer Science 1593 Springer 1999: 553–562.

[Oguchi 1999b] M. Oguchi and M. Kitsuregawa, Dynamic remote memory acquisition for parallel data mining on ATM-connected PC cluster. In: *Proceedings of the 1999 International Conference on Supercomputing*, June 20–25, 1999, Rhodes, Greece. ACM, 1999: 246–252.

[Oguchi 1997] M. Oguchi, T. Shintani, T. Tamura, and M. Kitsuregawa, Characteristics of a parallel data mining application implemented on an ATM connected PC cluster. In: B. Hertzberger and P. Sloot (Eds.): *High-Performance Computing and Networking, International Conference and Exhibition, HPCN Europe 1997*, Vienna, Austria, April 28–30, 1997: 303–317.

[Oguchi 1998] M. Oguchi, T. Shintani, T. Tamura, and M. Kitsuregawa, Optimizing protocol parameters to large scale PC cluster and evaluation of its effectiveness with parallel data mining. In: *Proceedings of The Seventh IEEE International Symposium on High Performance Distributed Computing (HPDC '98)*, 28–31 July, 1998: 34–41.

[Padmanabhan 1998] B. Padmanabhan and A. Tuzhilin, A belief-driven method for discovering unexpected patterns. In: *Proceedings of the ACM SIGKDD International Conference on Knowledge Discovery and Data Mining*, 1998: 94–100.

[Padmanabhan 2000] B. Padmanabhan and A. Tuzhilin, Small is beautiful: Discovering the minimal set of unexpected patterns. In: *Proceedings of the ACM SIGKDD International Conference on Knowledge Discovery and Data Mining*, 2000: 54–63.

[Park-Chen-Yu 1995] J. Park, M. Chen, and P. Yu, Efficient parallel and data mining for association rules. In: *Proceedings of International Conference on Information and Knowledge Management*, 1995: 31–36.

[Park-Chen-Yu 1997] J. Park, M. Chen, and P. Yu, Using a hash-based method with transaction trimming for mining association rules. *IEEE Transactions on Knowledge and Data Engineering.*, 9(5) (1997): 813-824.

[Parthasarathy-Zaki-Li 1998] S. Parthasarathy, M. J. Zaki, and W. Li, Memory placement techniques for parallel association mining. *Proceedings of International Conference on Knowledge Discovery and Data Mining* 1998: 304–308.

[Liu-Lu-Yao 1998] H. Liu, H. Lu, and J. Yao, Identifying relevant databases for multidatabase mining. In: *Proceedings of Pacific–Asia Conference on Knowledge Discovery and Data Mining*, 1998: 210–221.

[Liu-Lu-Yao 2001] H. Liu, H. Lu, and J. Yao, Toward multidatabase mining: Identifying relevant databases. *IEEE Transactions on Knowledge and Data Engineering*, 13(4) (2001): 541-553.

[Liu-Motoda 1998] H. Liu and H. Motoda *Feature Selection for Knowledge Discovery and Data Mining*, Kluwer Academic, Hingham, MA, July 1998.

[Liu-Motoda 2001] H. Liu and H. Motoda, *Instance Selection and Construction for Data Mining*. Kluwer Academic, Hingham, MA, February 2001.

[Massey-Newing 1994] J. Massey and R. Newing, Trouble in mind. *Computing*. May 1994: 44–45.

[Ng 1994] R. Ng and J. Han, Efficient and effective clustering methods for spatial data mining. In: *Proceedings of the Twentieth International Conference on Very Large Data Bases*, September 12-15, 1994, Santiago de Chile, Chile. Morgan–Kaufmann, 1994: 144–155.

[Oguchi 1999a] M. Oguchi and M. Kitsuregawa, Dynamic remote memory acquiring for parallel data mining on PC cluster: Preliminary performance results. In: P. Sloot, M. Bubak, A. Hoekstra, and B. Hertzberger (Eds.): *High-Performance Computing and Networking, seventh International Conference, HPCN Europe 1999*, Amsterdam, The Netherlands, April 12–14, 1999, Proceedings. Lecture Notes in Computer Science 1593 Springer 1999: 553–562.

[Oguchi 1999b] M. Oguchi and M. Kitsuregawa, Dynamic remote memory acquisition for parallel data mining on ATM-connected PC cluster. In: *Proceedings of the 1999 International Conference on Supercomputing*, June 20–25, 1999, Rhodes, Greece. ACM, 1999: 246–252.

[Oguchi 1997] M. Oguchi, T. Shintani, T. Tamura, and M. Kitsuregawa, Characteristics of a parallel data mining application implemented on an ATM connected PC cluster. In: B. Hertzberger and P. Sloot (Eds.): *High-Performance Computing and Networking, International Conference and Exhibition, HPCN Europe 1997*, Vienna, Austria, April 28–30, 1997: 303–317.

[Oguchi 1998] M. Oguchi, T. Shintani, T. Tamura, and M. Kitsuregawa, Optimizing protocol parameters to large scale PC cluster and evaluation of its effectiveness with parallel data mining. In: *Proceedings of The Seventh IEEE International Symposium on High Performance Distributed Computing (HPDC '98)*, 28–31 July, 1998: 34–41.

[Padmanabhan 1998] B. Padmanabhan and A. Tuzhilin, A belief-driven method for discovering unexpected patterns. In: *Proceedings of the ACM SIGKDD International Conference on Knowledge Discovery and Data Mining*, 1998: 94–100.

[Padmanabhan 2000] B. Padmanabhan and A. Tuzhilin, Small is beautiful: Discovering the minimal set of unexpected patterns. In: *Proceedings of the ACM SIGKDD International Conference on Knowledge Discovery and Data Mining*, 2000: 54–63.

[Park-Chen-Yu 1995] J. Park, M. Chen, and P. Yu, Efficient parallel and data mining for association rules. In: *Proceedings of International Conference on Information and Knowledge Management*, 1995: 31–36.

[Park-Chen-Yu 1997] J. Park, M. Chen, and P. Yu, Using a hash-based method with transaction trimming for mining association rules. *IEEE Transactions on Knowledge and Data Engineering.*, 9(5) (1997): 813-824.

[Parthasarathy-Zaki-Li 1998] S. Parthasarathy, M. J. Zaki, and W. Li, Memory placement techniques for parallel association mining. *Proceedings of International Conference on Knowledge Discovery and Data Mining* 1998: 304–308.

[Parthasarathy-Zaki-Ogihara-Li 2001] S. Parthasarathy, M. Zaki, M. Ogihara, and W. Li, Parallel data mining for association rules on shared-memory systems. *Knowledge and Information Systems*, 3 1(2001): 1–29.

[Piatetsky 1991] G. Piatetsky-Shapiro, Discovery, analysis, and presentation of strong rules. In: *Knowledge discovery in Databases*, G. Piatetsky-Shapiro and W. Frawley (Eds.), AAAI Press/MIT Press, 1991: 229-248.

[Piatetsky-Matheus 1992] G. Piatetsky-Shapiro and C. Matheus, Knowledge discovery workbench for exploring business databases. *International Journal of Intelligent Systems*, 7(1992): 675–686.

[Prodromidis-Chan-Stolfo 2000] A. Prodromidis, P. Chan, and S. Stolfo, Meta-learning in distributed data mining systems: Issues and approaches, In: *Advances in Distributed and Parallel Knowledge Discovery*, H. Kargupta and P. Chan (Eds), AAAI/MIT Press, 2000.

[Prodromidis-Stolfo 1998] A. Prodromidis and S. Stolfo, Pruning meta-classifiers in a distributed data mining system. In *Proceedings of the First National Conference on New Information Technologies*, 1998: 151–160.

[Provost-Kolluri 1999] F. Provost and V. Kolluri, A survey of methods for scaling up inductive algorithms. *Data Mining and Knowledge Discovery*, 3(2) (1999): 131–169.

[Rasmussen-Yager 1997] D. Rasmussen and R. Yager, Induction of fuzzy characteristic rules. In: H. Komorowski, and J. Zytkow (Eds.): *Principles of Data Mining and Knowledge Discovery*, Lecture Notes in Computer Science 1263 Springer, Trondheim, Norway, June 24–27, 1997: 123–133.

[Ribeiro-Kaufman-Kerschberg 1995] J. Ribeiro, K. Kaufman, and L. Kerschberg, Knowledge discovery from multiple databases. In: *Proceedings of the First International Conference on Knowledge Discovery and Data Mining* (KDD-95), AAAI Press, Montreal, Canada, August 20-21, 1995: 240-245.

[Rusinkiewicz-SK 1991] M. Rusinkiewicz, A. Sheth, and G. Karabatis, Specifying interdatabase dependencies in a multidatabase environment. *IEEE Computer*, 24(12) (1991): 46–53.

[Savasere-Omiecinski-Navathe 1995] A. Savasere, E. Omiecinski, and S. Navathe, An efficient algorithm for mining association rules in large databases. In: *Proceedings of International Conference on Very Large Data Bases*. 1995: 688–692.

[Savasere 1998] A. Savasere, E. Omiecinski, and S. Navathe, Mining for strong negative associations in a large database of customer transactions. In: *Proceedings of the 1998 International Conference on Data Engineering*. 1998: 494–502.

[Shintani-Kitsuregawa 1998] T. Shintani and M. Kitsuregawa, Parallel mining algorithms for generalized association rules with classification hierarchy. In: *Proceedings of ACM International Conference on Management of Data*, 1998: 25–36.

[Silverstein 1998] C. Silverstein, S. Brin, R. Motwani, and J. Ullman, Scalable techniques for mining causal structures. In: *Proceedings of ACM SIGMOD Workshop on Research Issues in Data Mining and Knowledge Discovery*, 1998: 51–57.

[Smyth-Goodman 1991] P. Smyth and R. Goodman, Rule induction using information theory. In: *Knowledge Discovery in Databases*, AAAI/MIT Press, 1991: 159–176.

[Srikant-Agrawal 1996] R. Srikant and R. Agrawal, Mining quantitative association rules in large relational tables. In: *Proceedings of ACM International Conference on Management of Data*, 1996: 1–12.

[Srikant-Agrawal 1997] R. Srikant and R. Agrawal, Mining generalized association rules. *Future Generation Computer Systems*, 13 (1997): 161–180.

[Srivastava 2000] J. Srivastava, R. Cooley, M. Deshpande, and P. Tan: Web usage mining: discovery and applications of usage patterns from Web data. *SIGKDD Explorations.* 1(2) (2000): 12–23.

[Su-LWZZC 2001] K. Su, X. Luo, H. Wang, C. Zhang, S. Zhang, Q. Chen, A logical framework for knowledge sharing in multi-agent systems. In: *Proceedings of COCOON*, 2001: 561-570

[Suzuki 1997] E. Suzuki, Autonomous discovery of reliable exception rules. In: *Proceedings of International Conference on Knowledge Discovery and Data Mining*, 1997: 259–262.

[Suzuki 1996] E. Suzuki and M. Shimura, Exceptional knowledge discovery in databases based on information theory. In: *Proceedings of International Conference on Knowledge Discovery and Data Mining*, 1996: 275–278.

[Ting-Witten 1997] K. Ting and I. Witten, Stacked generalization: When does it work? In: *Proceedings of International Joint Conference on Artificial Intelligence*, 1997: 866–871.

[Toivonen 1996] H. Toivonen, Sampling large databases for association rules. In: *Proceedings of International Conference on Very Large Data Bases*, 1996: 134–145.

[Tsikrika-Lalmas 2001] T. Tsikrika, M. Lalmas, Merging techniques for performing data fusion on the Web. In: *Proceedings of CIKM*, 2001: 127-134.

[Tsumoto 1999] S. Tsumoto, Rule discovery in large time-series medical databases. In: J. Zytkow, and J. Rauch (Eds.): *Principles of Data Mining and Knowledge Discovery*, Third European Conference, PKDD '99, Prague, Czech Republic, September 15-18, 1999: 23–31.

[Tung-Han-Lakshmanan-Ng 2001] A. Tung, J. Han, L. Lakshmanan, and R. Ng, Constraint-based clustering in large databases. In: *Proceedings of International Conference on Database Theory*, January 2001.

[Turinsky-Grossman 2001] K. Turinsky and R. Grossman, A framework for finding distributed data mining strategies that are intermediate between centralized strategies and in-place strategies. In: *Proceedings of Workshop on Distributed and Parallel Knowledge Discovery at KDD-2000*, 2000: 1–7.

[Webb 2000] G. Webb, Efficient search for association rules. In: *Proceedings of ACM International Conference on Knowledge Discovery and Data Mining*, 2000: 99–107.

[Wolpert 1992] D.H. Wolpert, Stacked generalization. *Neural Networks*, 5(1992): 241–259.

[Wrobel 1997] S. Wrobel, An algorithm for multi-relational discovery of subgroups. In: J. Komorowski and J. Zytkow (eds.) *Principles of Data Mining and Knowledge Discovery*, 1997: 367-375.

[Wu 1995] X. Wu, *Knowledge Acquisition from Databases*, Ablex, Norwood, NJ, 1995.

[Wu 2000] X. Wu, Building intelligent learning database systems, *AI Magazine*, 21(3) (2000): 59–65.

[Wu-Lo 1998] X. Wu and W. Lo, Multi-layer incremental induction. In: *Proceedings of the 5th Pacific Rim International Conference on Artificial Intelligence*, 1998: 24–32.

[Wu-Zhang 2003] X. Wu and S. Zhang, Synthesizing high-frequency rules from different data sources. *IEEE Transactions on Knowledge and Data Engineering*, 15(2003), 2: 353–367.

[Wu-Zhang-Zhang 2002] X. Wu, C. Zhang and S. Zhang, Mining both positive and negative association rules. In: *Proceedings of Nineteenth International Conference on Machine Learning*, Sydney, Australia, July 2002: 658–665.

[Wu-Zhang-Zhang 2004] X. Wu, C. Zhang and S. Zhang, Database classification for multi-database mining, *Information Systems*, accepted, forthcoming (Available online).

[Yan-Zhang-Zhang 2003] Xiaowei Yan, Chengqi Zhang and Shichao Zhang, Towards databases mining: Preprocessing collected data. *Applied Artificial Intelligence*, 17 (5-6) (2003): 545–561.

[Yao-Liu 1997] J. Yao and H. Liu, Searching multiple databases for interesting complexes. In: *Proceedings of Pacific-Asia Conference on Knowledge Discovery and Data Mining*, 1997: 198–210.

[Zhang 1989] S. Zhang, Discovering knowledge from databases. In: *Proceedings of National Conference on Artificial Intelligence and Its Applications*, Beijing, 1989: 161–164.

[Zhang 1993] S. Zhang, Premonitory dependency based on historical data. *Chinese Journal of Computing Technology*, 20(3)(1993): 50–54

[Zhang 1999] S. Zhang, Aggregation and maintenance for databases mining. *Intelligent Data Analysis: An International Journal*, 3(6) (1999): 475–490.

[Zhang 2000] S. Zhang, A nearest neighborhood algebra for probabilistic databases. *Intelligent Data Analysis: An International Journal*, 4(1), 2000: 29-49.

[Zhang 2001] S. Zhang, *Knowledge Discovery in Multi-databases by Analyzing Local Instances*. PhD Thesis, Deakin University, November 2001.

[Zhang-Liu 2002] S. Zhang and L. Liu, Causality discovery in databases. In: *Proceedings of ICAIS'2002*, 2002.

[Zhang-Qin 1997] S. Zhang and Z. Qin, A robust learning model. *Computer Sciences*, 24(4) (1997): 34–37.

[Zhang-Qiu-Luo 1999] S. Zhang, Y. Qiu, and X. Luo, Weighted values acquisition from applications. In: *Proceedings of Eighth International Conference on Intelligent Systems*, 1999: 24–26.

[Zhang-Wu 2001] S. Zhang and X. Wu, Large scale data mining based on data partitioning. *Applied Artificial Intelligence*, 15(2) (2001): 129–139.

[Zhang-Wu-Zhang 2003] S. Zhang, X. Wu, and C. Zhang, Multi-database mining. *The IEEE Computational Intelligence Bulletin*, 1(1) (2003): 5–13.

[Zhang-WZS 2003] S. Zhang, X. Wu, C. Zhang and K. Su, Identifying quality knowledge from different data sources. In: *Proceedings of ICDM '03 Workshop on Foundations and New Directions of Data Mining*, Melbourne, FL, November 19, 2003: 234–242.

[Zhang-Yan 1992] S. Zhang and X. Yan, CTRCC: An analogical forecast model. In: *Proceedings of ICYCS'91*, 1991: 553–556.

[Zhang-Zhang 1998] S. Zhang and C. Zhang, A method of learning probabilities in Bayesian networks. In: *Proceedings of ICCIMA'98*, Australia, 1998: 119–124.

[Zhang-Zhang 2001a] S. Zhang and C. Zhang, Mining small databases by collecting knowledge. In: *Proceedings of DASFAA01*, 2001: 174–175.

[Zhang-Zhang 2001b] C. Zhang and S. Zhang, Collecting quality data for database mining. In: *Proceedings of the Fourtennth Australian Joint Conference on Artificial Intelligence*, 2001: 593–604.

[Zhang-Zhang 2001c] S. Zhang and C. Zhang, Estimating itemsets of interest by sampling. In: *Proceedings of the Tenth IEEE International Conference on Fuzzy Systems*, 2001.

[Zhang-Zhang 2001d] S. Zhang and C. Zhang, Pattern discovery in probabilistic databases. In: *Proceedings of The Fourteenth Australian Joint Conference on Artificial Intelligence*, 2001: 619–630.

[Zhang-Zhang 2002a] C. Zhang and S. Zhang, *Association Rules Mining: Models and Algorithms*. Lecture Notes on Computer Science, Volume 2307, Springer-Verlag, New York, 2002.

[Zhang-Zhang 2002b] C. Zhang and S. Zhang, Database clustering for mining multi-databases. In: *Proceedings of the Eleventh IEEE International Conference on Fuzzy Systems*, 2002.

[Zhang-Zhang 2002c] S. Zhang and C. Zhang, Anytime mining for multi-user applications. *IEEE Transactions on Systems, Man and Cybernetics* (Part A), Vol. 32 No. 4(2002): 515–521.

[Zhang-Zhang 2002d] C. Zhang and S. Zhang, Identifying Quality Association Rules by External Data. In: Proceedings of the International Congress on Autonomous Intelligent Systems, Geelong, Australia, 12-15 Feb. 2002.

[Zhang-Zhang 2002e] S. Zhang and C. Zhang, Discovering causality in large databases. *Applied Artificial Intelligence*, 16 (5) (2002): 333–358.

[Zhang-Zhang 2004] S. Zhang, C. Zhang, and J. Yu, Mining dependent patterns in probabilistic databases. *Cybernetics and Systems*, 35(2004): 1-26.

[Zhang-Zhang-Webb 2003] C. Zhang, S. Zhang, and G. Webb, Identifying approximate itemsets of interest in large databases, *Applied Intelligence*, 18(1) (2003): 91–104.

[Zhang-Zhang-Yan 2003] S. Zhang, C. Zhang, and X. Yan, PostMining: Maintenance of Association Rules by Weighting. *Information Systems*, 28(7), October 2003: 691–707.

[Zhong-Yao-Ohsuga 1999] N. Zhong, Y. Yao, and S. Ohsuga, Peculiarity oriented multi-database mining. In: *Principles of Data Mining and Knowledge Discovery*, Lecture Notes in Computer Science 1704 Springer, Prague, Czech Republic, September 15-18, 1999: 136–146.

Subject Index